The Human Use of Signs
or: Elements of Anthroposemiosis

John Deely

ROWMAN & LITTLEFIELD PUBLISHERS, INC.
Lanham • Boulder • New York • Toronto • Plymouth, UK

ROWMAN & LITTLEFIELD PUBLISHERS, INC.

Published by Rowman & Littlefield Publishers, Inc.
A wholly owned subsidiary of The Rowman & Littlefield Publishing Group, Inc.
4501 Forbes Boulevard, Suite 200, Lanham, Maryland 20706
www.rowmanlittlefield.com

Estover Road
Plymouth PL6 7PY
United Kingdom

Copyright © 1994 by John Deely

All rights reserved. No part of this publication may
be reproduced, stored in a retrieval system, or transmitted
in any form or by any means, electronic, mechanical,
photocopying, recording, or otherwise, without the prior
permission of the publisher.

British Cataloging in Publication Information Available

Library of Congress Cataloging-in-Publication Data

Deely, John N.
The human use of signs, or, Elements of anthroposemiosis / by John
N. Deely.
p.   cm.
Includes bibliographical references.
1. Semiotics. 2. Linguistic anthropology. 3. Criticism.

I. Title.
P99.D399   1993   40'.41—dc20   92-37605   CIP

ISBN 0-8476-7803-2 (cloth : alk. paper)
ISBN 978 0-8476-7804-4 (paper : alk. paper)

*This book is dedicated
to the first professional historian
who became a member of the
Semiotic Society of America*

Peirce's representation of the labyrinth of signs, c. 1909, as centered probably on his dog Zola symbolically substituting for the Minotaur. Photograph courtesy of Joseph Brent.

Omnis doctrina vel rerum est vel signorum, sed res per signa discuntur. Proprie autem nunc res appellavi, quae non ad significandum aliquid adhibentur. . . .

Illis qui haec scribimus non intelligunt, hoc dico: me ita non esse reprehendendum, quia haec non intelligunt; tamquam si lunam veterem vel novam, sidusve aliquod minime clarum vellent videre, quod ego intento digito demonstrarem; illis autem nec ad ipsum digitum meum videndum sufficiens esset acies oculorum, non propterea mihi successere deberent. . . . Non enim si possum membrum meum ad aliquid demonstrandum movere, possum etiam oculos accendere, quibus vel ipsa demonstratio mea, vel etiam illud quod volo demonstrare, cernatur.

Augustine of Hippo on the Scope and Limits of Semiotics
DE DOCTRINA CHRISTIANA (c.397AD)
Book I, Chapter 2, and Prologue, Paragraph 3

Contents

List of Figures	ix
Preface	xi
Preliminaries *Paragraphs 1–29*	1
Part I. Signification *Paragraphs 30–133*	11
Part II. Textuality *Paragraphs 134–191*	53
Part III. Critick *Paragraphs 192–284*	83
Part IV. Otherness *Paragraphs 285–311*	121
Paragraphal Glosses	135
Appendix: The Ethics of Terminology	173
References	175
Index of Persons Mentioned	199
Index of Conceptions	202
About the Author	241

List of Figures

1	¶173:	Roman Jakobson's Factorial Model of Poetic Language	72
2	¶173:	Roman Jakobson's Corresponding Scheme of Functions	72
3	¶173:	Preliminary Model of Textuality	73
4	¶176:	Karl Bühler's Organon Model of Speech	73
5	¶176:	Thomas Sebeok's Morley Triangle Model of Communication	74
6	¶180:	The Pyramid of Anthroposemiosis	76
7	¶183:	Terry Prewitt's Attempted Three-Dimensional Reduction of Johansen's Pyramid to a Regular Trigonal Dypyramid Model	77
8	¶183:	Terry Prewitt's Segmented Discourse Model	78
9	¶224:	The Abductive Spiral of Experiences	96
10	¶270:	The Planes of Semiosis within Discourse (Segmentation of Johansen's Pyramid)	114
11		Gloss 47 (Second on ¶293): Aquinas's Derivation of Properties and Types of Being *from within* Being as *Primum Cognitum*	164

Preface

In *Introducing Semiotic* (Deely 1982), I argued in passing that the reduction of culture to social system characteristic of British and American anthropology in the wake of Radcliffe-Brown was the result of an inadequate understanding of semiosis as it occurs through specifically human language. I also argued, likewise in passing, that the doctrine of signs as formally consisting in irreducibly triadic relations provided a new way of understanding the ancient distinction between understanding and sense perception, and that this distinction was of a piece on the organismic side with the distinction between social organization and culture on the side of the objective world.

Tom Sebeok, in his Foreword to that work, was the first gently to point out that all this would have to be seen, as he put it, "in developments yet to come". The present book is my attempt to lay fully on the table the considerations and arguments necessary to vindicate these essential suggestions of the earlier work as to the uniquely human use of signs—the elements, as I think of them, distinguishing anthroposemiosis.

Yet since 1982 time has not stood still, and the present investigation focuses on anthroposemiosis more proximately against the background of the general extent and grounds of semiotics outlined in my book *Semiótica Básica* (São Paulo: Ática Éditora, 1990), published almost simultaneously in English (actually about two months earlier, and with some additional refinements) as *Basics of Semiotics*. Whereas direct explanation of the terms delineating the full scope of semiosis as I understand it—physiosemiosis, phytosemiosis, zoösemiosis, and anthroposemiosis—are provided in the chapters of that book, here I am concerned rather with a more detailed and deeper investigation of the knowledge that corresponds specifically to study of the action of signs as it bears on our species, that is to say, anthroposemiotics. In this sense, the present essay expands upon Chapter 5 in particular of *Semiótica Básica*, deepening it overall.

Myrdene Anderson, Robert Corrington, and Júlio Jeha provided many useful suggestions in reading several of the early drafts toward this book. Nathan Houser, like Max Fisch before him, proves ever ready as a sage consultant on arcana of the Peirce materials. Eugen Baer, whom I have never read or heard without learning, directly inspired ¶s 38–52, 55–58, and 60 in Part I with his "Via Semiotica" review essay (Baer 1992). Michael Herzfeld proved an essential guide to some key anthropological readings. And Richard Parmentier provided an essential stimulus for this work (noted in Gloss 28) with his twin insistence—doubly correct—on the absence of the notion of code in Peirce and on the importance of the concept for anthropology. Thanks for help in proofreading and final manuscript preparation go especially to Lynn Gemmell, Brooke Williams, Sujata Guha, and Mitchell Johnson.

Essays of mine that have appeared since *Introducing Semiotic* that are especially germane to the central thesis and thrust of the present work are cited in these pages, but the main one is "Philosophy and Experience" (Deely 1992a), which directly addresses in the context of modern philosophy the problem of in what exactly experience consists. That experience is the sole ground of human knowledge is all but universally recognized. But what experience is remains subject to the most widely varying expositions—most of them, traditionally, too narrow to encompass even the most rudimentary of everyday experiences of discourse in community. We confront in this issue the dividing line between modernity and postmodernism.

This book is the best argument I can make to date that the perspective required to develop a doctrine of signs in the fullness of its proper possibilities implies also an understanding of human experience that will be for the first time integral and adequate to the task of providing the measure of human knowledge in the whole of its extent, as distinguished from imposing upon experience and systems of belief some ideological measure designed to dismiss large parts thereof a-priori. To minimize the difficulty of the argument, the book has been set up in such a way as to emphasize the autonomy of the paragraphs.

The present work is published in the hope especially of drawing other workers into the labor of understanding the human use of signs, recognizing all the while that the work perforce advances along an asymptotic curve ill-suited to dogmatic beliefs of any stripe. A community of inquirers cannot escape from the need to provide its own authority, and at the same time to ground that authority critically on the nodes and intersections of objective being with physical being.

With this much prologue, I turn to the task at hand, with the reader's good assistance.

John Deely
completed with a Pelikan 120
at Gallmans' Farm, Indiana
9 March 1993

Preliminaries

1. As its title openly suggests, this is an essay in anthropology. As such, it is not an empirical study but a foundational one. More specifically, it is an attempt to explain the claim once made by a prominent semiotician to the effect that semiotics is "the first true anthropology".

2. For anthropology is the science constituted through the systematization of discourse concerning *anthropos*, the human creature, and so seeks to describe and explain what that creature is so designated specifically in its contrast to the many other creatures and types of creatures comprising the physical and objective universe around us.

3. This science has its own focus, therefore, like every disciplined study; but what this focus is itself requires some focusing. For action not only follows upon being and provides our only point of access to a knowledge of what some being or other is in its proper nature (that is, as a source of actions and a nexus of relationships in the world, apart from which it cannot exist). Action is coextensive with being and sustenative of it: *Esse dependet ab actionibus et relationibus resultantibus*. Only logically is being prior to and presupposed by action: existentially, a being is only so long as and through the actions (and resulting relationships) it entertains, both actively and passively, with its surroundings, whether objective or physical. Hence also only logically do structures "exist" apart from actions. They exist actually only as virtualities of the action itself which sustains being, and—especially—as the patterns of relations resulting from those virtualities *as* sustenative.

4. The patterns of relations, thus, are what are decisive. Apart from the relations—resultant, yes, but *concomitantly* resultant, logically posterior while existentially simultaneous—there neither is nor can be being. "To be" is to act, but "to continue to be" hangs from the relations actions dimanate,[1*] in what the being undergoes no less than in what the being does. For just this reason "models of structure exhibit tendencies in action". Structures are not just residues of action, but platforms which actions sustain insofar as the structures have being; and, through their being, structures, like individuals, transcend the particular moments of their establishment, with this difference: the (socio-cultural) structures are ultimately expressions of relationships resulting from antecedent as well as sustenative actions, webs in which individuals are caught and by which individuals are formed, but to which they cannot be reduced. Karp and Kendall (1982: 267) attribute this lesson especially to Giddens: "Structure, he tells us, is both the medium in terms of which actions take place and the unintended consequence of action."

5. The fabric of relations sustaining the individual is like a living thing, and indeed participates the individual's life: it can change constantly, be rent or sundered, but the individual it sustains cannot subsist independently of it nor be understood apart from it save as an empty center: a "substance" in contrast to an individual subsistent, a being-in-a-world, be that world objective or merely environmental.

6. The sustaining network of relations through which being is held onto by its individual members and instances is thus not homogeneous. Not only does it involve relations of different kinds, but even of different orders. Certeau (1984: xi) practices rather anthropomorphism than anthropology with the claim that a relation is "always social". The relationships by which the individuals sustain their being as such are by no means always social: they may be merely environmental and physical, as among asteroids and atoms (assuming these not to be living individuals) or also vital, as among plants, and *further* social as among some animals, or *even* cultural, as among human animals. What remains true is that the relations determine the intelligibility of their terms, and that "each individual is a locus" in which an "often contradictory plurality of such relational determinations interact".

---

* Superscripts in the text refer to paragraphal glosses that are placed at the end of the text.

7. To say that this situation makes the individual *incoherent* (Certeau, loc. cit.) is, strictly speaking, an exaggeration, because the intelligibility of a term is correlative to the foundation or fundament from which the relation arises in the first place and on which it rests. But this situation does make the individual multifaceted, aspectually inconsistent, and hence partially opaque. No one standpoint "makes full sense" of the individual existing: hence its opacity. The several standpoints required to understand its continuing existence (as long as it lasts) may, indeed, be mutually inconsistent logically considered. But from the standpoint of existence the several standpoints are far from incoherent. On the contrary, they prove necessary to understanding the sustenance of existence and ultimately its loss. Thus prima facie logical incoherence often has as its existential counterpart sustenance through conflict. Far from being wholly exclusive, logical inconsistency and existential sustenance provide a contrast which serves to underscore the difference between being objectively taken and physically given. A "science of singularity" thus comes into view in terms of "the relationship that links everyday pursuits to particular circumstances" (Certeau 1984: ix), while the individual in its totality of relationships continues to verify the maxim of the Latins: "de singularibus scientia non datur".

8. To speak of any being objectively taken is to speak of some being which belongs to its environment also through cognition and emotion, as well as physically and through the structure of a body as such. This is a very important point, and the point which is ultimately foundational for anthropology. Objective relations, even when they are social, also contain and express more than the social, either on the side of the physical environmental relations which the social only imperfectly transcends, or on the side of the cultural relations which the social relations (in the case of anthropos) sustain but never absorb fully. The cultural transcends the social even more than the social transcends the simply physical, but the *objective* includes all three.

9. Accordingly, take cognizance right from the start of the contrast and conjunction here of the terms "objective" and "physical". Both are technical terms throughout the present discussion, to be defined adequately by the discussion. In particular, while "subjective" is a synonym for "physical" or "psychical" alike, "objective" is not a binary opposition term with "subjective", as it is commonly (mis)taken to be in usage today. For what is

subjective may *also* and *at the same time* be objective, and conversely, though not necessarily so: we are not dealing here at all with simple antonymy.² Yes, in this particular, as in others that do not immediately concern us, the customs of natural language have developed in a way that actively opposes the development of the true science of *anthropos*. But that is hardly cause for despair, or for the clever construction of a deconstructive void. Let us rather, in view of our purpose, seek simply to set the usage straight. Whatever is known as such, let us say henceforward, is objective, regardless of whether it is also and further physical. We shall see as we go along that this is a change in usage more or less imposed by the requirements of adopting systematically a semiotic point of view, the only point of view intrinsically suited to the "morally, politically, even epistemologically, delicate" and technical task of bridging "the gap between engaging others where they are and representing them where they aren't" (Geertz 1988: 130), the task of Giddens' "double hermeneutic", which is nothing else than the task of species-specifically human interaction, as *also* of anthropology (which, after all, adds to such interaction only the reflexive element of critical control to the objectification "in which", as Karp exactly notes [1986: 134], "the observer attempts to make an account which incorporates the agents' subjectivity and intentionality into an explanatory model that uses terms derived from the life world of the observer").

10. Ethnographic study is not the issue for a foundational anthropology, but rather how such a thing as ethnography is possible in the first place as a mode of critical inquiry (the critical control of objectification, to be precise). Fabian's question (1983) of "how anthropology makes its object", after all, is only a particularization of the question of how objects of whatever type are constituted in the first place, and that is a matter of semiosis from the first and of anthroposemiosis only later on. Here, of course, it is this "later on" that interests us. Even "those of us who like to season our propositions with a dash or two of verification" (Basso 1976: 107) are dependent first on knowing what it is that is to be verified, and this is in every case an objective structure first of all.

11. Note in particular, therefore, that the human being, *anthropos*, is only biologically physical. That is, it is not so much as a component of the physical environment that the *anthropos* specifically distinguishes itself (although it does this too) as it is through the artifactual transformation of that environment revelative of the objective content of its thought and experience, its "interior dimension". This objective content embodied in artifacts is also embodied in an a priori way, though less clearly from an observational standpoint, in "behavior", especially such specifically anthropic behavior as dickering in a marketplace, choosing one's wardrobe, saluting a flag, genuflecting in certain churches, or bowing toward Mecca, etc.

12. In short, the human being, like every being, can exist and be known only through actions and consequences of actions; and, more specifically, it can be known *as* human only through the distinctively, the "species-specifically", human component or dimension of those actions even when they also involve, as they must and always do, many other components and dimensions which are anything but species-specific to the anthropic animal.

13. Every new age in philosophy introduces a new definition of the rational animal. And so it is with semiotics. From the semiotic point of view, *anthropos* appears first and pre-eminently as the linguistic animal. It can be argued that this is only a first approximation to the more basic nature of the *anthropos* which explains especially its linguistic manifestations, namely, its existence as the *codifying* animal.[3] And, most importantly and fundamentally, that is to say, more broadly, the distinctive codifying behavior manifested pre-eminently in linguistic exchange *itself already* appears as *dependent* upon and a variety of an action radiating in every direction looking from or to *anthropos*, namely, the action of signs in nature, or *semiosis*. Yet this relation to a broader context does not gainsay the pre-eminence of the linguistic code in all that concerns the species-specifically anthropic: the postlinguistic cultural codes depend for their being on the prior network of relations constituting the linguistic code as such.

14. The definition of *anthropos* as the codifying animal, semiotically considered, therefore requires that we conjure up in our theoretical understanding a model of a being sustained and developed through a distinctive semiosis, *anthroposemiosis*, in contrast to the semioses distinctive of merely cognitive or animal nature (zoösemiosis), life in the most general sense (phytosemiosis), or even that vast contingent of physical nature—embracing stars, various planets, and the reaches of cosmic rays and dust between—which appears to have no life at all (physiosemiosis). In this semiosis, moreover (anthroposemiosis), language appears as central but neither autonomous nor terminal.

15. The focus of anthropology, then, is not just a certain kind of being. It is rather a certain kind of action, constitutive of a certain kind of being *through which* the human individual and all other elements of the physical universe alike are known and knowable in the first place, namely, the being proper to experience. It is not an organism that we study in anthropology first of all, nor even the distinctive products of the activity of a certain organism (*Homo sapiens sapiens*, for instance). First of all we must study rather the activity through which there supervenes upon a certain organismic type a network of relations of a most distinctive kind, namely, a network of relations wherein both the organism itself and its surroundings first become accessible objectively and remain so. That is to say, we must bring into view the distinctive network of relations and kinds of relations (both mind-dependent and mind-independent, we shall see, but in every case and always triadic) that causes the environment to exist actually as knowable in contrast merely to being and interacting physically and in a merely potentially knowable form.

16. This distinctive network, part, as we have said, of a much larger series of networks ultimately coextensive with reality itself in its total being, at once objective and physical, is aptly characterized as *the semiotic net* or *web*. It comprises that network of relationships wherein are caught and held up for study all the elements that enter into the experience of the human organism. Precisely as catching and rendering objective those various elements, as we shall see, this network constitutes experience in its irreducible and proper being. Whatever is known or knowable, self or other, natural or cultural, insofar as it is verifiably known, is sustained by this web.

17. We will see that *criticism*, the evaluation of specific units of discourse according to selected criteria, or *cannons of readership*, is only one of the language-dependent activities unique and proper to anthroposemiosis (science and morality being others). We will also see that criticism has a scientific and an ethical side as well as a literary one, being, in general, the modality of critique essential to the evaluation of culture as such, in whatever modality of existence the anthropic content receives embodiment. For this reason, in speaking of the analysis and evaluation of codes in whatever dimension (linguistic, behavioral, embodied in material artifacts) or modality (literary, ethical, scientific, historical, etc.), we shall be speaking of criticism in terms of its very ground, and in a sense broader than, but including, the various specific types of criticism (such as literary criticism, textual criticism, behavioral critique, etc.). For this we may borrow from Locke's *Essay* (1690: 362) the term Critick, since indeed it is the very term originally proposed for labeling the domain of the new sort of critique in matters epistemological which we could expect to result from the systematic development of the perspective proper to a doctrine of signs.

18. Similarly, literature itself and the criticism thereof, as a highest form of anthroposemiosis, need be no less imaginative for being scientific, nor can the literature of human science ("Geisteswissenschaften") as a particular semiotic web be cut off from its origins in the network of semiosis, where natural science as well (as a specific modality or form of anthroposemiosis) has its origin. It is a question, with semiotics, of the common origin of all knowledge and of the possibility of a critical perspective applicable to the whole of knowledge and belief.

19. At the same time, by the very nature of our situation as finite knowers, the composition of this web, the lattice and angle of its strands which reveal and constitute by their intersection the objective as such in its difference from the merely physical, is inherently labile and reformable along new lines. The semiotic web, sustained within and by the larger network of semiosis tying anthroposemiosis itself to the biosphere (through its zoösemiotic and phytosemiotic strands) and to the physical environment at large (through its physiosemiotic strands), constitutes the reality of all that is experienced, but suchwise as to ensure that that reality cannot be divided in a final way into what is and what is not independent of the cognition. Such a division as final is precluded for the excellent reason that every act of understanding not only rebounds upon the contours of perception and the perceived as such but also immediately or prospectively redefines the margins of the line separating what is and is not independent of awareness as a "here and now" moment of experience. The "double break" by which Bourdieu explained first the origin and then the limits of "objectivism" through the "*dialectic of the internalization of externality and the externalization of internality*" (1977: 3, 72) is actually a twofold fissure built into anthroposemiosis from the start, both in its species-specific difference from zoösemiosis and in its generic dependency on that larger semiosis wherein zoösemiotic activity itself extends and completes anthroposemiotic experience and ties it back into its ground in the physical environment and the conditions of life generally.

20. Thus the object of anthropology is perforce always a model more or less complete, seeking to account for and incorporate into itself the objective elements of experience given and redefined more or less slightly differently by each individual semiosis in the community of inquirers participating in the experience we call "being human", and which we must seek to characterize with both exactitude and generality in the paragraphs to follow. The present essay is a first attempt, then, to refocus the object of anthropological study, by isolating the elements of anthroposemiosis within the larger semiosic networks upon which it depends in its very further specification of an otherwise common process—the action of signs giving being to the universe actually (that is to say, objectively) as well as virtually (that is to say, physically).

21. The notion of modeling system is thus central to anthropology semiotically—which is to say, integrally and properly—conceived. The most general model capturing the being proper to experience (the animality of the codifying animal) is the one first worked out by Jakob von Uexküll, namely, the *Umwelt*. The original semiotic idea of a modeling system, of course, was much more restricted and specifically linguistic—the "primary modeling system" of the Tartu school (mislabeled, as it proved: see Sebeok 1987).

22. The merging of these two notions, the one biological, the other linguistic, into the specifically semiotic notion of experience as a web of objective relationships is largely owing to Thomas A. Sebeok. The critique, expansion, and modification of Sebeok's decisive merger of the biological and the linguistic (into the properly and integrally semiotic) notions required to adumbrate the proper focus of anthropology, therefore, is the task of the paragraphs to follow, the successful completion of which, it is hoped, will result in a better delineation of the elements of anthroposemiosis and of the proper focus of anthropological investigation than has heretofore been possible to achieve.

23.   I will proceed in four parts.

24.   In Part I, I will examine the generic element in the semiotic definition of *anthropos* as *animal linguisticum*, that is to say, what is common to zoösemiosis and anthroposemiosis through the action of signs in the building up of "experience" as something in its own right superordinate to the brute secondness of environmental interactions. This I do under the heading of Signification. And here, following up on Sebeok's suggestions, we will see how the basic notion of modeling system extends much wider than the linguistic base assigned to it by the Tartu school.

25.   In Part II, under the heading of Textuality, I will examine, so to say, the linguisticization of the world of experience—that is, the species-specific element of experience that makes the human modeling system, or experience anthroposemiotically considered, different from the modeling system of animals employing communication systems lacking the code constitutive of the *signum expertum ad placitum* (the sign experienced linguistically, let us say). This sign will appear as ultimately rooted as such in the relation of signification grasped and deployed in its distinction from the perceptible sign-vehicle and the content signified. We will thereby see how textuality, virtual in the Umwelt, becomes actual through the indefinite decompositions and recompositions of experience linguistically construed by means of the establishment of a praeterbiological code which no longer, as in Sebeok's notion (cf. Baer 1981: 183), adequates the Uexküllian notion (1940) of "meaning-plan", because textuality breaks the proportion between biological heritage and object as such experienced. In a word, we confront in the codes whereby experience is textualized the differentiating factor in the semiotic definition of *anthropos* as *animal linguisticum*.

26.   This examination of code will bring us to the third element in this modeling of anthroposemiosis—Part III of the essay, examination of the curiously detached domain called "Critick" in the wide and generic sense explained above (¶ 17) as taken from Locke's *Essay*, wherein that equally curiously detached exercise called "criticism" takes place according to various forms. Therein, at one and the same time, what is most distinctive and what is most feeble in anthroposemiosis coincide to create that illusion whereby the literary aspect of semiosis is raised to the pinnacle of intellectual achievement and treated perversely as a self-contained and autonomous exercise of semiotic competence. Here we will make explicit a point that will have been established virtually in the two previous stages of the discussion: the critical function and faculty is a subspecies of semiotic competence rather than identical with semiotic competence. Subordinate to and subtended by much broader processes of semiosis, criticism in any specific sense owes its validity to its connection with, rather than to its misleading appearance of autonomy within, those processes. It is a question of appreciating the expanse of the framework and depth of the foundation that belongs to semiotics today by birthright as an offspring of the doctrine of signs gestated by the Iberians after 1529 (Soto's *Summulae*), crystallized thematically in Poinsot's *Treatise* of 1632a, named by Locke in 1690, and implemented by Peirce in its wholesale possibilities with the essay on categories of 1867 and in the many essays thereafter until his death in 1914.

27. Once the expanse of the framework has been grasped, it will be possible, in a few concluding remarks (Part IV on "Otherness"), to show how "constituting the other" is not unique to anthropology but is rather the basic activity of human intelligence essentially dependent on linguistic means. What is unique and uniquely interesting about anthropology is simply that "the other" is, normally, a conspecific whom we encounter only after socialization to maturity has occurred on the basis of cultural rules and expectations alien to our own socialization.

28. "Conspecific" here must be understood in a semiotically and not biologically specific way. Inasmuch as the capacity for language lies at the heart of anthroposemiosis and at the foundation of culture as the totality of postlinguistic systems, the capacity for language constitutes and defines a conspecific anthropologically conceived. In this way, our essay prepares the ground even for the eventual encounter with extraterrestrial linguistic forms, which belong (or will belong, to be exact) to the "object" or "subject matter" of anthropology no less than do such biologically conspecifics as the Yoruba, Trobriand islanders, Balinese, or even New Yorkers.

29. I begin with signification, the condition proper to signs, as being the most fundamental item in our attempt to sketch a model of anthroposemiosis.

Part I. Signification

30. In our fourfold plan of discussion, "sign" is the most fundamental notion. The reason is that the notion of a text—our second discussion plane—is inconceivable apart from the notion of *critick*—our third plane—which is in turn predicated on the *possibility of* analysis and evaluation of texts, and the notion of "other" depends for its explication precisely on textuality. While there may be other things besides signs, there are no texts without signs, and criticism of whatever sort loses its object in the absence of texts.

31. There are signs, and there are other things besides: things which are unknown to us at the moment and perhaps for all our individual life; things which existed before us and other things which will exist after us; things which exist only as a result of our social interactions, like governments and flags; and things which exist within our round of interactions—like daytime and night—but without being produced exactly by those interactions, or at least not inasmuch as they are "ours", i.e., springing from us in some primary sense.

32. The first and most radical misconception to be addressed is the notion that there are other things besides signs, as if signs were an item within our experience which has its place among other things besides. For, when we speak from the strict standpoint of experience (which of course we must in all contexts where we hope to avoid delusion), the sign is not by any means one thing among many others: the sign is not any thing at all, nor is it even first of all a distinct class of objects. As a type of object or objective structure contrasting with other objective structures, the sign is singularly unstable and derivative, precisely because signs are not objects first of all. Signs are presupposed to there so much as being whatever objects there are in the content of experience in general and at any given time.

33. For just as objects are what things become in experience, so signs are what objects become; but while objects as such do not in every case presuppose things, objects and things alike do presuppose signs within experience. Objects are not what the things are in their being prior to and independent of experience; objects are what the things become once experienced—that is, once they take on the existence proper to experience. The status of objects as signs vis-à-vis other objects is unstable not because of a deficiency in the sign but rather because of an instability in the status of the object as such, regardless of whether a given object (a star, say, or a vampire) is also a physical element as such in the environment.

34. We shall see that every type of object, every objectivity and objective structure as such, owes its being within experience to the sign. The derivative and unstable status of signs considered within the order of experience objectively constituted, by contrast, is owing to the fact that any object can become a sign of any other object, and every object in experience begins as, or quickly becomes, a sign of several other objects, which ones depending on context and changing over time. What does not change, what remains invariant at the base of experience, is the role of the sign as giving being to objects of whatever type in the first place.

35. We need not go beyond the boundaries of experience in order to clarify, in its contrast both to objects and to signs, this notion of "thing" introduced here. It is a notion that arises inevitably early in the experience of each of us, through the resistance we meet to our desires and, indeed, our expectations with such regularity that there is no adult real or conceivable who does not have the idea of an environment surrounding him or her which is comprised of a great variety of objects possessing a being or existence which exceeds the individual's experience of them in precisely the sense that much of this variety anteceded the individual me, much of it is unknown to me (it is full of surprises, welcome and unwelcome), and much of it will survive my demise. At least, such is our original conception of thing. To this notion traces the "opinion" lamented by Berkeley as "strangely prevailing amongst men, that houses, mountains, rivers, and in a word sensible objects have an existence natural or real, distinct from their being perceived by the understanding" (1710: 1 sec. 4). Things, in this most general sense, are whatever in my experience is experienced as not reducing to my experience of it and as having an embodiment, moreover, in the environmental structures such that it is not a mere figment of thought or imagination but has also an existence proper to itself physical or real that obtains apart from my thinking of it. Things have bodies, in a word.

36.   But not only things have bodies. Embodiment is a general phenomenon of experience, inasmuch as whatever we encounter, learn, or share through experience has about it an aspect which is accessible by some sensory modality, be it only the physical being of marks or sounds subsumed within language and employed to create some text (a literary *corpus*, we even say) wherein resides and is conveyed some object of consideration which, we learn on occasion while at other times knowing from the start, has no other body besides a textual one, such as the medieval unicorn, the ancient minotaur, or the celestial spheres which gave occasion for the condemnation and imprisonment of Galileo.

37.   In this way we are required to distinguish within our notion of the things experienced the notion also of objects which may or may not be things. Nor is the notion of thing, "that which exists regardless of being known here and now by any finite mind", quite as straightforward as might appear.

38.   Even though a thing is thought through the concept of what exists independently of me, our arrival at this concept—its arising within us under the pressure of secondness, the physical interaction of ourselves with our environment as irreducible to and corrective of our experience of it—is far from a matter independent of experience. This irreducibility is, in certain regards, the very essence or "paradigm case" of experience—"ist ipsamet experientia", as the Latins said (Poinsot 1632a: 306/13-307/4, esp. 306/19-20; see Deely 1992a).

39.   What we take to be a thing, moreover, is not the *type* of a thing, its abstract concept, but a *token* of thing, an actual

instantiation of the type in or as a concrete object of experience here and now. And this token already and necessarily transcends the notion it purports to instantiate. While the thing introduces itself as what *need not be* or least *need not have been* an object of experience, it cannot escape doing so precisely in the guise of an object here and now, for, by definition, an object exists as such through its relation to a knower, through being known, whereas a thing as such, by definition, exists independently of such a relation (even if it happens to be in such a relation at the moment).

40. The paradox is that in order to be a *known* thing, the thing must be an object, whereas precisely as object it need not be a thing. We can talk of what exists outside of our knowledge of the universe in general, but not in particular. If asked to name one such thing, one single actual existent, one concrete particular, of which we have no knowledge at all, we choke on the question. It demands the impossible. It is "unreasonable" in the strictest sense.

41. Perhaps because of its very "unreasonableness", this is a question that philosophers have seldom tried to face. Less understandable is the failure of philosophers generally to face clearly an inverse formulation of this question which, far from unreasonable, can very well be handled rationally: under what aspects of experience have we reason to posit that we are directly in contact with mind-independent being in its physical aspect—in other words, with aspects of objects which have a necessary coincidence with the being of things as interacting with the knower? The following text shows that the requirements of the question in this form were recognized at least as early as Aristotle (c.330BC: *De anima* 417b19-28):

> In the case of what is to possess sense, the transition is due to the action of the male parent and takes place before birth so that at birth the living thing is, in respect of sensation, at the stage which corresponds to the *possession* of knowledge. Actual sensation corresponds to the stage of the exercise of knowledge. But between the two cases compared there is a difference; the objects that excite the sensory powers to activity, the seen, the heard, & c., are outside. The ground of this difference is that what actual sensation apprehends is individuals, while what knowledge apprehends is

universals, and these are in a sense within the soul. That is why a man can exercise his knowledge when he wishes, but his sensation does not depend upon himself—a sensible object must be there. A similar statement must be made about our *knowledge* of what is sensible—on the same, viz. that the sensible objects are individual and external.

42. What the Greek commentators made of this point I do not know. But I can say that, among the Latins, the idea conveyed here became for some a central problematic of philosophical reflection (see esp. Deely 1985, 1992). Thomas Aquinas and those strongly influenced by him over the twilight Latin centuries—which in this regard would exclude Occam and the Nominalists, as well as the Scotists, so far as I know, and certainly Suárez, who became the almost sole pervasive influence on the early moderns—pinned the *idea* of thing within experience to the one channel of apprehension relative to which there are no grounds whatever for postulating the functional presence of an idea, namely, the channel of sensation *analytically prescissed within and considered in its distinction from* perception.

43. For while perception, like understanding, exhibits an indifference to the physical presence or absence of its objects, sensation technically prescissed consists in the idea of an interaction here and now between two bodily existents of which one at least is so constituted as to be capable of registering an immediate aspect of the other as conveyed in and by the interaction cognitively or apprehensively, thus making of it an element of experience.

44. Otherness, then, in the sense of a physically opposed other, an alternate subjectivity, not thematically seized upon as such, to be sure, but given as such nonetheless in the actual encounter, appears as an *element* of experience: that element which is irreducible to experience of it. Otherness, more precisely, *at this level*, is that element in the experience as a whole which demonstrates that experience as a whole is not reducible to the existence of things, and the existence of things is not reducible to our experience of them.

45. Perception, by contrast, and a-fortiori understanding, knows no such constraint to the here and now in its essential contour, in its difference from sensation as such. Bare elements of sensation are mere threads in the fabric of objectivity as perceived or understood. This fabric makes the supposedly no-longer-existent-past alive and operative as an influence on the present and the supposedly not-yet-existent-future a partial influence here and now on the experience of objects (for of course just the partial existence of the future as influencing the partial influence of the past constitutes the present in its everchangingness).

46. Small wonder that we can be mistaken about things. It is not a question of the general notion of a thing. It is a question of the concrete particular: this thing here and now, is it real or not? Is it really a thing we are considering? Or have we fallen into that ever present trap of mistaking what is not for what is?

47. We see thus why the primordial idea of thing is bound up with embodiment (only bodies act upon sense), but also why things of experience involve more than bodies and more than what merely exists prior to and independently of us. The Arc de Triomphe or the Coliseum is indeed a thing, that is, an object of our experience—we living today—which is experienced as something that anteceded our existence and something that we expect will survive our passage (if some terrorist idiocy of nature or culture does not intervene).

48. Suppose that were so. Suppose that not only we now living have died but that we have left no surviving progeny. Suppose the earth just as it shall have been in the year 1993, but with all human beings departed. There still stands the Arc de Triomphe, the Coliseum, the Hoover Dam, and quite a few other "things" besides, such as turtles and metals buried in the earth, but none of them, now, objects, or at least not objects of *anthropo*semiosis, for, on our supposition, that particular semiosis has regionally ceased.

49. We are confronted, in our hypothesis, not only with things, but with two kinds of things: things produced in and by anthroposemiosis, and things anthroposemiosis never got to touch—some of the metals buried in the earth, for example (though not, since the Viking Lander, the sands of Mars).

50. So we can resolve what is paradoxical about the notion of thing. The notion arises in the experience of each of us, indeed, but there it is bound up normally with objects produced in and by anthroposemiosis, and almost never, under conditions of contemporary existence, with objects whose physical constitution itself, or at least whose context of appearance, has not been structured by human intention. Of course, things *wholly* untouched by anthroposemiosis are *wholly* unknown to our species, like Pluto in the middle ages or the rings of Saturn before the telescope.

51.   In distinguishing things from objects, we need to add, as Baer suggested (1992: 352, emphasis added), "that things are accessible only by becoming signs—*that is, by becoming representations of 'subjects of physical interaction'*."

52.   What Baer steers us away from is too simple a drawing of the distinction between objects and things. Even though a thing experienced and an object of experience are far from wholly the same, the division between objects which are also things and objects which are merely objects is an aspectual one, not a total distinction. Of course, every thing *experienced* is by that very fact *also* an object of experience—a dynamic object as well as an immediate one. But not every object of experience, by any means, is also a thing in the sense of having an existence prejacent to the human community and independent of an embodiment within that community, such as experience indicates to be the case with much of nature. The distinction is of capital importance, so some illustrations emphasizing it should be useful.

53.   Objects are sometimes identical with physical things according to this or that aspect, as the north star names a unique natural entity contextualized to a specifically cultural but also magnetic and planetary frame of reference. At other times objects are identified with physical things without achieving a unique identity therewith—as the boundary for a certain stretch between Iowa and Illinois "is" the Mississippi River, or the President of the United States was first identified with Washington, later with a whole string of successors. At other times physical structures are made to instantiate objectivity without by any means being identical with the object locally embodied, as a statue of Romulus and Remus as founders of Rome or a statue of the minotaur has the physical aspect of a thing without that physical aspect being at all what is proper to its objectivity, unlike the mountain stream, which enters experience as an object

with a physical being precisely proper to its objectivity. So, too, many objects of experience have no physical existence in addition to their embodiment within texts. Cinderella, we think, along with her glass slipper and pumpkin coach, are purely objective, as the rocks and stars are not. The celestial spheres, long thought to embody the very stars, turn out not to embody them at all—the stars being the bodies while the spheres proved objects in the merest sense of fictions cut from the whole cloth of experience by the understanding, which confused their objectivity with the physical existence (or *subjectivity*) proper to things become object, that is, experienced.

54. We see thus that the world of experience as experienced is through and through objective, the leprechaun no less than the cancer cell or silver bullet or mountain stream. We see too that the physical universe exists within and as part of the objective universe of experience, indeed, as its lining and skeleton, so to speak. But we see also that the objective and physical worlds are by no means coterminous, as each extends in its own way well beyond the confines of the other. Of course, only the objective world, strictly speaking, in all its diversity mixed with physicality, exists *as* experienced. The physical surroundings may or may not also so exist—i.e., objectively, or as experienced. At least, this is the notion of physical being and existence that experience imposes on each of us: the notion that there is more to what we experience in its aspect of embodiment than reduces down to our experience of it (the dynamic object expresses itself within without reducing itself to the immediate object, we could also say), so that there are no doubt "things we have yet to learn and things we may never know".

55. We also see that objects of experience can never be merely things, as to be merely things they would have to be stripped of their relation to the knower, and *eo ipso*—or "presto chango"—they would cease to be *objects* and settle back into their physical subjectivity and interactions as potential seconds. Yet we also see that objects of experience as such are always representations, regardless of whether or not they are taken to be also things or of whether or not they are taken to be signs of other things. This fact is disguised through the circumstance that, as objects, the "things of experience" are *self-representations*.

56. Hence it is that objects can present themselves "as if" they were simply things, which is also the reason why we can be mistaken (and too frequently are, as both individual and social, as history too well illustrates) about which objects or aspects of objects are also "things" and which are not. This problem never arises as a theoretical issue for animals other than anthropos. Those animals, "using signs without knowing that there are signs", deal with objectivity only as a practical matter of survival.

57.   The difference on which semiosis depends—and hence which is of most direct concern to semiotics—is not expressed in the distinction between things and objects or between representations and signs but, as Baer iterates (1992: 353), in the distinction between objects and signs—that is, in the distinction between self-representations, whether or not false, and representations of what is other, whether or not existent. On this difference does experience depend, for only through the action of signs to begin with do things become objects, and only through objects do we discover the difference between objects and things, on the one hand, or between objects and signs, on the other.

58.   In Baer's words (ibid.): "representations are objects of experience and if representations are just themselves, they are what they are, objects. If, however, they refer in addition to something else, they become signs." This formulation holds for every object of experience as such without exception, regardless of whether the experienced aspect is also physical or purely objective. We see then why Peirce could say, and was right to say (1905b: L387, p. 277), that "to try to peel off signs & get down to the real thing is like trying to peel an onion to get down to onion itself" (see also Gloss 15 on ¶ 116 below).

59.   A particularly interesting aspect of the requirement that objects have an embodiment, be it only "textual" or linguistic in the sense of conveyance by some sensible *moyen* subsumed into the order of language, comes into view in those cases where the objects discoursed about are by definition independent of the world of bodies entirely, as in the case of supposed spirits or of the deity of Western religious conviction. Here the objective embodiment—the texts explaining and arguing about the nature and reality of these beings—is precisely denied to be of the essence of the object experienced through the discourse about it. (This case is in sharp contrast, say, to the unicorn, which only contingently proved to want for a bodily form beyond the discursive, or textual, corpus.) In the later medieval tradition, the term

"physical" was transferred to these objective entities, as well as to the likes of rocks, bugs, and stars, in order to emphasize that objective existence *tout court* stands in contrast to the physical existence whereby experience is exceeded precisely on the side of the objects experienced through some avenue and by some thread of embodiment, however slender (such as sounds, marks, or movements understood as representing something other than themselves and other than any per se sensible phenomenon of experience, actual or possible).

60. We thus see how the notion of "thing" as physical existent, originally given with and through the experience of bodily interactions, implicitly transcends that original context of given. For once the concept is grasped, it comes also to be seen that no contradiction follows upon some things not having bodies, even though we first come to know of things only through bodies, including our own (our own involvement in secondness), within objectivity. Materialists are frequently outraged by the logical licitness of this implication in the notion of thing because they hold the belief that there are in fact no physical existents which are not bodily existents. But ideology is one thing, logic quite another. And logically, the notion of thing involves no more than an existence independent under this or that aspect here and now of being apprehended by any finite mind, even though it may in fact be being so apprehended. So "things" *may be* material existents or spiritual existents, logically speaking, regardless of our *belief* as to whether there are in fact spiritual existents.

61. These considerations hardly exhaust the variety of ways in which objectivity and physical existence or being compenetrate and interweave. But they are perhaps sufficient to make unmistakable the point that the contrast between objective and physical being in what we experience is a fundamental contrast between two orders or frameworks which are not identical at every point, even when they happen to coincide. The objective and the physical depend upon one another without being coextensive and without being articulated in the same way. This last point is extremely important to take fully into account. The structure of experience and the structure of nature are because of it relatively independent variables.

62. Let us recall as an example the arcane consideration of physical entities which have ex hypothesi no bodies: the angelic beings of Christian belief, the general idea of a "spirit world", or of a unique divine being than which no greater can be conceived. Even more than mythical animals or legendary heroes, these entities are, from the standpoint of experience, purely objective beings. Not even statues can be made on their behalf which will properly illustrate what they are objectified as being, for to embody them is to contradict their fundamental nature, understood as having and able to have in their proper existence no bodily form (hence, e.g., the orthodox Jewish interdiction of graven images intended to portray Yahweh). Yet even these beings are known within experience, and regardless of whether their independent existence beyond experience and discourse—their subjectivity—is accepted or denied or considered undecided, they yet exist within experience, sometimes even influencing human conduct, as objects of consideration always through some thread of embodiment, at base linguistic (marks or movements seen or felt, sounds heard), often amplified, supplemented, and enhanced by artistic works of art and music.

63. We thus have a general rule: physical being, while it reveals itself within experience as involving a dimension which exceeds experience, also reveals itself on the material side as providing for experience a necessary lining. That is, experience, without being reducible to the points where physical and objective being are coincident, consists formally in an objective structure embodied through a lattice of physical relations which would not be just what they are apart from experience, but which are not the whole of experience either. The objective world (the world of experience) at once enfolds in part and restructures in part the physical environment within which it sustains itself.

64. In this discussion the sign has not appeared as a perceptible element as such within our inventory of experience, nor will it. For the sign has no existence in itself, but only in what other things become. It is the lattice, not the objective terms, of experience.

65. Even the classical formula "a sign is anything that stands for something else" (*aliquid stans pro aliquo*) can be misleading in this regard. "A", for example, stands for the first letter in our alphabet in capitalized form, or for an indefinite article opening a new sentence. But you see at once that a relation of "standing for" requires a specified context: one thing stands for another only *in some respect or capacity.* So the sign is not a thing as such, not a physical element merely existing in the environment, like a rock or a toad, but something as doubly related: A stands for B in context C. Let us suppose that A is a physical object: as such, it is not a sign. It is a sign only as doubly related in the required sense: what makes a sign is neither its physical being as thing nor its experienced being as object, but its experienced being as doubly related in the required sense. The being thus doubly related, not A in itself, is what formally constitutes the sign in its existence as sign.

66. Yet we are still in danger of misconstruing the case. To say the sign is "doubly related" is not to say that it is constituted by "two relations", but to say rather that one "thing" is related to two other "things" at one and the same time by *one single relation*. It is not a question of two relations, one between A and B, and another between A and C, for, even supposing there to be such, neither such relation taken independently nor both such relations taken together would constitute A as a sign. The relation constituting A as a sign is a single relation with three terms—sign, signified, and specified context or ground within and on the basis of which the sign signifies this signified rather than some other, or rather than not signifying at all. The physical mark A is constituted as sign not by its physical "reality" or being as such, nor by its being objective as such, but by its being the intermediate term in a triadic relation of the type Jakobson (1974; 1980) aptly named *renvoi*—a relation which has an intermediate term that sends the mind beyond itself to a signified according to a specific context. (After all, a thing may represent itself and nothing more, in which case it is an object rather than a sign.)

67. According to a *specific* context: What makes the sign stand in this rather than that capacity or respect to what it signifies so as to achieve a "proper significate outcome"? What constitutes a specific "context" as specific with regard to signification? This cannot be explained simply by the "context and circumstances" in which the sign occurs generically considered, but requires specifically something within the sign itself, an element or factor at work in the signifying which determines within the general context and circumstances what specifically is relevant to the signifying, what makes the context *specific* to what is signified, so that the sign signifies this rather than that (cf. Deely 1990:

Chapter 3). This third term in the sign-relationship Peirce called the *interpretant*. This term first appears in his writings in March of 1866 (Kloesel 1983: 111-112), but it is only later defined in terms of "the proper significate outcome of a sign" that "need not be a mental mode of being" (c.1906: 5.473), although it is this when it "creates in the mind of that person" to whom the sign stands for something else "an equivalent sign, or perhaps a more developed sign" (c.1896: 2.228).

68. The theoretical need for the interpretant as a third term essential to the sign-signified linkage was firmly established in semiotics long before Peirce coined the name, inasmuch as the Iberian semioticians of the 16th and 17th centuries had firmly established that the relationship in which a sign consists must be as such triaspectual (Araujo 1617, Poinsot 1632a; cfr. Beuchot 1980).

69. As regards *the cases where the interpretant is a mental representation*, these thinkers had meticulously established that for one object of perception to function as sign relative to another object, a concept in the mind is necessarily presupposed to ground the relation of signification (Poinsot 1632a: 271/22-42). The most striking feature of this earlier demonstration was its determined generality, that is to say, the demonstration that the requirement holds true not only in the obvious case of cultural symbols but equally when, in the case of so-called natural signs, a causal relation is also supposed to obtain between the sign (say, smoke or clouds) and the signified (say, fire or rain to come), so that, in every case without exception, the relation of signification is other than any dyadic relation of cause-effect (ibid.: 137n.4):

> Those relations by which a sign [i.e., a sign-vehicle] can be proportioned to a signified are formally other than the sign-relation itself. For example, the relation of effect to cause, of similitude or image, etc., even though some recent authors confound the sign-relation with these relations, but unwarrantably: because to signify or to be caused or to be similar are diverse exercises in a sign. For in signifying, a substitution for the principal significate is exercised that that principal may be manifested to a power, but in the rationale of a cause or an effect is included nothing of an order to a cognitive power; wherefore they are distinct fundaments, and so postulate distinct relations. These relations,

moreover, can be separated from the sign-relation, just as a son is similar to the father and his effect and image, but not a sign. The sign-relation therefore adds to these relations, which it supposes or prerequires in order to be habilitated and proportioned to this significate rather than to that one.

70. As regards *the cases where the interpretant is not a mental representation*, the essential clue that the interpretant need not be mental had already been uncovered prior to Peirce, as has been demonstrated (Deely 1990: Chapter 6) from Poinsot's formula (1632a: 126/3-5): "It suffices to be a sign virtually in order to signify in act".

71. But no thinker before Peirce, as far as I know, had gone so far as to assign a name to this silent partner or third term essential to the sign-signified linkage, or explicitly envisage its ambit of covering the *semeion* no less than the *symbolon* even when explicit mental representation is not involved. Hence the inclusion of the interpretant as a thematic factor of such an ambit in the analysis of signs was thus a major theoretical advance in the development of semiotics as a body of knowledge. The role of the interpretant in the semiosic structuring of experience, as a result, had never, prior to Peirce, been analyzed in sufficient detail to appear as an instance of a more general phenomenon—as a species of Thirdness, as we shall see (¶ 78 below).

72. Eco and Bierwisch (1986: I, 387) conclude that "the very richness of the category of interpretant lies in the fact that signification, as well as communication, by means of continual shifts that refer a sign back to another sign or string of signs, circumscribes cultural units in an asymptotic fashion", making of the sign, as Peirce said (1904: 8.332) "something by knowing which we know something more". This "repetition of renvois", each at least slightly different from the previous one, enables us to see that the "proper significate outcome" of a sign is not something static and fixed but rather a moment or phase in a continual growth of understanding (cf. Peirce c.1902a: 2.292, c.1904: 8.191; Liszka 1990: 26ff.). At the same time, it is essential to see that the "cultural units" circumscribed by the notion of interpretant are more than merely cultural, inasmuch as the interpretant is often a natural unit recognized as such in the cultural achievement of a critically controlled objectification.

73. What then is the sign? It is simply the element that is *playing the role* of a standing-for at any given time. Insofar as this element is something sensible—a red octagon, say, with a four character string on it in white—it is merely a physically instantiated object. What makes of that object, any such object, a sign is not that it is a sensible element as such, but only that it is a sensible element serving as the intermediate one of three terms in a relation of *renvoi*, a relation whereby an observer is made to attend to something other than the so-called "sign" identified with the sensible element. Were we from the wrong culture, the red octagonal white-marked thing would still exist as an object that could be ostended. Only after the requisite information had been gleaned, however, would the object in question reveal itself as also a sign regulating specific types of behavior, particularly as pertains to the operators of motor vehicles.

74. Considerations such as these have taught contemporary semioticians to speak rather of "sign-vehicles" than of signs when intending objectified physical entities—be they marks or sounds or cultural artifacts of whatever type—functioning in the role of signs. Signs, strictly speaking, that is to say, signs as signs, are not as such perceptible entities at all. Signs are rather certain patterns of relationships—always triadic, as we have seen—into which perceptible entities as such enter upon actually being perceived or understood, that is to say (in either case), objectified. Semiotics is not the study of sign-vehicles: the physics of acoustical phenomena is not the science of spoken language, for all that spoken language involves such physics, any more than the physics of light waves is the study of written language, for all that written language involves light waves; the physiology of optic nerves is not the study of reading, for all that reading normally involves optic nerves; and so on. But we could perhaps say that semiotics is the study of sign-vehicles *as such*, i.e., in their biaspectual tri-relative guise.

75. When objects of experience are looked at in a certain guise, we find that they relate to other objects in a distinctive way, specifically, in a way that leads to awareness of things other than themselves. This is the behavior or action peculiar to signs, an action distinguished by the causing of one thing to lead to an awareness of other things besides itself, and distinct from the many other types of activity in which perceptible objects engage, notably interactions of brute force which directly and immedi-

ately change the material structures involved. The action of signs, by contrast, is involved in such changes but does not consist in them.

76. Consider the text through which Cinderella's coach became a pumpkin: on the side of physical existence, that is to say, insofar as it is a kind of thing and item within the physical environment insofar independent of our experience of it, that text is a mere set of markings, sustained by chemical and atomic interactions of a variety and extent not exhausted by our best awareness. As an object experienced, that same text, while remaining an element of the physical environment, also becomes as such a vehicle for making present to us events and entities which contrast most decidedly with the thing which the marks are in their physical dimension. The marks are not a pumpkin and a pumpkin is not a coach, but through some now singular chemistry these marks bring us to think of a coach—which the marks are not—and this coach in turn—which is not a pumpkin—makes us think of itself becoming a pumpkin. So we have, in addition to the physical chemistry whereby the marks have a continuing existence in the environment experimentally identifiable within our experience, some other kind of chemistry whereby these same marks become identified with quite other objects foreign to the physical being of the marks. These other objects are themselves—coaches and pumpkins—able indeed to be physical beings in their own right (though the tale might have been of some strange spirits or a divinity not able to have a body proper to itself), but they are able also to be signs of other objects in ways other than they are able to exist physically.

77. This remarkable other chemistry, whereby physical elements of the environment are first of all taken up into experience as objective elements and then further transformed within experience into vehicles representing and conveying what they themselves are not, is called semiosis. Semiosis is the name for the action of signs, in sharp contrast to the action of bodies whereby physical effects are produced. In the physical interaction of bodies, material modifications directly result and objective changes occur only secondarily or may not be involved at all. In semiosis, it is just the opposite: material modifications are merely presupposed and at the periphery, while objective transformations and interconnections constitute the whole essence of the interaction. C. S. Peirce (c.1906: 5.484) draws the contrast between the action of signs and the action of bodies in this way:

All dynamical action, or action of brute force, physical or psychical, either takes place between two subjects (whether they react equally upon each other, or one is agent and the other patient, entirely or partially) or at any rate is a resultant of such actions between pairs. But by "semiosis" I mean, on the contrary, an action, or influence, which is, or involves, a cooperation of *three* subjects, such as a sign, its object, and its interpretant, this tri-relative influence not being in any way resolvable into actions between pairs.[4]

78. Peirce also called dynamical interaction *secondness*, in contrast to the realm of pure possibilities, or *firstness*, on the one hand, and to the realm of the manifestations or results of an action of signs, or *thirdness*, on the other hand (see Houser 1989). Semiotics, then, is the study—or rather, the knowledge gained by the study—within experience of Thirdness as the manifestation or result of an action of signs.

79. J. Poinsot—Peirce's precursor in the work of clearing and opening up what we now call, following the terminological suggestion on this point of J. Locke (1690: 361), "*semiotic*, that is, the doctrine of the essential nature and fundamental varieties of possible semiosis" (Peirce c.1906: 5.488)—sees the contrast between the action of signs and the action of bodies as deriving from two principles (Poinsot 1632a: 195/3-9; 195/18-29):

> The first is that an object, insofar as it exercises an objective causality in respect of a power and represents itself, does not do so productively, but functions only as an extrinsic form which is applied to a cognitive power by some other efficient cause and is rendered present to the cognizing organism by means of a specifying form.
>
> The second principle is that a sign falls under the notion of and is substituted in the place of an object precisely in this line and order of an objective cause, . . . not indeed as if it were an instrument of an agent producing a physical effect, but as it is a substitute for an object, not informing as a specifying form but representing from the outside.

80. So we come to the heart of the problem, the action proper to signs in the interplay between objective and physical being which constitutes experience. We must divine if we can what the nature of signifying must be in order to play precisely this mediating role, beyond the dynamics of physical interaction (whether material or psychological and psychic, as Peirce points out). The two principles proposed by Poinsot as key to understanding semiosis have as their key this peculiar notion of *objective causality* as a subspecies or variety of the general notion of causality and cause.

81. The narrow early modern notion of causality as physical production is not immediately helpful in this regard, for the causality proper to signs is clearly not the causality which pertains primarily to the realm of brute secondness and dyadic interaction, as does transient efficient causality, the agents or agencies bringing a material change about or a material individual into being.

82. The slightly later, even narrower still, modern conception of cause as a constant conjunction or concomitance of events within experience, developed by and after Hume, would appear at first blush to be much more promising as a framework for understanding semiosis. The action proper to signs is precisely an action whereby, without any efficiency in the productive sense, one object accompanies another, and this would seem to be just what transpires through the "association of ideas" according to the doctrine of associationism.

83. Associationism has long been a central doctrine of modern philosophy and a shaping influence on the establishment of psychology as a science in the modern sense (Gannon 1991: 37-60). It is only to be expected that such a puissant doctrine should be extended and applied to semiotics, and indeed that has been the case. In the case of semiotics, associationism, dominated from within by the power of the voluntary, often goes by the fashionable name of "deconstruction".

84. Unfortunately, insofar as deconstruction relies on the principle of universal analogy and sympathy—the principle (Eco 1990: 24) "not only that the similar can be known through the similar but also that from similarity to similarity everything can be connected with everything else, so that everything can be in turn either the expression or the content of any other thing"—it leads not to an understanding of semiosis but to a process of drift.

In itself, associative drift, "Hermetic drift", in Eco's deft allegorical characterization of it, is a comparatively aimless process, and in this sense endless. The "form of drift" that is "extolled by deconstruction" (Eco 1990: 32), "Derridean drift", as we might say, is something else again, a free reading in which the interpreters take advantage of the ever-present within-text mechanisms of Hermetic drift to follow unexpected lines of possibility which the text can be made to disclose, or even to impose their own will on a text so as to force it to say, in spite of itself, through a play of terminal cleverness, what the interpreters want it to say, even if that be in the end to "prove" that the text says nothing at all.

85. Deconstructive drift thus depends upon Hermetic drift without reducing to it, while inevitably, as Kintz (1987: 157) noted of Derrida's own efforts to explain deconstruction, the deconstructionist "falls back into that old problem of 'intent'" but now by raising the question of *his or her own intent*, i.e., the intent of the deconstructive interpreter, which, if that intent goes so far as to suppress, respecting the text interpreted, not only any question of authorial intent but even of contextual boundary, becomes what Eco has called (ibid.: 29-30) "an instance of connotative neoplasm", inasmuch as "in cases of neoplastic growth . . . no contextual stricture holds any longer". The problem with such a process is, however, that we confront a process which knows no limits outside itself, a process wherein autism and solipsism coincide.

86. But this absence of external check is precisely why "drift" in whatever form cannot by itself constitute the process of semiosis. Proceeding toward the infinite is not the only characteristic of semiosis, and not the defining one.[5] What defines semiosis is not *how far* it proceeds in any given case or *how far* it proceeds from the point of view of the individual and the community of inquirers, but *how* it proceeds in each case. Assuming the pragmatic maxim that a conception is defined accurately by all the conceivable experimental phenomena which it implies, Eco observes that (ibid.: 40), in each case, "the process of interpretation must stop—at least for some time—outside language—at least in the sense in which not every practical effect is a semiosic one".[6] Similarly (ibid.: 38), "it is irrefutable that in the act of indication (when one says *this* and points his fingers toward a given object of the world), indices are in some way linked to an item of the extralinguistic or extrasemiotic world."

87. Semiosis is not a self-contained but rather an assimilative process, wherein and whereby nature and culture compenetrate within experience, and understanding progresses, not simply grows. Semiosis can involve cancerous mental processes and can degenerate into cancerous forms, but it is not itself a cancer so much as a progress in time. In semiosis, a sign brings something not semiotic into the semiotic realm: it makes of a thing an object signified, a significate,[7] leading in turn to further signifieds, many of which are often new. "The key to understanding the apparently puzzling infinities involved", Ransdell notes (1986: 676), is to realize that "they pertain to the object-sign-interpretant relation considered *in abstracto,* whereas in the concrete application of semiotic conceptions there will always be legitimating reasons for regarding certain signs as the first signs of the object and certain interpretants as the last interpretants" in an account "that satisfies whatever intellectual motives instigate the concrete inquiry or specific line of inquiry."

88. Eco (1990: 28) considers it a fundamental principle in Peirce's semiotics that "A sign is something by knowing which we know something more" (Peirce 1904: 8.332). According to Poinsot (1632a: 117/12-17, second emphasis added), this is a fundamental principle of semiosis itself:

> Indeed the manifestative element *of a sign* is found both with an order to another [as in the case of associationism or "drift"] . . . and *with a dependence on that other* to which it is ordered, because a sign is always less than what it signifies and is dependent thereon as on a measure.

Thus Eco points to a fundamental difference in a process in which, by the knowing of one thing, we merely know something *else,* and a process in which, by the knowing of one thing, we are led thereby to know something *more.* In other words, semiosis exhibits the central notion of the more classical and comprehensive analyses of causality, that of a *dependency in being* of sign upon signified, rather than a mere reversibility of association between the two.

89. The process of being-led-to-something-more is irreducibly triadic; the process of being-led-to-something-other may or may not be. Insofar as it happens to be triadic, as where the will of the interpreter imposes itself as the hidden interpretant violently dominating the text under the cover of cleverness, association provides at best an anemic form of semiosis. In itself, semiosis is something more than association of ideas, whether free or forced, and indeed is a process whereby the mind, through and in its own products, is involved with something more than itself and its products. Understanding is that form of semiosis whereby the world in its totality gets to know something of itself, not only as but as including mind. Thus Peirce remarks (c.1909: 6.324) that thought "needs the existential facts, but regulates them. It is only imitation-thought"—i.e., a mental process, such as drift, which does not imply and does not regulate brute fact—"to which the adjective 'mere' is appropriate."

90. The notion of causality as the *dependence in being* of a thing or aspect of a thing upon another thing or aspect of a thing was objectified by Aristotle in four forms. Dependency in being, he pointed out, may be efficient (or dependency in respect of production), final (or dependency in respect of outcome), material (or dependency in respect of composition), and formal (or dependency in respect of arrangement or pattern).

91. We have already seen that the notion of productive or efficient cause, while no doubt involved in semiosis, hardly explains the semiosis in what is specific to it as an action of signs, for the action of signs is triadic whereas the efficient cause is essentially dyadic and dynamical. For much the same reason we can rule out the dependency in being proper to material causality, for material causality is inseparably bound up with the subjective being of a cause or an effect in its constitution as an element of the environment (of the physical world in its proper being as physical), regardless of whether it is also objectified.

92. All spatio-temporal entities similarly have a material structure and formal architecture, that is, they are made out of something and made out of it in a definite way. Dependency in material structure is the notion of *material cause*: what something is made out of gives it definite properties affecting all that it is and can do. In the case of organisms, for example, what substances count as food and what as poison, what tissues or organs can be transplanted and what can not, etc., all this is determined by a material dependency or *dependency in type of matter*. Similarly in the case of artifacts: cardboard may be suitable for constructing a model of a building, but an actual building so constructed will fare ill in adverse weather. And so on. Aristotle called this aspect of dependency in being, accordingly, *material cause*. Note that efficient and material cause are, respectively and determinately, the one extrinsic and the other intrinsic: just as efficient or productive causality is always extrinsic to the effect as such produced, so material causality is always intrinsic to the effect and defines or limits the range of activity. Material causality, like efficient causality, is undoubtedly involved with semiosis: the sign-vehicle illustrates such causality par excellence. But, just as the sign-vehicle is not the sign formally considered, so material causality is not the causality which explains the action of signs as signs, for, like efficient causality, material causality pertains essentially and wholly to the order of subjective being, whereas the proper significate outcome of the sign as such is always objective.

93. In general, we can say that no notion of cause which is wholly bound up with the subjective being of an effect can be the cause which explains semiosis in what is proper to it. Nor can the cause we seek be wholly extrinsic to the being of the effect, as is the case with the efficient cause. We need a cause which at once constitutes and transcends the given physical effect, the given material structure, with which it is involved. In fact, of Aristotle's four causes as originally presented, only the final cause meets this requirement *prima facie*.

94. The notion of final cause, or *teleology*, in Aristotle is already presented as twofold, intrinsic or extrinsic.

95. An intrinsic dependency obtains in the case of individuals that develop from an initial primitive state to a mature adult state (Ashley 1952). This notion applies especially to living organisms: the course of growth and development is plainly not random but follows a plan, and that plan is the mature state toward which the development tends at each stage. This inner directed tendency is also called today *teleonomy* (Simpson, Pittendrigh, and Tiffany 1957; Pittendrigh 1958; Mayr 1974, 1983), to distinguish the biological datum from the many illegitimate uses which have been made of it and irresponsible inferences which have been drawn from it over the centuries, but particularly in modern times, in apologetic contexts by defenders of religious belief.

96.   An extrinsic dependency in outcome obtains in the case of one individual using something else to achieve the user's ends. Thus the production of artifacts of whatever kind, all works of art or technology, exhibit a dependency of this kind: acorns grow on trees through a process of intrinsic final causality, but forks as eating implements come into being only through manufacture, an external agency which shapes them according to a plan of the agent. Extrinsic final causality is at work, for example, in deconstruction;[8] whence, for reasons already examined, we must conclude that extrinsic final causality, frequently verified in relation to anthroposemiosis, yet fails to explain what is proper to that semiosis as an action of signs.

97.   Intrinsic final causality exists as a developmental tendency. "Now, something can tend toward something without ever actually attaining that toward which it tends", as Ransdell notes (1986: 683). But, wherever there is a real tendency there is teleology, whence Ransdell, following Peirce, infers that "semiosis processes are thus telic in overall form", and points out (1977: 163) that Peirce expressly "thought of semiotic as precisely the development of a concept of a final cause process and as a study of such processes". Modern commentators on Peirce seem to have found this fact "an embarrassment, a sort of intellectual club foot that one shouldn't be caught looking at, much less blatantly pointing out to others", which would explain "why the topic of final causation is so strangely absent in criticisms and explanations of Peirce's conception of semiotic and semiosis", despite its centrality in Peirce's own reflections and explanations.

98.   Final causality is clearly more relevant to the action of signs, to semiosis as such, than either efficient or material causality. In its intrinsic form, teleology is coextensive with life, and this consideration motivated Peirce to go so far as to consider an hypothesis of panpsychism to explain the ubiquity of the action of signs in nature. In this area Peirce seems never to have said his final word, and to have suffered considerable confusion to boot. Thus, in his "Minute Logic" (c.1902b: 1.204-272) we have a lengthy analysis of what he calls "ideal" or "final" causality. Initially, Peirce assimilates these two terms as descriptions of the same general type of causality (ibid.: 1.211, 227). But, in successive analyses (ibid.: 1.211, 214, 227, 231; and similarly in 1903a: 1.26), it emerges that causality by ideas constitutes the more general form of this sort of explanation, inasmuch as final causality, being concerned with mind, purpose, or quasi-purpose, is restricted to psychology and biology (c.1902: 1.269), whereas ideal causality in its general type requires as such neither purpose (1.211) nor mind or soul (1.216).

99. Here we find an important theoretical opening which Peirce did not sufficiently exploit. For if there is another cause besides the final cause which meets the double criterion of at once constituting and transcending a given physical effect (a given material structure) with which it is involved, and if it does this in a more general way than the final cause, we will have the cause proper to semiosis as such without the need for considering panpsychism.

100. Now in fact we find in the Latin world of Medieval and, especially, Baroque and Renaissance times, a developed analysis of the Aristotelian *formal cause* which shows that a version of dependency respecting formal arrangement exactly meets the proposed criterion required to explain the action of signs, and does so more fully than does any final cause.

101. The activity or function of an effect, indeed, its very being as effect, is limited by the manner in which it is put together or composed of whatever material it may be that the effect is composed of: the pattern according to which it is and is recognizable as the effect that it is. This is so-called formal causality, the dependency in being of something respecting formal arrangement. This intrinsic dependency upon the pattern or form exhibited in the effect as such is called the *formal cause*. When something is produced, when it has come into existence as something distinctly distinguishable from other factors surrounding it, whether as an individual in its own right or as a change within an existing individual (say, a rotten spot in the wood of a door frame, or a symptom of a malady in an organism), the effect as such exhibits a pattern or formal structure, an "architecture", as it were, according to which it holds together and functions as a distinct effect. When this pattern dissolves, for whatever reason and in whatever way, the effect ceases to be in its own right. The formal cause, thus, in one respect is always embodied in the effect, specifically, as constituting the being of the effect correlative with the material cause. In this respect the formal cause is unlike the final cause, which has no internal correlate constituting the being of the effect, and hence can fail while the effect survives as a physical entity.

102. The Latin analyses emphasized the extrinsicality of the final cause to the effect and the intrinsicality of the formal cause to the effect, because the formal cause together with the material cause constitutes the being of the effect as an entity in its own right,[9] whereas the efficient cause and the final cause alike are extrinsic to that entitative reality in a very important sense: the effect often remains—and hence the formal cause remains operative—when the productive cause ceases and remains when the final cause fails (the effect may fall short of the final state while still existing in its own right).[10] Thus matter and form were considered *principles as well as causes* of natural things, whereas efficient and final factors were considered *causes but not principles*, because their absence left the entity in being as an effect.[11]

103. The fact that the formal cause is always intrinsic to effects in a proper and direct way (is a principle of being and becoming as well as a cause thereof), whereas the final cause is not, is an extremely important point theoretically, because it ties intelligibility to the intrinsic constitution and being of an entity, whether the entity be natural or artifactual. As we will see, for this reason semiotics cannot be confined to the order of culture alone, but, like semiosis itself, constitutes an interface between the two orders.

104. This crucial difference between formal cause as always pertaining to the intrinsic intelligibility of an effect and final cause as not always so pertaining must not prevent us from seeing how the formal cause is yet like the final cause in that, even though the embodiment of the formal cause is itself an intrinsic dependency, formal causality can also be exercised according to an extrinsic, and indeed a nonexistent, source.

105. The first and obvious way in which a formal cause can be extrinsic to an effect, and the way which was principally considered in the history of the discussion of these questions, is found in the case of artifacts: the architect constructs a building out of materials and according to a plan which he has drawn up, and this plan is then embodied in the building, so that it becomes a "Mies van der Rohe building", for example, an instance and illustration of a definite architectural style and school; the artist creates a painting as an expression of something within the artist, or models the work, a statue, say, or a portrait, on something external which the artist nonetheless wishes to represent.

Even when the work is called "non-representative" and so strives to be a mere object with no significant power, as an expression it fails, in spite of itself, to be without significance. Extrinsic formal causality in this first sense came to be called *ideal* or *exemplary causality* among the Latins; but this is clearly not the sense of "ideal causality" that Peirce initially confused with final cause.

106. The Latins recognized, however, a second way in which a formal cause can be extrinsic to its effect. This second type of extrinsic formal causality is much more interesting, and actually much more important for science and philosophy, despite its comparative neglect in the history of these questions. As a matter of fact, historically speaking, it appears that, among the Latins, the variety of formal causality I am here trying to describe received attention thematically only in the context of epistemological questions (the term "epistemology", of course, is a much later coinage[12]), that is to say, in proximately semiotic context, where it received the name of *specifying* or *objective causality*.

107. This is the "causality", that is to say, the dependency in being, that knowledge as such has upon the object known. The object *specifies* the knowledge as being of this rather than of that. "Object", in this sense, of course, means the *subject matter* or *content* of the knowledge: biology as distinct from psychology (or psychology as a subdivision of biology), physics as distinct from chemistry, history as distinct from political science, etc. Peirce was unaware of Poinsot's analyses on this point, both in general and in the specific context of the doctrine of signs.[13] Yet, as I pointed out some years ago (Deely 1985: 493), a close examination of Peirce's texts on his so-called "ideal" causality reveals it to be what is in Poinsot's Latin text extrinsic formal, objective, or specifying causality, particularly as verified in real relations. By the Third and Fifth rules of the "Ethics of Terminology" (Peirce 1903: esp. 2.226),[14] as well as by the Sixth, which proscribes introducing terms which interfere with an existing term (and, we have seen, the Latins had already appropriated the expression "ideal causality" to extrinsic formal exemplary or prototypical causality), the late Latin scholastic name of *objective* or *specifying cause* is the terminology we ought to adopt.

108. Extrinsic formal causality of this second type, that exercised by an objective cause, is far removed from considerations of art or artifact, even though it pertains to such considerations

PART I. SIGNIFICATION 37

insofar as they involve questions of knowledge. Objective causality occurs in nature itself wherever there are instances of relationship—that is to say, it occurs everywhere in nature. The dinosaur, long dead, is present in the fossil bone as its extrinsic specifier, which enables the scientist—paleontologist, in this case—definitely to classify a bone as belonging to a brontosaurus rather than a pterodactyl, etc. Objective causality occurs equally throughout culture, again wherever there is a question of relationships, which (again) is everywhere. The question of "style" is a matter of extrinsic formal causality in the objective sense; deconstruction, as noted in the Gloss 8 on ¶ 96 above—when (as in the best cases) it is more than the willful imposition of a psychological subjectivity upon a text through the selection and construction of devices which transform the targeted text into a vehicle of objectification of a will to power—is an exercise in tracing patterns of extrinsic formal cause relative to a text; detective work is a matter of determining the extrinsic formal patterns which clues provide for the detective (and which patterns, by including this or that sensible element, constitutes a clue—a sign-vehicle—in the first place).

109. The situation is not as difficult to grasp as might at first seem against the background of the abstract discussion of causality according to the various modes of dependency in being. Think simply of an actual conversational situation. The words spoken provide a physical sign-vehicle in the soundwaves which strike the ear as the efficient cause of the nerve reactions in the speaker. The relation of these spoken words to an objective content, conveyed along with the soundwaves but superordinate to them and differentiating them from "mere noises", makes of them linguistic signs rather than "sounds signifying nothing". This objective content gives the discourse its specific form as about this rather than that, and this form of the discourse in turn focusses the attention of the hearer. Here the objective content of the discourse functions as the extrinsic formal cause specifying the listener to attend to this. If the information thus conveyed was "a word of advice" and the hearer heeds the advice in some subsequent action, the objective content of the advice is now functioning for the actor as an exemplary cause, an ideal type or model against which the action is being measured. We see in this way that extrinsic formal causality of both the specifying type and the ideal or exemplificatory type are at work all the time in animal life, and that objective causality as underlying all understanding (and indeed cognition generally) is actually far more fundamental to human culture than the efficient causality which is otherwise a blind force of nature.

110. Because formal causality ties intelligibility to the intrinsic constitution of an entity, whether the entity be natural or artifactual, the objective exercise of this causality in semiosis through the action specifically proper to signs ensures that semiotics cannot be confined to the order of culture alone, but, like semiosis itself, constitutes an interface between the two orders. At this interface, the sign manifests itself not at all as a physical thing, nor even as a peculiar type and variety of object. The sign appears, rather, as the linkage whereby objects, be they bodily entities or purely objective, come to stand one for another within some particular context or web of experience. And semiosis appears as the process whereby phenomena originating anywhere in the universe signify virtually in their present being also their past and their future and begin the further process of *realizing* these virtualities—especially when life intervenes and, within life, when cognition supervenes. The process does not begin with the advent of cognitive organisms, but merely enters a further phase—a new magnitude of thirdness. At the level of anthroposemiosis, semiosis finally reveals itself for what it has been all along, a task that can be accomplished only in community and over the indefinitely long run. Furthermore, in the case of anthroposemiosis, the preservation and generation of culture is future-oriented *beyond* mere biological propagation, a point that completes the grand view of a progression through past-future relations from physiosemiosis to anthroposemiosis. "In other words," to borrow the summation of Santaella Braga (1992: 313), "where there is a sign, there is a temporal process, seeing that the action of the sign is to develop itself in time."

111. Life is more than semiosis, and, conversely, semiosis is more than life. But of the two, semiosis is the more general process, and broader overall. Moreover, when it comes to living beings, the causality proper to signs is so completely interwoven with the fabric of interactions whereby life develops, so delicately maintained in the specification of the other channels of causality that structure that interaction, that to separate it in analysis from vital activity is already an achievement of intellectual abstraction in the scientific sense. Nonetheless, "everything whose being consists in active power to establish connections between different objects . . . is everything which is essentially a Sign—not the mere body of the Sign, which is not essentially such, but, so to speak, the Sign's Soul, which has its Being in its power of serving as intermediary between its Object and a Mind" (Peirce 1908a: 6.455).

112. So it is important to grasp explicitly the fashion in which objective causality can be virtually operative specifically within the channels of the productive, efficient, or dynamic interaction of secondness (and here recall the definition of *dimanation* from Gloss 1). Given that signs themselves consist in triadic relations grounded in some (in principle) sensible, physical vehicle (whence semiosis lies outside the order of productive causality, as we have seen) and that relations as such cannot be acted upon except through their physical ground, Poinsot emphasizes the important distinction between the materially representative element or factor in the sign (normally perceptibly objectifiable), which is the *foundational* principle in the sign or the sign *foundationally considered* (the sign-vehicle, as we have said), and the formally constitutive relation, which is superstructural to this foundation as the *formal* principle in the sign or the sign *formally considered*. The former is Peirce's "Body of the Sign, which is not essentially such", the latter "the Sign's Soul, which has its Being in its power of serving as intermediary". It is then clear that signs are inserted into the dynamical processes of secondness never formally as signs but through their "bodies", i.e., their foundations as sign-vehicles. This makes possible a virtual action of signs within nature even outside the boundaries of an actual experience where semiosis as such is formally at work: "For since the rationale of moving or stimulating [productively] . . . comes about through the sign insofar as it is something representative even if the relation of substitution for the signified does not remain, the sign is able to exercise the functions of substituting without the relation" (Poinsot 1632a: 126/13-18; see Deely 1990: Chapter 6).

113. The actual process has been best clarified by Baer. Citing the proposition (from Deely 1990: 87) that "before there are actually signs, there are signs virtually", Baer comments as follows (1992: 356-357):

> What is the difference? Actual semiosis always involves some sort of cognition in which objects point to other objects and/or things. To be sure, such objects need not be

actually existing things. A sign can signify an upcoming bridge that is no longer there. But what is actual even in inferences of not actually existing things is the inference itself in and through which the semiosic relation is actualized. This is not the case in virtual semioses. Here all we need have is a pattern of knowability, a pattern of potential inferences which at one point or other in time may or may not become actualized. The fossilized bone contains such a pattern. It contains a certain amount of codified information about the Pleistocene deeply buried in the garden, lying there to be discovered or never to be seen at all. When the gardener [ignorant of paleontology] finds it, this virtual semiosis is not actualized. It remains virtual until the appropriate interpretant of the paleontologist actualizes it.

114. With these distinctions in mind, we find in Ransdell (1986: 677) a quite helpful general method for representing the processes of semiosis at work in the universe at large:

Considered dynamically, the representation relation is the basic form—repetitively occurring and overlapping—of a linked process of semiosis without any determinable absolute beginning or end. This can be likened intuitively to a chain interminable in both directions, starting from any given point within it, though conceivable from without as originating in an ultimate ancestral object and as terminating in an ideal final interpretant. That is, one might devise a method of representation of a semiosis process by beginning with such a picture or—as Peirce would say—"icon" of the semiosis process. This would then have to be complicated by taking into account the fact that:
(1) any given "link" in the chain might represent a sign (which, bear in mind, is always also an interpretant) having two or more sign values, which would have to be represented by a corresponding number of branchings at that point;
(2) any two or more given chains might merge into a single chain through an interpretant-sign which is a result of signs in different chains having cooperated conjointly in producing that interpretant (much as premisses conjoin in producing a conclusion);
(3) any two or more given chains might originate ultimately from the same ancestral object (from which any number of chains may emanate); and

(4) the individual "links" in the chain are always potentially analyzable into innumerably many possible sub-links and sub-sub-links (within sub-chains and sub-sub-chains), since a sign is not a "logical atom" but only something which it happens to be intellectually profitable to treat as a unit at a certain point in an analysis, though always analyzable in principle into sub-signs if or when the analytic project should require it, and which may itself be a sub-sign within some more exclusive sign.

Moreover, a sign may be inclusive both of what we would identify as the text and the context, or, on the other hand, it might be more profitable intellectually to retain the distinction between the two in a given analysis.

115. The semiotic web, thus, even through the causality proper to semiosis itself, turns out to be coextensive with the whole of nature and embraces not just the living world (the biosphere) nor even just the realm of cognizing organisms. The so-called physical world exists within the world of experience, but it is not *as* experienced that the physical world is properly called physical: *as* experienced, as we have seen, it is properly called *objective.* Within the objective world two further discriminations experientially impose themselves. A difference emerges among objects of experience between those which are *also* physical existents and those which are *only* objects of experience (although embodied perforce in instruments of social interaction, such as roadways, monuments, legal documents, and the like). A difference also emerges between those objects of experience which have in their own right as objective a physical embodiment and those which have in their own right as objective only the accompaniment of some physical structure or structures through which they are accessible to sensory modalities without being reducible as objectivities to what is thus accessed. The engrained dichotomy between the subjective on the one hand, which is all that is essentially private or illusory, and the objective on the other hand as what is public, real, and independent of the observer, fails when duly weighed and considered in the light of the only instrument we have for discriminating the true (or more sound) from the false (or less sound). A trichotomy is necessary, and a trichotomy of a most peculiar kind. The essential category for the experienced as such is the category of the objective: whatever exists in any way as felt or known. Opposed to the objective in this sense is both the physical in the sense of the things of the environment prejacent to and able as such to survive the demise of experience, and the subjective in the sense of the psychological or psychic depths of the individual insofar as they are not available at the level of public experience (which is a matter of degree, not of kind). In other words, we have a trichotomy where the subject stands at the center of a web of relationships comprising precisely an objective world. Within this world the subject sustaining the web is, through the web, entangled in other networks also subjectively sustained and spun (whether psychically or physically) but objective in what their skeins catch and hold up for scrutiny. Each of the subjects sustaining an objective network is itself already a kind of thing in that it too has as cognizing organism a bodily dimension through which it exists as an element active in the physical environment below and beyond the ways in which the subject experiences that environment and reconstitutes it structurally as an objective world sharable with some others.

116. With this in mind, it will perhaps not be misleading to make our approach as spare and trim as possible, the better to avoid losing stragglers along the path of discussion of the being proper to signs.[15] Following Peirce in this matter (c.1906: 5.474), "I omit all I possibly can; but there is one fact extremely familiar in itself, that needs to be mentioned as being an indispensable point in the argument. It is that every man inhabits two worlds", an Innenwelt, as we say in semiotics today, and an Umwelt.

117. The concept of the Umwelt is an extremely important one for the doctrine of signs. In its original formulation at the hands of the brilliant nineteenth-century biological researcher Jakob von Uexküll, this notion was linked conceptually to the philosophy of mind of Immanuel Kant, in particular to his *Kritik der reinen Vernunft* (1781, 1787), as being not only the dominant work of classical modern philosophy in general and German philosophy in particular, but also the first major work of the philosophical mainstream to seek to provide a systematic account reconciling the notion of necessity in our experience of nature with the construction of phenomena within experience according to species-specific modalities and forms. The environment selectively reconstituted and organized according to the specific needs and interests of the individual organism constitutes an Umwelt. The Umwelt thus depends upon and corresponds to an Innenwelt, or cognitive map, developed within each individual. This map enables that individual to find its way in the environment and to exist as a base station or node within a network of communication, interest, and livelihood sharable especially with the several other individuals of its own kind.

118. Each Umwelt, thus, in its totality, is accessible only to conspecifics. Partially, there is nothing to prevent sufficiently similarly constituted organisms of diverse species from establishing Umwelts that intertwine and overlap at various points. At the extreme, sufficiently dissimilar organisms, while each inhabiting and depending in various ways upon a common physical environment, yet inhabit mutually invisible objective worlds. One organism may destroy another entirely, without at any moment entering into the Umwelt of the organism destroyed: here the interaction between the species would be purely physical and of the nature of brute force, without becoming even for a moment objective. At other times, two species direly opposed in the order of physical being would yet form cathectically opposite objective factors within the other's Umwelt, as is the case where the species are related as predator and prey. At still other times a threatening physical relation may itself become objectified but only on one side, and action might be taken consequently to preserve the threatened species as now part, but a mainly contemplative part, of the other species' Umwelt, as in the case of the snail darters once threatened by a project of the Army Corps of Engineers, or in the case of any endangered species on whose behalf environmental statutes are enacted.

119. The above enumeration of possible ways in which specifically diverse Umwelts intersect and bear upon or are borne upon by physical interaction should be sufficient to make the point that the Umwelts of the many life forms are like so many soap bubbles cascading about on the physical surface of the earth (no doubt, one would think, on many other planets elsewhere as well, though the fact remains to be proved as a matter of direct experience), sustained throughout by a lining of physical being and shared whether within or across specific lines by material (i.e., sense accessible) media, but irreducible to the physical as such and superordinate to it.

120. The concept of Umwelt is notoriously difficult to translate, as is normally true of basic philosophical concepts introduced in whatever language. Because the term is German, the illusion is inevitable that it would be easier to grasp were one a German speaker. This is far from being true. In fact, in my own opinion, being steeped in the German tongue is normally an impediment to the full unfolding of what is proper to this concept, because it exacerbates the entanglement with Kantian idealism (an entanglement ultimately counterproductive for the understanding of the Umwelt as it applies species-specifically to our own life form) and tends to make of the distinction between object and thing a diremption rather than a difference often able partially to coincide experimentally. Indeed, this possibility of coincidence actually realized within experience and indefinitely expandable through the critical control of objectification lies at the heart of science. The partial coincidence of objective structures with structures of physical being within sensation and perception is the zoösemiotic basis and ground for all studies and experimentation properly termed scientific. Through the linguistic framing of this base and the application to it of instruments in critically controlled experiments, the human Umwelt becomes a uniquely malleable one, open to reconstitution along alternative lines of objectification in ways no other Umwelt on this planet is open.

121. Partly for this reason, the notion of primary modeling system introduced into contemporary semiotics by Soviet thinkers ought properly to be identified with the notion of Umwelt rather than with the notion of language. In this view, the primary modeling system is the Umwelt, different for each species, in ways determined first of all by a species' biological constitution, as this channels what and in what ways physical interactions within the trans-specific physical environment become objectified, and to what degree. Language, the aspect of modeling unique to the human species, becomes thus a subordinate or "secondary" modeling system, the instrument whereby—specifically, through verbal markers—the functional cycle through which all other biological forms relate to the physical world by the movement to extinguish the physical stimulus in its objective protrusion into the Umwelt (by fleeing a hostile factor or devouring a sought one) is transcended. In this way language makes possible the consideration of alternatives divorced from the immediate needs of biological interaction, and opening the way to possible worlds different from the actual one of the Umwelt here and now.[16] Such alternatives underlie the perception of "neutral objects", in J. von Uexküll's phrase (1940: 27ff.), which are nonetheless even as such capable of being, as T. von Uexküll notes (1981: 163), sign vehicles for anthroposemiotic enterprises of natural science.

122. As a result, the Umwelt as it is structured by linguistically mediated social interaction becomes freed from over-determination by biological heritage, enabling the formation of what I have called (1982: 111ff., after Morris 1946) the post-linguistic (or "tertiary" modeling) system, the semiotic equivalent of what anthropologists heretofore have termed simply culture—a semiotic system postlinguistic in nature but presupposing language both in order to come into being in the first place and in order to be understood in what is proper to it (see also Deely, Williams, and Kruse 1986: xii-xv). The establishment of government among human groups is a different matter from the social establishment of leadership roles among primates. Monarchy is perhaps the most closely derived form of government based on primate social interaction. But its hereditary aspect is predominantly cultural, just as are the alternatives of popularly determined representation in the many constitutional forms—by no means exhaustive of the possibilities—that have since ancient times, but especially since the French Revolution, come into historical being.

123. The Umwelt is thus a "model world" from the point of view of possibility, one of the infinite variety of possible alternatives according to which the bare physical furnishings of the environment can be arranged and incorporated into an architectural superstructure of possible experiences, supposing especially this or that biological form. But from the point of view of its inhabitants, an Umwelt is the actual world of experience and everyday reality, in comparison to which the prejacent physical in its proper being is secondary, derivative, and not necessarily recognized according to the intrinsic requirements of its own being at all. We think today, for example, generally, that a human Umwelt which incorporates the institution of slavery is a less acceptable species-specific habitat than one which is free of slavery. The "model world" of the twentieth century is sharply different in this regard from the "model world" acceptable to and inhabited by the ancient Greeks, Saint Paul, medieval man, etc. The Umwelt of Sparta differed sharply from that of Athens, and much physical appropriation of physical resources within the shared environment was put to the use of determining which objective model should dominate over or even supplant the other. Rome sought to destroy not the physical lining of the Carthaginian Umwelt so much as the Umwelt itself as sustained by that lining. *Delenda est Carthago.*

124. A change in fashion, a change of age, a major triumph at arms, amounts to a remodeled world.

125. In the human Umwelt, uniquely, one aspect of the social system takes for its cultural aim precisely the objectification—that is, the modeling—of physical aspects of the environment in that exact dimension of their objective being which extends beyond and outside of what is sustained primarily by human experience. This aspect of the socio-cultural system, which we call "hard science" (in distinction from the older use of "scientia" as a generic name for the realm of knowledge in all its objective diversity, including that specific realm which seeks to understand the physical relations among environmental objects according to their properly physical and not merely objective being), precisely tries to model how the world is in those dimensions which we experience exactly as not reducible to our experience of it. The Ptolemaic system can be physically instantiated in a model solar system no less than the Copernican or Newtonian system; and planetaria today with a marvelous complexity model the night sky as we understand it must have been objectively for a conspecific observer 2,000 years past or 2,000 years future—a model objectively different in appearance experienced from either today's sky itself or the model of today's sky projected by those same planetaria. In the microscopic realm, Riordan's story (1987) of the contemporary quantum physics' "hunt for the quark" exhibits quite spectacularly the modeling aspect of science within the human Lebenswelt.

126. The regions of so-called "human sciences" no less clearly exhibit the modeling procedure. Thomas More's *Utopia* and Plato's *Republic* provide alternative models for consideration in further remodeling of the experienced world of human beings, the actual Umwelt. The *Code Napoléon* objectified future experience within the French Empire along lines divergent from those of previous times; and in general legal systems are precisely objective structures seeking to channel how the environment will be experienced by individuals in various present and future circumstances. Jurisdictional boundaries, whether within or between states, similarly are purely objective phenomena which nonetheless constrain and articulate human interaction and impart an inevitable quality, for better or for worse, to the experience of individuals living within or falling subject to those jurisdictions. Contemporary feminism constitutes an objective structure for remodeling human consciousness and experience of biological gender as a prejacent given.

127. This brings up a problem with the term "model" and "modeling system" as a proposed translation or "synonym" for Umwelt. The notion of model often suggests a representation in miniature of something else which is by comparison real. This connotation of the term "model" and "modeling system" applies to the Umwelt only insofar as it harbors virtually scientific theories in the specific sense described, i.e., in the sense that it includes "neutrals" among its objects, or, in the most general terms, insofar as it is anthrposemiotically as well as zoösemiotically constituted. The "model world" of the dragonfly is not primarily a representation of something else more real by comparison. To the extent that world contains—inevitably as Jacob points out (1982: 56)—elements representing as such physical aspects of the dragonfly's surroundings, these elements are not more real than the Umwelt itself, but considerably less real, and derive their interest, moreover, specifically from their place in the larger objective whole which precisely does not at all points correspond objectively to physical elements in the surroundings. In this respect, the Umwelt of the dragonfly is not a model world, it is the real world, wherein the dragonfly lives and moves and has its being.

128. What has just been said of the dragonfly Umwelt holds as a general point. Only from an external point of view can we speak of an Umwelt in its totality—as distinct from the scientific enterprise subspecific to the human Umwelt—as a "modeling system". From within any given Umwelt, that Umwelt is the reality for the specific individual. It is not a model world, it is the objective world of experience, with respect to which physical being comprises only a part which may or may not be modeled in what is proper to it by any given construct of understanding. The notion of reality and the notion of the Umwelt are, from the point of view of experience, thus inseparable. What is distinctive about experience within the human Umwelt is, quite precisely, the notion that Umwelt and reality are yet not coextensive.

From this bare suspicion of the understanding in its difference from sense arises, as I have tried to indicate elsewhere (Deely 1982), on the one hand, the whole enterprise of science and technology, and, on the other hand, morality as distinct from mores.

129. We see then what is required of the sign: it needs to be a means of establishing connections, and not in any bare physical sense: experience is not needed for smoke to be an effect of fire, but it is needed if smoke is to become a sign of fire (an extremely important point: see Poinsot 1632a: 137 note 4, and ¶ 69 above). The sign in its proper being requires an understanding of how there can be connections established in an objective sense which yet does not preclude incorporating whatever of the physical as such may happen to be objectified within the larger totality of the species-specific lifeworld. It is here that the doctrine of signs departs from the dogma of Kantian criticism and dictates in the process of appropriating semiotically the Uexküllian notion of Umwelt some remodeling of the very notion from within.[17] We need to know how the sign functions so as to enable the merely physically existent—both the others than the subject knowing, and the knowing subject as well in its organismic dimension as also a bodily element of the physical surroundings and in its psychical subjectivity—to become also partly objective. We need further to know how, once become, the objective throughout is itself further and further diversified internally by one object standing or coming to stand for and convey another in a continuing semiosis that incorporates into and sustains within its objectivity at each moment elements of the physical surroundings both as lining for experience and as objective elements contributing to the diversity of experience—especially at those points where the objective reveals itself as resistant to the actions of the cognizing organism. Each pure object, already given through signs, dissolves more or less quickly into a cascade of signs.

130. The problem of the sign, therefore, is, fundamentally, the problem of the common source of all Umwelts, the emergence of objectivity *in its difference realized* from the physical environment as such. There are forms of semiosis, to be sure, already at work in physical nature itself anterior to the advent of anything living and independent of it.[18] But only with the Umwelt do we encounter in its full actuality—that is, as transcending, not just virtually (as in the laws of physics and chemistry) but actually, the dynamics of physical interaction—the first phenomenon of semiosis, the explicit realization of the function essential to the sign: aliquid stans pro aliquo. An environmental factor existing prior to and independent of the cognizing organism is now additionally present in some or other of its aspects to the organism as an object apprehended. As apprehended, it is no longer a thing only, but a thing become object. As thing merely, it existed ex hypothesi in its own right independently of being cognized; as object also, it exists only for the cognizing organism and is precisely dependent thereon. Fairly immediate is the abductive inference to an intraorganismic factor on the basis of which the thing exists here and now in apprehended relation to (i.e., as object for) the organism apprehending it. This factor, a percept, say, is not the object apprehended[19]—still less the thing anteriorly existing. Neither is it the relation between organism and environmental aspect or thing. It is solely and only the foundation or basis, the ground upon which the relation in question supervenes. The percept functions to relate organism (one kind of thing at the environmental level) with object (another kind of thing at the environmental level) not in the manner of brute force and secondness, but in the manner of semiosis, precisely by making present in awareness something that it itself is not.

131. This point is among the most fundamental points to be made in the doctrine of signs, and possibly the single point least understood: there is no object which does not depend in its objectivity on the simultaneous action of the sign as making present in experience something other than itself, something that it itself is not. Beneath every object presented as this or that—friendly or hostile, familiar or novel, puzzling or plain—stands a sign (more normally, a complex of signs); and within every object stands an indefinite series of further signs. The object, in its turn, as experienced, inevitably links up also with other objects, as like or unlike them in various ways, as suggesting also this or that, so that, among the objects experienced, there arise further series of relations of "standing for" without end (the "unlimited semiosis" of Eco), but always presupposing what does not appear (it is objects that "appear"), namely, the sign in its proper being as the triadic relation whereby objects integrally exist as such—the relation constitutive of experience as such—in the first place:

> The rationale of an object formally and directly respects or is respected by the cognitive power of an organism in such

a way that the respect between the two is immediate; but the rationale of a sign directly respects a signified and a power indirectly, because it respects the thing signified as that which is to be manifested to a cognitive power. Therefore there is a different line and order of respecting in an object inasmuch as it is an object, and in a sign inasmuch as it is a sign, *although for it to be a sign, an object must be presupposed* [Poinsot 1632a:136/49-137/7, emphasis added; see also Gloss 15 on ¶ 116 above].

132. This fact, that every sign in its proper being consists as such in a relationship for which an object is presupposed, explains how the sign relation (the relationship constitutive of a sign as such) differs from a bare physical relationship, which presupposes simply two things, not a thing and an object. This fact further explains why the sign as such is not something that directly appears in experience—why a sign as such is never a thing on the one hand or an object simply on the other. It is never an object simply, for an object simply represents itself within awareness, while a sign simply makes something other than itself present in awareness. Hence an object need not be a sign in some given respect, and, when it is also a sign, it is so only in the respect that it stands for some other object. If the object in question happens to have within the experience where it exists as object also as such a body or embodiment proper to itself, such that, pointing—a sign-vehicle—to this body, we say "There is a sign" (as happens, for example, with billboards, or with the red octagons we employ for regulating traffic flow, or with the notices posted along highways, etc.), what we are pointing to is the sign fundamentally, whereas formally the sign is not that to which we are pointing but that for which that to which we are pointing stands. The sign as such consists in the relation between the two, the *renvoi* of the one to the other. Dines Johansen, who has worked explicitly to incorporate literary semiotics within the major tradition, makes this point quite clear (1985: 231): "The sign as an existent material entity (called the sign-vehicle by Morris [1971: 96]) only makes sense if it is related to other elements in the signifying process: semiosis."

133. Every relation consists in a connection or linkage between two or more, be they things or objects. The relation is neither the one nor the other, but precisely the connection between, grounded or founded, to be sure, in some aspect or characteristic of the one and terminating at or respecting some aspect or characteristic of the other (in which the "phenomenal being" of the object will principally consist when it is a question of physical elements objectified). The one or the other may be accessible to sense, but the connection as such taken in abstraction from both is something that cannot be perceived, it can only be understood. The consequence of this has been best expressed in a work by Maritain (1957: 52-54). On the one hand, animals other than humans make use of signs, but they do not know that there are signs. On the other hand, the birth of language consists in the grasp of the relation of signification as such, that is, as distinct from the sign vehicle or sensible embodiment of the sign as ground of semiosis, and as distinct from the object signified (whether present in or absent from the physical world), and as distinct also from the exaptation of language into speech for communicative ends. For "what defines language is not precisely the use of words, or even of conventional signs; it is the use of any sign whatsoever as involving the knowledge or awareness of the relation of signification"—in which formally and strictly, as distinct from fundamentally and perceptually, the sign as such consists in its proper being—"and therefore a potential infinity; it is the use of signs in so far as it manifests that the mind has grasped and brought out the relation of signification". This feat opens the possibility of a text.

Part II. Textuality

What exactly is textuality? Texts are strings of signs that are in principle exchangeable (substitutable) with other signs in accordance with a given code. Texts are thus translatable and transformable from one set of objects to another, precisely because their "being" resides not in things or objects, but "in-between" them. Hence the concept of textuality entails that any object can be "used" to actualize the relation of signification.

. . . what is commonly called "culture" is an umbrella term for texts precisely in this sense of the stipulable sign. Texts conventionalize the objective world as naturally determined and insert into the natural order a degree of freedom, impressively demonstrated by a great variety of cultural, including literary, codes.

—Baer 1992: 355-356—

134. Once the relation of signification has been grasped on its own as distinct from a particular object signifying a particular object signified, it becomes possible, theoretically, to understand that ideas or concepts, as including percepts and "mental images", are themselves signs. And, as an independent practical matter, it becomes possible to detach a sign relation from any particular objective sign vehicle and to attach it instead to some other object which will now serve, by choice, in lieu of the original vessel—i.e., which will now serve as ground for a relation originally grounded elsewhere. With the awareness enabling such a choice, a new kind of sign and a new mode of signifying comes into existence objectively, the *stipulable*[20] sign, of which what we call "linguistic signs" are a specific variety.

135. Such signs are arbitrary in their prospective ground. But they consist in relationships no less than, and precisely as do, social signs embodying connections which are physical before becoming also objective and social (such as the connections between clouds and rain or smoke and fire), or connections which are objective associatively rather than physically (such as the connections between candlelight and lovers, napkins and meals), or manipulative (such as pressing a lever and receiving a pellet of food) rather than stipulative. By reason of this unified and unifying rationale, even arbitrarily grounded signs, if they are experienced in their signifying (i.e., grasped correlative to their significates at the same time that they are being perceived as objects through this or that sensory channel or combination of channels), they are experienced as natural, on a par with any other object significatively apprehended.

136. The ability to grasp such signs, we may say, is what is meant by the linguistic understanding of signs. For to grasp such signs—i.e., to experience their proper correlation with a signified despite their ground as incidental simultaneously to, *first*, the physical composition of the signified (which need by no means but may be, as we have noted, an incorporeal being, purely objective, like an archangel or the square root of a negative number), *second*, the physical composition of the sign-vehicle, and *third*, the physical composition (i.e., the biological heritage) of the apprehendor—is just what is meant by "intelligence" in the species-specific sense of linguistic competence. Intelligence as linguistic competence is that particular "subspecies of semiotic competence" overlaying the biological species-specific competence with a developmental and historical dimension and introducing into the objective world of the species the permeating element of textuality.

137. Using (along with conceptual premises which are pre-zoösemiotic) the older terminology of images and ideas—meaning by the former an intraorganismic factor grounding a relation between an organism and an object of its experience regardless of the animal species to which that organism belongs (i.e., including human animals), and by the latter an intraorganismic factor grounding a relation between a human organism as such and an object of its experience—Maritain attempted thus to describe the situation (1957: 53):

> Normally in the development of a child it is necessary that the idea be "enacted" by the senses and lived through before it is born as an idea; it is necessary that the relationship of signification should first be actively *exercised* in a gesture, a cry, in a sensory sign bound up with the desire that is to be expressed. *Knowing* this relationship of signification will come later, and this will be to have the *idea*, even if it is merely implicit, of that which is signified. Animals and children make use of this signification; they do not perceive it. When the child begins to perceive it (then exploits it, toys with it, even in the absence of the real need to which it corresponds)—at that moment the idea has emerged.

138. But this description fails in its purpose, unless it is *further* made clear that the detachment of the relationship from the related elements is achieved in such a way that the relation in its proper being as imperceptible can be made a foundation or basis which, as such—that is, *as* imperceptible—is able *further* to serve to stand for and represent some *other* relationship yet again. (Whether that other relationship terminate at an object which is *also* imperceptible in turn is not what matters, although such a case does emphasize what is distinctive to the semiosis in question, namely, its transcendence of being limited to purely perceptual modalities and consequent capacity for processing to infinity.) It is at this moment that the "perhaps metaphysical sense" ascribed by Sebeok to semiosis as unlimited (1991: 82) is realized in anthroposemiosis (cf. Poinsot 1632a: First Preamble, Art. 2, esp. 60/7-62/18, and Art. 3, 68/35-72-17). For a dog, for example, wanting to be let out, can indeed learn to fake the need to evacuate as a way of manipulating its master "even in the absence of the real need to which it corresponds" (cf. ibid.: First Preamble, Art. 3, 66/46-67/34): and yet, at that moment, an idea in the sense in question—the anthroposemiotic sense—has not emerged, no matter how playful the dog may become in its efforts.

139. At the heart of the difference between the human Umwelt and the Umwelt of other animals lies the "idea" in this specifically semiotic sense of the relationship itself constituting signification, grasped according to the being relation has as distinguishable both from a given signified and from a given sign-vehicle, and therefore as detachable from any given vehicle and attachable to any other vehicle, and as directable to some other object as well, or to the same object only, in its new attachment. This difference makes for the possibility of a text as such, with the result that only in the human Umwelt do texts exist actually, as also language in the abstract sense of the model of a system of objective relations exaptable for communication "positing an indifferent sender and receiver" (Bourdieu 1977: 25).[21]

140. Texts exist not, of course, as objects experienced in a primarily physical dimension (the dog can see the contents of the bookshelf as well as I). They exist rather as objects experienced in what is proper to them as a network of relations originated in, even when for the purpose of controlling, the objectivity experienced by an animal which, besides perceiving—say—marks on paper or carvings in stone, grasps their relation to objects not on the paper nor in the stone physically but nonetheless signified and conveyed by those marks according to a convention or *code* which makes of them signs. The code transforms the otherwise merely physical manifestations into the foundation for a complexus of relations to a corresponding objective structure understandable but not perceptible in the marks or carvings as physical objects given in perception.

141. We see, then, that texts are not only literary. They can be any physical structure at all made objectively to embody ideas in the semiotic sense. What makes a text of a perceptible physical structure is the fact of its grounding a relationship or network of relationships as terminating in an objective structure whose contours are controlled by the difference between signs whose relation to what they signify is reducible to associations among perceptible objects as such and signs whose relation to what they signify, over and above associations among perceptible objects, is grounded in the codes of an apprehension socialized through free play among objects-understood-in-their-detachability from the specific perceptible means whereby they—the objects in question—are brought into experience in the first place or in any given case.

142. The whole of culture, in this radical sense (cf. Danow 1987, 1991), is a text, a network of signs whose lattice of articulations is chosen at critical nodes, though not at all nodes (which would be impossible, an outer limit of the intelligible, pushed, for example, in Joyce's *Finnegans Wake*). These critical nodes are chosen differently and to different degrees in individual cases, with the effect that they are also, as chosen, gradually expanded (and sometimes even detached) from the initial choices over their course of becoming *naturalized* through the habit-patterns of a community as "conventions" in the strong sense of "the way we do things here". The network exhibits a hierarchical or quasi-hierarchical structure relative to the physical side of the objects experienced within its frame.

143. Thus, a technological artifact embodies critically controlled relativities no less than does an artistic or a literary creation, and all three would serve as documentary evidence to some future anthropologist or to an extraterrestrial seeking to understand, by a "reconstruction", the contemporary human objective world, our Umwelt. But the objective relations embodied in the technological device directly relate also to its physical constitution as such in order for it to function as an instrument, whereas the objective relations embodied in an artistic structure dominate the physical constitution of the whole in quite another fashion. Finally, the objective relations constitutive of the literary work tend to be a variable relatively free respecting their embodiment, i.e., their sensorially accessible base. This is why the written word tends to function as the primary analogate for our understanding of text. Here the relation of signification is exhibited not only as subject to critical control but in the cultural form most subject to critical control (the linguistic form) compatible with permanence in the exhibition (the written in contrast to the spoken word).

144. Powell, in seeking to explain the freely chosen dimension of reality whereby the objects of human experience become textual as well as natural in their totality, resorts to the improbable language of "real and unreal relations" as being equivalent in the sign. This equivalence, of course, being the very being proper to signs as such, is as true of signs in the Umwelts of animals other than the human as it is true of linguistic and postlinguistic signs in the human Umwelt. But the point which Powell makes is that it is the making of *this difference itself* between "real" and "unreal" an object of experience that distinguishes the human case, that makes of the objective world in its totality, as including nature through experience, a "text". Thus, for example, signs can signify indifferently what is present and what is absent, what is physically existent now and what is no longer so existent, what exists in nature and what does not or did never exist, what could exist physically and what could never so exist, and so on. This indifference of the sign as such, derivative from its rationale as formally relative, explains precisely why, for all species, the objective world is not the same as, and is divided up differently from, the physical environment, even though something of the physical environment as such is incorporated into the structure of the Umwelt.

145. But to create a text is to become aware of the difference between physical surroundings and objective world and to play with that difference, thereby erecting perforce a system of signs expressly in consciousness of the difference and enhancive of it. To create a text is to come to understand that "the role of the object in the semiosis is", as Johansen puts it (1985: 235), "not confined to being an element in an experiential situation interpreted to tell if a symbol applies or not".[22] Accordingly, to create a text is to proceed in the use of signs freely to structure objectivity in a contour and manner accessible only to a conspecific in the precise sense of another organism able to share understanding of the contrast between objective being and physical surroundings (between "unreal" and "real") and to grasp signs fashioned on its basis, that is, encoded according to patterns neither reducible to nor accessible within the perceptible dimension, the physical being, of the sign structure as such. Text creation is a function of musement, for the understanding of which function two terms must be clarified: code and idea.

146. The need for the clarification is well exhibited in Peirce's quasi-description (1904a: 251) of the situation of the first human animals begotten of ancestors jointly or separately capable only of perceptual apprehension (parents, in our terms, restricted to an Umwelt in its difference from objectivity textualized): "The real universe began in many individual minds, strangers to one another, but gradually becomes the common thought of the whole community". Whether regarded from the point of view of belief or strictly of language,[23] the notion of reality itself is already an instance of what Corrington has felicitously termed "semiotic convergence" (1987: 48), the primary *phaenomenon explanandum* of the present case.[24]

147. How, then, does semiotic convergence around the notion of reality become possible in the first place? Notice two points. This notion in its bottom line consists of an experiential content: the contrast given in secondness between what does and what does not reduce to my experience of it, the precipitation within experience of "things" as objects in their contrast with the purely objective as a thirdness grounded in dynamic interactions. Second, there is no place in the initial anthropological moment for interpreting speech from the side of language (cf. Bally 1965; Bourdieu 1972). The "model of all possible routes" with which one anthropos confronts another in order to "point out" the objectification of reality is nothing more nor less than the individual Innenwelt as, *ex hypothesi*, lacking at this moment *any* possible route given in advance (any avenue of exchange in accordance with which the Umwelt has already been exapted to communicate the difference of the environmental factors of physical being as such objectified within an Umwelt from the Umwelt itself as such—as an objective world with a structure of relations that incorporates environmental relations without consisting of them exclusively and without being hence merely "a world of things").

148. It may seem at first glance that what we are calling for here is no different than Bourdieu's aim (1972: 3-4) "to make possible a science of the *dialectical* relations between the objective structures to which the objectivist mode of knowledge gives access and the structural dispositions within which those structures are actualized and which tend to reproduce them," to carry out "a new reversal of the problematic which objectivism has to construct in order to constitute the social world as a system of objective relations independent of individual consciousness and wills".

149. In fact, our problematic here is just the opposite, and more fundamental. Bourdieu's critique of Saussure (1977: 25) on the ground that his standpoint is forced "to neglect the functional properties the message derives from its *use* in a determinate situation and, more precisely, in a socially structured interaction" would be quite out of place here. To begin with, in the original anthroposemiosic moment or moments we have hypothesized, *la langue* as a communicative exaptation of the anthropic *Innenwelt* has yet to be achieved. But, more fundamentally, the question here to be faced concerns what it is about the structure of objectivity itself that makes possible such an exaptation in the first place, *only after and supposing the success of which* is there so much as a horizon against which Bourdieu's complaints might be envisaged.

150. The practical functions to which signs are anthropically put, indeed, "are never reducible to functions of communication or knowledge", as Bourdieu rightly says (1977: 24). But neither are these functions of communication or knowledge simply identical with the practical functions. The fact of a symbiosis hardly privileges the practical over the communicative or displaces the theoretical. On the contrary, in the case of human practice, what makes of it anthropic and not merely one other variety of pure zoösemiosis is precisely the fact that it occurs in a context of a communcative *moyen* which conveys always tacitly and often expressly the residue of an objectivity which is not only itself. This is why, exactly as Baer said (1979: 173), from the standpoint of community and inquiry, "a thing cannot ever appear at all except insofar as it appears within *some* kind of story", which is to say, within an anthroposemiosis in its difference realized from zoösemiosis.

151. The "sacred remains", to borrow Parmentier's expression (1987), are what is left over in experience from the experience of it; they are the reason, in Baer's formula (1977), that "things are stories", and are the beginning of morality as well as science, mythology as well as history—in a word, of all that will emerge in anthroposemiosis as "distinctively human" in the transcendence of zoösemiotic modalities, *especially* communicative ones. The purpose is not "to grasp the function of these historicizing signs in particular contexts of social action" (Parmentier 1987: 305) but to see how a historicizing sign is possible *on the side of the sign* and as a result of *its* structure. It is a question neither of social practice nor "objectivism" as a practice of science (a "theoretical" practice) but of objectivity in its proper being. It is a question of how the Umwelt becomes from within differentiated in an anthroposemiotic way, not in general, but specifically so as to reveal and constitute language in its species-specific uniqueness, whence are enabled the postlinguistic structures whose virtualities transform the social order of human animals, again from within, into a cultural world—a text which includes in its textuality whatever there is of nature as well woven into the fabric of anthropic experience, the ground of many worlds and the common measure of every world so far as it can be taken in discourse. Like every animal, the human animal wakes up in an Umwelt first of all.

152. Every Umwelt is, as such, conspecifically shared. The problem, therefore, is how a universe, begun as an idea in an individual mind, comes to be a universe common to other individuals as well. How ideas might be private is not the problem. The problem is how are objects known on the basis of private ideas (ideas as subjective modifications of the individual psyche) rendered common to the experience of individuals in whom the ideas did not originate, in particular that singular (and singularly opaque) notion or "object", the anthroposemiotically unique objectification elusively termed "reality".

153. When the term "ideas" is defined semiotically—that is, as the individual discovery of relation as such as the connection and difference between sign and signified—the question becomes: how is such a discovery shared? How is a relation of signification, seen for itself as detachable from this sign-vehicle and attachable rather to that one, communicated in its difference? That is the question to which the term "code" is proposed as answer. In other words, *"idea" is to Innenwelt as code is to Umwelt as species-specifically* (and regardless of planetary location) *human*. To understand what a text is, and to understand the human lifeworld in what is specific to it, are the same.

154. The human Umwelt, like every Umwelt, is a biological sphere of life. But the human Umwelt, unlike every other Umwelt, is a biological sphere of life capable of recognizing and incorporating into itself physical objectivities without having to move toward extinguishing—from the standpoint of experience—their environmental source.[25] This is the meaning of "intelligent life" in the sense that radio astronomers earnestly search for among the physical stimuli rendered objective by their remarkable (if no doubt remarkably primitive) instruments. It is improbable that such a lifeworld, a radically flexible and open Lebenswelt such as Husserl showed at the base of the sciences and the humanities, in contrast with the *Umwelts* at best partially flexible and finally encapsulated wholes of other species, has evolved only once and at one place in the physical totality of the prejacent surroundings. Be that as it may, it is from within the Umwelt of such a species, a species able to mark for subsequent contemplation physically objective protrusions into its sphere, that the understanding of the sign, in contrast to its bare use, must begin. In other words, the understanding of semiosis begins inevitably from within human experience, which is to say, as a moment of anthroposemiosis.

155. From this point of view, thoroughly experiential, and therefore liable to some success in sorting out the true and false, the totality of the Umwelt is experienced, precisely as we have pointed out, as objectively (though far from "clearly and distinctly") divided between two rather different sorts of objective beings. Peirce describes the experimental point of departure within anthroposemiosis for a doctrine (as distinct from an employment) of signs thus (c.1906: 5.487, original emphases):

> Every sane person lives in a double world, the outer and the inner world, the world of percepts [see the discussion of percept in Gloss 19] and the world of fancies. What chiefly keeps these from being mixed up together is (besides certain marks they bear) everybody's well knowing that fancies can be greatly modified by a certain non-muscular effort, while it is muscular effort alone . . . that can to any noticeable degree modify percepts. A man can be durably affected by his percepts and by his fancies. The way in which they affect him will be apt to depend upon his personal inborn disposition and his habits. Habits differ from dispositions in having been acquired as consequences of the principle . . . that multiple reiterated behaviour of the same kind, under similar combinations of percepts and fancies, produces a tendency—the *habit*—actually to behave in a similar way under similar circumstances in the future. Moreover—*here is the point*—every man exercises more or less control over himself by means of modifying his own habits; and the way in which he goes to work to bring this effect about in those cases in which circumstances will not permit him to practice reiterations of the desired kind of conduct in the outer world shows that he is virtually well-acquainted with the important principle that *reiterations in the inner world—fancied reiterations—if well-intensified by direct effort, produce habits*, just as do reiterations in the outer world; *and these habits will have power to influence actual behaviour in the outer world*; especially, if each reiteration be accompanied by a peculiar strong effort that is usually likened to issuing a command to one's future self.

156. The difference between an Innenwelt able to engender an Umwelt which makes for an objective reality imposing itself without question (a truly "given"—wherein it is not a question of "belief", that is, one way or another) and an Innenwelt able to engender an Umwelt which makes for an objective reality which is in some measure a "freely chosen reality", as Powell puts it (1983), is the difference between an Umwelt in which beliefs function without question and an Umwelt where beliefs precisely can be questioned and, as a result, modified. In other words, texts presuppose the species-specific difference between a model world which is what it is in the course of experience because of its provenance from and attachment to a biological heritage as such (and so can evolve only in a quasi-Darwinian fashion), and a model world which is what it is not only because of such provenance and attachment but also as the result of the secondary modular *detachment* of objectivity in its proper being through the introduction of arbitrary signifiers (stipulated signs). The consequent florescence of linguistic and postlinguistic objective structures is what is commonly referred to as "culture" (and is transmissible by quasi-Lamarckian means, the habits which grow up around stipulated signs as conventions, in contrast with habits reducible only to associations between sense-accessible objects experienced as such).

157. The perceptions of an animal which learns through experience alone vis-à-vis the beliefs of a human animal as subject to rational criticism as well are the key to textuality as the species-specific human form of objectivity. We distinguish among "fancies" the two distinct iconic forms of *images*, derivable from and reducible to a correlation between objects sensorially accessible as such given a specific biological endowment, and *conceptions or ideas*, which express relations of signification in the being proper to them as relations, that is, as indifferent to their subjective ground and consequently detachable *from* any given sign-vehicle as object for attachment *to* an objective ground elsewhere and otherwise.

158. Ideas in this sense, conceptions *within* perceptions of the world, are unique to and species-specifically definitive of anthroposemiosis. But in order to establish the basis for *shared* conceptions, these ideas must be embodied in a publicly accessible objective structure, which is not the case as long as their only embodiment is the cerebral cortex of the individual for whom a given idea has taken form (Peirce 1901: 2.303):

If, an interpretant idea having been determined in an individual consciousness, it determines no outward sign, but that consciousness becomes annihilated, or otherwise loses all memory of other significant effect of the sign, it becomes absolutely undiscoverable that there ever was such an idea in that consciousness; and in that case it is difficult to see how it could have any meaning to say that that consciousness ever had the idea, since the saying so would be an interpretant of that idea.

A given objective relation, seen in its detachability, must not only be detached but *attached elsewhere*: it must be *assigned* a new ground in such a way that that new ground can in turn be experienced as a sign-vehicle relative to the objectivity originally grasped elsewhere. The code is the correlation and proportioning of a sensibly accessible element to an objectivity which is *understood* as correlated thereto. For the code to be established, an idea must be correlated with some physical element within experience taken to serve as ground for the relation in which the idea expressly consists. That correlation is what constitutes a *code* in its difference from an idea.

159. Code and idea alike are logical interpretants, but the logical interpretant considered now on the side of Innenwelt (idea), now on the side of Umwelt (code). A code thus channels and directs relations among objects in a publicly accessible way. A mastery of the encoding will result in a partial duplication (a sufficient overlap, we might say) within the decoder of the ideas behind the original encoding, imposing thereby a *common conception* (an *intersubjective moment*) within and beyond the perceptually shared objectivity. In this way, an idea arising in one mind engenders an objective relation that can be detached from its subjective ground and correlated with some objective sensible to serve as vehicle for conveying another mind to an awareness itself engendering in turn, under the stimulus of the objective correlate (i.e., through the specifying influence of an extrinsic formal causality), a conception of what arose in the other.

160. The Umwelt, in itself perceptual through and through according to the species-specific constraints of a biological inheritance, is now modified and restructured from within by further objective relations not themselves constrained directly by the biological heritage. As a result, the Umwelt is *experienced differently* from how it had been prior to the intervention of the arbitrary sign (the stipul*able* sign) understood in its encoded reality as objective (the stipul*ated* sign).

161. Eco rightly insists (1977: 38, original emphases) that "we must make a distinction between the elements of a *system* bound by reciprocal relationships and the *correlation* which one can apply to the elements of this system and the elements of another system. *Only this correlation has the right to be called code*". But as far as the code constitutive of textuality in our sense is concerned, i.e., as far as it is a question of stipulable signs in their proper being as anthroposemiotic phenomena, it is not enough to establish reversibility operations (ibid. 40). One must also distinguish further between the reversibility that might be established associatively between the percept apple and the mark or sound apple, on the one hand, and the reversibility that can only be established stipulatively between an object in principle imperceptible and the mark or sound conveying that object in its precisely imperceptible being. Only this latter sort of reversible association pertains to code in our sense, *even when it is a question of objects not in principle imperceptible*. Thus the stipulable link between apple and apple, rather than the perceptual link, is at the heart of anthroposemiotic coding, in its distinction from possible notions of zoösemiotic code (cf. Deely 1982: Part II and Appendix II).

162. Code, on this analysis, belongs to the object experienced, idea to the organism experiencing. Both alike serve to ground, channel, and define or specify the relationships of dependency that comprise the objective world in its integral being subsumptive of the physical, but from quite different vantages. "In all general inquiries about signs", Peirce observes (1907: 9), "nothing is of more lively importance than maintaining a clear and sharp distinction between the object, or proposed cause of the sign, and the meaning, or intended effect". He continues: "experiences seem to me to be rather the object of a conception than its meaning, for they are too external to the mind to be meanings". Hjelmslev's remarks apropos of naive realism pertain here (1961: 22-23):

> Naive realism would probably suppose that analysis consisted merely in dividing a given object into parts, i.e., into other objects, then those again into parts, i.e., into still other

objects, and so on. But even naive realism would be faced with the choice between several possible ways of dividing. It soon becomes apparent that the important thing is not the division of an object into parts, but the conduct of the analysis so that it conforms to the mutual dependences between these parts, and permits us to give an adequate account of them. In this way alone the analysis becomes adequate and, from the point of view of a metaphysical theory of knowledge, can be said to reflect the "nature" of the object and its parts.

When we draw the full consequences from this, we reach a conclusion which is most important for an understanding of the principle of analysis: both the object under examination and its parts have existence only by virtue of these dependences; the whole of the object under examination can be defined only by their sum total; and each of its parts can be defined only by the dependences joining it to the other coordinated parts, to the whole, and to its parts of the next degree, and by the sum of the dependences that these parts of the next degree contract with each other. After we have recognized this, the "objects" of naive realism are, from our point of view, nothing but intersections of bundles of such dependences. That is to say, objects can be described only with their help and can be defined and grasped scientifically only in this way. The dependences, which naive realism regards as secondary, presupposing the objects, become from this point of view primary, presupposed by their intersections.

163. Semiosis, in the fullest sense of the action of signs, extends, as we have noted in passing, well beyond the boundaries of culture, as also well beyond the boundaries of animal societies to include the dynamics of plant life and even the dynamics of chemistry and physics down to the quantum level insofar as there is a question of *future outcomes* and *law governed interaction*—in other words, thirdness. Our concentration has been on the explicit absorption and redistribution of elements of physical environment within the relational network of objective world through cognitively mediated experience—the construction of species-specific Umwelts corresponding to Innenwelts—for the purpose of providing the proximate genus in contrast to which the specific difference of a human world might become visible. That difference, we now see, is textuality: in the precise sense of the introduction through understanding of relations into the objective world which are not grounded in the perceptible elements as such of that Umwelt as correlated with a species-specific biological heritage. These relations alter the objectivity itself experienced and add to that experience the element of critical control. This is not control in the bare sense of something modified or modifiable through the muscular effort and plan of the organism, such as, for example, the beaver contemplating a mountain stream before and after building its dam, but control in the rich sense of a musement recognizing the possible in its objective being as distinct from the whole order of physical elements as such.

164. The exaptation of the human modeling system (let us say, language in the ground sense) through speech into a communication system is, therefore, only one aspect of textuality, specifically, that aspect wherein the communicative intention finds an embodiment distinct from the other purposes which enter in perforce when action is directed beyond language to the establishment of the postlinguistic structures of civil organization, shelter, trade, clothing, etc. These other systems, too, depend on the stipulable (the "conventional") sign in the fullest sense of the embodiment of the relation of signification grasped in itself, as distinct from any given subjective ground. But they are required to take account of their material embodiment as objects created to perform more than a communicative function (in the case of a house, for example, to withstand the elements; in the case of a machine, to work reliably; and so on), whereas the language as exapted to communicate through embodiment in a system of sense-perceptible elements needs to take no more account of the bodily form than is minimally necessary to the one function in its purity. For this one function, no more is needed than to carry the code, according to which the relations constituted by ideas in their anthroposemiotic difference from zoösemiotic images have been transferred from the Innenwelt to the Umwelt as determinative of the experience of others able to grasp the code precisely in its conventional being (its situation of being incidental to the sensible constitution of its immediate ground, its "arbitrariness" in happening to be this way from customs dimanated by stipulations). Thus the animals other than humans perceive the difference between the general's uniform and that of the private. But only the human animals have a chance to understand the difference not in its material effects (for the animals too experience social power relations) but in its formal constitutive (which is first of all cultural and only derivatively social).

165. In this sense we can agree with Barthes that "every semiological system has its linguistic admixture" (1964: 10; cf. Culler 1982: 21). At the same time, our point is more basic: *every linguistic system has its semiological surplus.* The language is not only not an autonomous system, still less "a semiotic into which all other semiotics may be translated" (Hjelmslev 1961: 109). The structural peculiarity of language is not unlimited in that sense, but in the sense of being able to draw all other semiotics (and semiosis) into the trajectory of the communicative intention freed from a species-specific *biological* inheritance. The "linguistic admixture", far from providing the foundation of all other semiotics, pertains rather to their surplus and perfection in community, a diaphanous medium and network of relations through which the objective world receives a texture of intelligence. By this texture the context of nature itself, and biosemiosis in particular, is enhanced and transformed according to objective possibilities not prefigured as such in the biological heritage of the species. These possibilities are, rather, opened up through the Lamarckian means of convention transmissible through the praeterphysical means of correlating codes embodied in physical elements reworked with understanding, including especially the physical elements of linguistic communication. Physical elements exapted to this capacity achieve a semiotic preeminence in the objective world as Lebenswelt by virtue of being independent of any specific purpose in order to be, in the context of communication, at the service of every other purpose. Language as a communication system—as a publicly available coding of the Umwelt—is the objective reflection of the freedom of the intellect as a growth in time.[26]

166. But the coding of the Umwelt is hardly restricted to linguistic coding. According to our anthroposemiotic definition of ideas, the coding of the anthroposemiotic Umwelt—its transformation into a Lebenswelt—is the *accumulation* of marks made by intelligence on the objective world *in whatever respect, and whether deliberately or as a concomitant attribute of intelligent action.* This means that the conventionalizing of objective relations makes of the context of Umwelt and environmental physical relations (here and now cognition-independent, even if originally provenating from apprehensive action, as Poinsot noted) the one texture of human experience. This one texture is the relational network assimilative to public life of environmental factors (i.e., physically subjective factors) and private conjectures (i.e., psychically subjective factors), transformed intersubjectively especially through the exaptation of language to communicative purposes at the level of stipulable signs actualized in community, but also consequently in the whole panoply of artifacts and customs which give an identity to a "civilization". Precisely through this intersubjective transformation is constituted, within experience, the network of *codes* in the broadest sense, with respect to which the linguistic codes are but a subset, albeit a privileged one.

167. The semiosis of the twofold assimilation of subjectivity to the intersubjective order of the objective world is not something actual or actualizable in only one way. It is rather something multiply actual (the diversity of natural languages and cultures) and only virtually universal. This virtual universality is destined always to be defeated in time by the actualizability called into being by specific circumstances on this planet and (we think) on planets elsewhere as giving rise through semiosis to a biosphere and intelligent life in the sense that we are speaking of here as anthroposemiotic. Nonetheless, by examining "institutions, exchanges, and aesthetic domains as elements in a web of decipherable communication" semiosically conceived (Joseph and Joseph 1987: 1), it is always possible in principle to decipher the relevant codes even when they have originated in a Lebenswelt foreign to our own.

168. In such a sense we can appropriate Eco's conclusion (1977: 52): "To see cultural life as a web of codes and as a continuous reference from code to code is to restore to the human animal its true nature". But we must well understand in making the appropriation that the "nature" we are restoring the human animal to is its nature as semiosic *in actu signato*, that is, its nature as an animal able to realize that, as inventor of the Rule, the anthropos is in dire need of being wary of the surrounding virtualities which provide a partial extrinsic measure, in every case, of how truly reasonable the "rule" is in the context of what humanity must depend on (such as the rain forests or the ozone layer) in order to pursue its seemingly (but not entirely in fact) "unlimited semiosis". Otherwise, we risk making a semiotics on the model of the Hobbesian King, answerable to nothing below, and hence immune to considerations of justice or injustice.

169. The code marks the environment in its objective being (sometimes, indeed, scarring it physically, where the "intelligent" behavior has become too free a variable respecting a local environing context, as in strip-mining). The code provides what von Uexküll called (1934: 50ff.) a "familiar path", but a familiar path for conceiving the world, not just for perceiving and acting within an environment objectified, such as is the "world" of a nonhuman animal. A code is, in semiotic terms, an *interpretant*, of the variety described by Peirce as "logical", i.e., as pertaining only to the being and results of ideas in the anthroposemiotic sense in their difference from zoösemiotic images and grounds of phytosemiosis or physiosemiosis. In another sense, no doubt, it is possible to speak of a "code" as defining a familiar path zoösemiotically (cf. Baer 1981: 183): there is a thirdness, an "ideal being", at work in all of nature, not, as Sebeok justly put it (1984a: 2), only in "that minuscule segment of nature some anthropologists grandly compartmentalize as culture". But code as we are here delineating it defines the anthroposemiotically "familiar path" in the manner of its partial discontinuity with the zoösemiotically familiar.

170. An interpretant in general need not be logical. It is the ground on which whatever object functions as a sign. Interpretants exist, consequently, at those points in semiosis where objects are transformed into signs or signs are transformed into other signs. Ideas are interpretants, but not all interpretants are ideas. Interpretants as such are indifferently physical or even mental. They define the points of innovation in semiosis. In other words, when an interpretant is introduced to explicate a sign, this is where the original sign is amplified into another sign. And the act of amplification is where the innovation takes place. To take an easy example within anthroposemiosis, if one says "I don't know what a dog is", and goes to a dictionary to look it up, the inquirer will find four-legged, animal, etc. At each point in the inquiry, every time there is an act of interpretation through which something new is learned, innovation takes place at that point in the sequence.

171. In this way, it is easy to spot the fallacy in the facile claim (e.g., Barthes 1964: 14) that the individual as such can neither create nor modify language, for in fact the individual does exactly both each time an actual understanding is achieved and shared with another individual. In just this way the *Lebenswelt* or human Umwelt gradually differentiated itself and stood apart from the network of Umwelts otherwise comprising the biosphere, as Peirce makes clear in the following text[27] where the logical interpretant is aspectually distributed among speaker, hearer, and community (1906: 196-197):

> There is the *Intentional* Interpretant, which is a determination of the mind of the utterer; the *Effectual* Interpretant, which is a determination of the mind of the interpreter; and the *Communicational* Interpretant, or say the *Cominterpretant*, which is a determination of that mind into which the minds of utterer and interpreter have to be fused in order that any communication should take place. This mind may be called the *commens*. It consists of all that is, and must be, well understood between utterer and interpreter at the outset, in order that the sign in question should fulfill its function.

172. The communicational interpretant in this sense, as embodied in the objective world, is precisely what we have called *code*, of which the linguistic code (no less virtual in its universality than any other code, be it noted) is a subspecies. Johansen comments on this text (1985: 38) that it "constitutes the nucleus in Peirce's theory of linguistic interpretation, because it is possible to arrange the other . . . divisions of the interpretant in relation to the communicational point of view". Our interest in this nucleus is that it allows us to see in what sense the "linguistic admixture" is at the heart of our notion of textuality, even though the city, the countryside, or the night sky as "text" is not reducible to Barthes' (or anyone else's) "world of language". What we see here is that all language is poetic language—that is, that all language, embodying a communicative purport in its possible relation to all other forms of semiosis as shaping the physical universe in the direction of an objective world (the real world of experience), is poetic in the precise sense of conveying an Innenwelt as basing an Umwelt in its difference from physical being taken as what is prejacent to or separable from the objective.

173. Thus, Jakobson's famous model of poetic language (1960: 350-377) does indeed schematize the factors inalienably involved in verbal communication, provided we understand that "verbal" here is a synonym for "linguistic". In fact, we can arrive at a model of textuality by the following series of hypothetical moves.

If we (1) combine into a single model Jakobson's factorial model (1960: 353)

Figure 1. Roman Jakobson's Factorial Model of Poetic Language

and his subsequent (ibid.) "corresponding scheme" of functions,

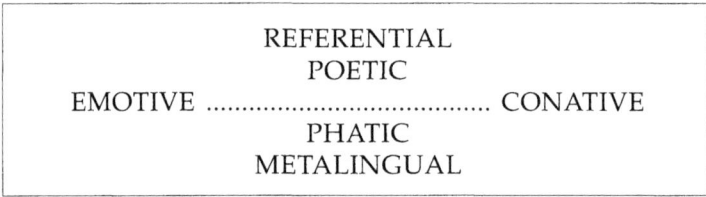

Figure 2. Roman Jakobson's Corresponding Scheme of Functions

with the factorial element indicated as substructural to the superstructural element of function; (2) redraw the separating line in this combined schema so that the asymmetry defining textual communication (now understood as the communication typical of inhabitants of a human Umwelt, or Lebenswelt, in contrast to the inhabitants of strictly perceptual Umwelts) becomes a matter of foreground; (3) invert the central column of the model as a whole so as to place iconic emphasis on the superstructural nature of the asymmetry constitutive of the code as dimanating the textual element in the overall situation; and (4) add brackets to indicate the objective dimension of relationality as such introduced into the Umwelt as remodeled by ideas, we then arrive at the model on the following page. In this model, emotion provides the motivation whence the "addresser" attempts (*conari*) to reach another with a unique conception (poetic message) by means of a sensory modality (*phasis*) in a context of existence by means of establishing a code or putting now into operation (with or without perceived modification) a pre-existing code.

PART II. TEXTUALITY   73

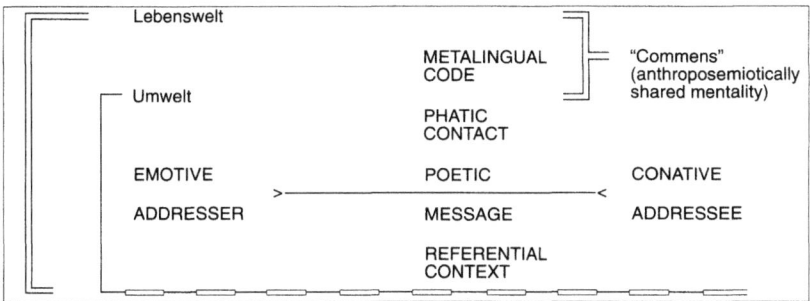

Figure 3. Preliminary Model of Textuality (after Jakobson)

174. The Lebenswelt, in short, as the species-specific but Lamarckian-structured human Umwelt, is precisely achieved as a *commens*, or socio-cultural institution, by bridging, and in the process altering the superstructure of, the originally biological species-specific but Darwinian-structured zoösemiotic Umwelt—zoösemiotic, indeed, but prospectively human through the further working of anthroposemiosis.

175. The above model represents the factors and functional outcomes well enough, but it is too simplistic to represent the dynamics of the process. Two attempts have been made to represent schematically the complexity of the process in its dynamic dimensions.

176. One is the attempt by Sebeok (1972: 14), directly based both on Jakobson's model and on Bühler's earlier triadic speech model (1934: 28):

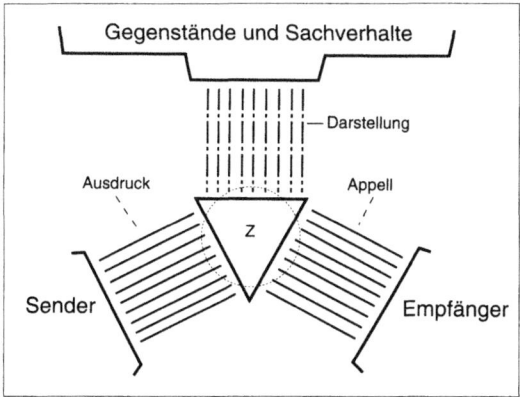

Figure 4. Karl Bühler's Organon Model of Speech

Sebeok takes the elements of Jakobson's and Bühler's models and embeds them in a Morley triangle, so as to bring out the essentially triadic nature of the semiosis which was not foregrounded as such in Jakobson's model:

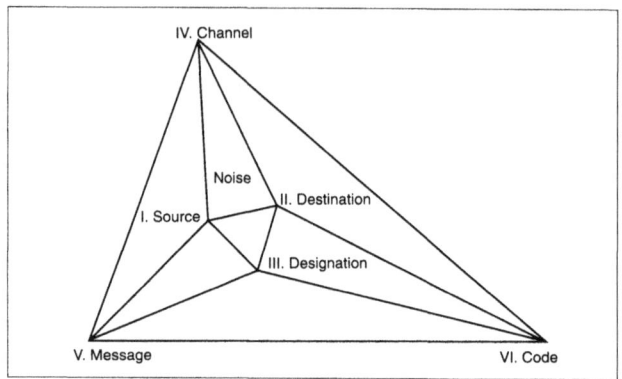

Figure 5. Thomas Sebeok's Morley Triangle Model of Communication

177. The Sebeok model nicely brings out the complexity of the dynamics, but it has a major drawback for our present concerns. Sebeok generalizes the notion of code to an abstract commonality of the species-specific biological rearticulation of environment into objective world through a relational network, in order to account precisely for the zoösemiotic component as such of communication as common to all animals, including humans. The notion of code as we have developed it here, however, is prescissed from the biological notion of code (biological heritage, especially genetic) in order to develop a notion proportioned exclusively to the anthroposemiotic component of the engendering of an objective world *in its difference* from a shared zoösemiotic objectivity. Whereas Sebeok stresses the element of code as channel in experience for the objectivization of relations insofar as code is *analogous* to Umwelt as such and Umwelt as Lebenswelt (i.e., as anthroposemiotically engendered as well as zoösemiotically), our stress has been on the *equivocal* element in the objectivization, *which alone we have designated "code"*.

178. The second attempt to model the dynamics of the process, which makes no reference to Jakobson's model or to any earlier models, is the original effort of Dines Johansen. This attempt is of particular interest by reason of having been formulated by a literary scholar expressly regarding the problem of situating literature (the anthroposemiotic phenomenon par excellence) and criticism within the more general purview of semiosis in the major tradition of contemporary semiotic development. Such an attempt is in welcome contrast to the usual attempts to develop literary semiotics primarily within the purview of the Saussurean minor tradition, with its emphasis on a dyadic notion of sign restricted to cultural semiosis in its difference from the broader semioses whereby anthroposemiosis in its integrity is linked not only to zoösemiosis but to phytosemiosis and the deeper currents of physiosemiosis in all its integrity.

179. Johansen works out a dynamic model derived principally from a consideration of the writings of C. S. Peirce. As a result, this model takes no express account of the notion of code, neither in the sense we have expressly developed above nor in any of the generalized senses made familiar within minor tradition semiotics, especially by epigones of Saussure, Barthes, and Derrida. As a result, to understand Johansen's model, which he calls "the semiotic pyramid", the reader needs to make some adjustments. Our above notion of code needs to be distributed among the five "poles" of the pyramid, by actively conceptualizing at each point the respective contributions of the ten axes and planes identified by Johansen to the formation and operation of the metalingual or "commensurating" code proper to anthroposemiosis in the unique dimension of textuality which characterizes in a permeating fashion the totality of human experience, of anthroposemiotic objectivity as virtually including the Umwelt of zoösemiosis.[28]

180. Johansen's model (1982: 473; more fully discussed in 1985: 266, and 1993: Chapter VI), stripped of its exclusively Peircean technical vocabulary, relabeled at each pole so as to suppress technical presuppositions not explicable terminologically within the limits of the current discussion, and enhanced by an explicit identification of the ten axes constituting the pyramid, may be introduced into the present discussion as in Figure 6 on the following page.

181. The complexity of this model obviously takes seriously Russo's rhetorical challenge issued in the same year in which Johansen first introduced his model. Russo's challenge (1982: 185) gently mocks the attempts of Eco, Riffaterre, and Walker Percy to bring a Peircean point of view to bear within literary semiotics,

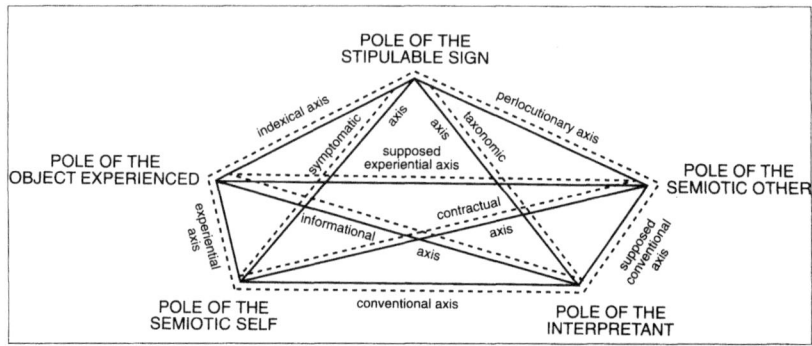

Figure 6. The Pyramid of Anthroposemiosis (after Johansen; see Figure 10 in ¶ 270 below, distributing this model into textual planes)

with the question: "Does a triangular diagram suffice to describe the play of displacements that complex mediation by an interpretant entails?"[29] Johansen's pyramid is comprised of no less than ten triadic planes (a ten-dimensional triangle, if you like) six of which radiate from the sign pole of the anthroposemiosis, while four more radiate (presuppositively and collaterally, as it were, and collaboratively) from the zoösemiotic and physiosemiotic dimensions of the object pole and interpretant pole—the "linguistic admixtures" as such within experience—intersecting the addresser and interpreter, the self and the other. These complexities, it needs to be noted, are demonstrated by Johansen as generated inevitably by the unique requirement of anthroposemiosis that it make some attempt to take account of the other as such in its irreducibility to the objective pole of individual experience, or, as Sebeok puts it, to mark linguistically (rather than simply to extinguish interactionally, as in von Uexküll's model) the stimulus intruding "physically" into the objective web of the Umwelt.

182. This last point, that the complexity of the model results from the requirement (unique to anthroposemiosis in differentiating itself from zoösemiosis simply considered) that a way of modifying objectivity so as to take account of the other in its otherness—that is to say, of noting and codifying objectively the apparent irreducibility of a given object to the experience of it—be represented in any model hoping for adequacy, is the crucial point in our consideration of the model. The impersonal aspect of logical relations within discourse, for example, is well represented by the propositional plane within Johansen's model (see ¶ 271 below).

PART II. TEXTUALITY   77

183.   Terry Prewitt (1991: 30) dauntingly describes what he calls "the Johansen/Deely model" as "a *four-dimensional* 'tetrahedron' (actually a decahedron turned in on itself somewhat like a polyhedral Kline bottle), the minimal four-dimensional geometric figure", and suggests (ibid.: 27-34) that "the selection of a 'four-dimensional' graphic" in this case "is an unfortunate complication" in view of the fact that "the four-dimensional decahedron easily converts to a [supposed easier to understand] three-dimensional figure, a trigonal dipyramid with lines mutually

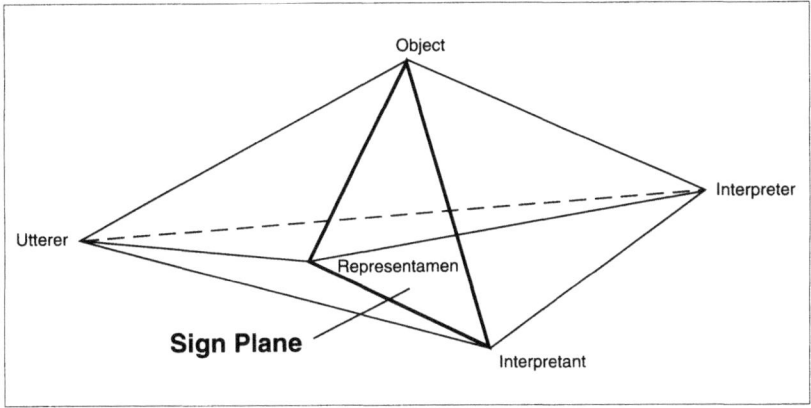

Figure 7. Terry Prewitt's Attempted Three-Dimensional Reduction of Johansen's Pyramid to a Regular Trigonal Dipyramid Model

connecting each of its five points", as in Figure 7. Prewitt adds a Solomonic segmentation of this reductive model to represent recognition of "the discursive imprecision we encounter on the level of meaning" as between any two individuals discoursing, ending up with what he calls the "Segmented Discourse Model", as in Figure 8.

184.   Two questions arise at this point, one only in passing. Is the result of the Solomonic segmentation not rather a veering again toward solipsism, in the typical trajectory of modern philosophy? This first question need not be resolved here (cf. Deely 1971a, 1978, 1981). A second question, however, is crucial, and bears on the very course our essay should take at this juncture: given the greater simplicity of Prewitt's model, is it to be preferred over Johansen's model for the representation of integral anthroposemiosis? Prewitt recognizes that "the symmetry of the three-dimensional form carries different graphic implications" from the original four-dimensional presentation, but he is inclined

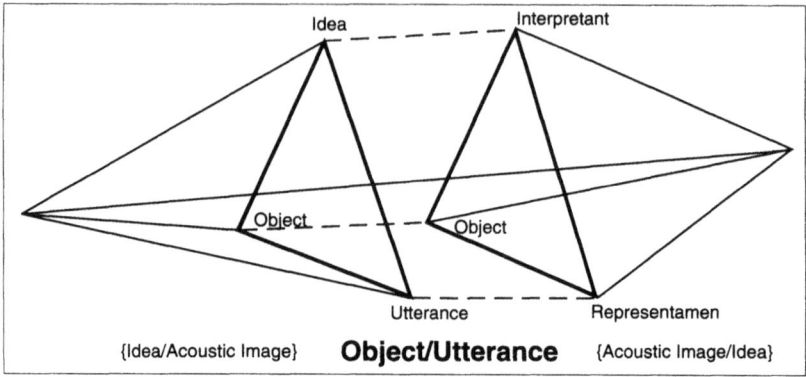

Figure 8. Terry Prewitt's Segmented Discourse Model

to dismiss the differential implications as superfluous to the point of the model. "The dimensionality of a model", he remarks, "can have direct logical implications, can be purely heuristic, or can constitute a kind of 'over-modeling'." His contention is that Johansen's pyramid is a case of 'over-modeling' remedied by the adoption instead of the "segmented discourse model".

185. However, to the contrary, a better case can be made that the dimensionality of Johansen's original pyramidal model is at least heuristic, probably with direct logical implications for the reality modeled, and is certainly not reducible to or equivalent with Prewitt's Solomonically derived segmented discourse model. Of the several differential implications that could be followed out, the implication crucial for present purposes is that the three-dimensional "simplification" Prewitt offers restricts the applicability of the model to anthroposemiosis in two essential ways: either (a) the model can be taken to represent the exchange between two *animalia linguistica* as conspecifics, i.e., as linguistic, in which case it is by no means a model of anthroposemiosis adequately considered (considered, that is, as including zoösemiosis formally and eminently) for it leaves out the crucial step whereby the exaptation of human language modifies the objectivity of the animal Umwelt from within through the actualization of the stipulability of this or that sign as naturally experienced; or (b) the model can be taken to represent the exchange between two *animalia sine sermone*, in which case it is by no means a model of anthroposemiosis at all.

186. In other words, the reduced model can be applied on its own terms ("univocally", as logicians say) either to zoösemiosis or to anthroposemiosis separately considered, but it can be applied to both at once as transpiring within anthroposemiosis only equivocally. Like Sebeok's Morley triangle model, it is well suited to no more than the common aspect of the dimensions of zoösemiosis and anthroposemiosis. For the "simpler representation" advocated by Prewitt "shows", in Prewitt's own words, "that the 'self' and 'other' perspectives on the sign plane are symmetrical" (ibid.: 32), whereas, as we have discovered, there is no way that there can be veritable symmetry of signification between occupants of Umwelt as biologically proportioned and occupants of linguistic Lebenswelt as culturally encoded, unless the differential between these two orders of objectivity is suppressed. For there to be symmetry in the manner postulated in Prewitt's model, the signification in question must be, within an objective world, either *animal ut animal ad animal simpliciter* or *animal linguisticum ut linguisticum ad animal linguisticum simpliciter*, but in neither case *animal linguisticum ut animal linguisticum ad alterum sive linguisticum sive non*. That is to say, in either case, we do not have a model adequate to anthroposemiosis in its integrity, but, at best, an equivocal model applicable only as indifferent either to what anthroposemiosis includes of zoösemiosis or to what constitutes zoösemiosis independently of anthroposemiosis. Such a model as Prewitt has arrived at by reduction has its merits only when the context of its application is restricted in a manner incompatible with a foundational anthropology.

187. Adoption of the segmented discourse model as fundamental risks all over again the confusion of what comes from the source with what comes from the destination—the fallacy of *Klüger Hans*—when analyzing (or attempting to analyze) communication with horses, whales, apes, and people—or people and any other species (Sebeok and Rosenthal 1981; Sebeok and Umiker-Sebeok 1980; Sebeok 1979). Concerning his simplified model proposed as an adequate substitute for Johansen's pyramid, Prewitt asks, for example, (p. 32), "does part of the model disappear" if we use it to explain "the 'discourse' of ape language research"? The ambiguity of the reduced model in this regard is fatal for its anthropological utility as a fundamental model, and the need for the question belies equivalence of the reductive model with Johansen's richer scheme. The case is not at all parallel with Prewitt's earlier discussion (pp. 27-29) of models indifferently two-dimensional or three-dimensional, in which points in the two-dimensional representation directly imply the three-dimensional form, which becomes accordingly "an unnecessary complication for many readers". In the present case, points represented in Johansen's pyramid disappear entirely in the segmented discourse model, so that everything represented in Prewitt's model is included in Johansen's, but from Prewitt's model much of Johansen's has disappeared. We move easily by way of reduction from Johansen's model to Prewitt's model, but in making the move we also find erased points necessary to find our way back, which reveals the complications to be neither unnecessary nor unfortunate but essential to what is being represented.

188. It does not help "to reduce our expressions to their simplest components" (Prewitt 1991: 33) when the simplest components are not what we are seeking to understand. The simplest component of anthroposemiosis is to be found at the physiosemiotic level, precisely where the concepts required to explain either zoösemiosis or anthroposemiosis alike are not needed at all. The reduction to simplest components as a fruitful approach always presupposes the question "simplest respecting what phenomenon"? Reduction to the simplest in the absence of such a question answered as guideline was known in ancient times as Atomism and in recent times as Positivism, ideologies neither of which provides an atmosphere conducive to a flourishing of anthropology.

189. Postulation of the adequate must always take priority over reduction to the simplest. The claim that "Deely's division of planes as 'six radiating from the sign-pole, four from the organismic poles of interpreter and utterer' is an artifact of his perspective on the original drawn graph" (ibid.: 30) will not stand up, inasmuch as the division in question is rather an implication of the original graph as drawn, a point that Johansen himself, in his most recent study expanding on the original pyramid (1993: 245-271) makes clear. And the original graph was drawn precisely to attempt to be adequate to the semiosis which, while incorporating (rather than abstracting from or reducing to) the dimensions of zoösemiosis, achieves superstructurally unique aspects constitutive of the higher processes of cultural coding (the species-specifically human encoding of the objective world) above and beyond merely the simplest performative codings common to socialization processes within the objective world of other species as well. The Johansen model attempts to represent not the simplest processes as such but the simplest processes as differentiative of anthroposemiosis.

190. The crucial requirement whereby anthroposemiosis takes exception to the rule (von Uexküll 1934: 10) that "The effector cue or meaning extinguishes the receptor cue or meaning" is nicely adumbrated in a text of Peirce which Johansen cites in relation to his model, a juxtaposition which has the happy effect of pretty well precluding the simplistic reading of Peirce's remarks as one more tired illustration of the solipsism characteristic of classical modern philosophy (see also Johansen 1993a). Following unknowingly in the footsteps of Poinsot before him, Peirce makes the point that, at the heart of the constructivity of consciousness, the role of the idea as sign is precisely to found relations which bring the other as other *thematically* (and not just ontologically) into the purview of individual awareness, with all the consequences for community[30]—starting with its nascent possibility in the idea of something "real"—that this uniquely anthroposemiotic prescission entails (Peirce 1907: 194, 198-199):

> The purpose of a sign is to supplement the ideas of the life of which I, the interpreter, am a part—ideas which I have drawn directly from my own life—with a copy of a scrap torn out of another's life, or rather from his panorama of all life, his [that is to say, a] general view of life, and I need to know just where on my own panorama of universal life I am to insert a recopy of this copied scrap.
>
> But the utterer has no ideas but his own ideas. . . . Let him try to specify a place on the interpreter's panorama, and he can only look over his own panorama, where he can find nothing but his own ideas. On that panorama he has, however, no difficulty in finding the interpreter's life, that is to say, his idea of it, and among the interpreter's ideas, that is, his own ideas of the interpreter's ideas, he finds an idea of that part of the interpreter's panorama to which he conceives this scrap should be attached and this he expresses in his sign for the interpreter's benefit. The latter has to go through a similar round-about process to find a place in his own life that seems to correspond with his idea of the utterer's idea of his life and with all these changes of costume there is much imminent danger of mistake. . . .

191.   *Eppur si muove!* We move from the idea of reality as an order of existence independent of the observer, no part of the Umwelt as biologically proportioned, to an idea of reality—the semiotic idea of "reality"—as including also the observer in all that is dependent on the observer along with whatever in experience reveals itself as a part of something—the old idea of "reality"—*independent* ("physical being" in its praeter-objective character as the *lining*) of experience. We move from the medieval and classical modern idea of reality as mind-independent being, *ens reale*, to the postmodern idea of reality as the text of specifically human experience. We move from communication in the service of biological ends to a communication system opening as well possible worlds beyond any species-specific objective one or any imaginary reductionistic purely physical one. Such is the movement from signification to textuality, which brings us to the matter of criticism, the method proper to *les sciences humaines*.

Part III. Critick

192. Here we arrive at a most delicate and important point in our analysis, a point which has been the locus of confusion and misapprehension on many sides, toward the clarification of which our analysis in this essay is intended to serve: the place or role of criticism within anthroposemiosis.

193. The coding of the Umwelt through the play of stipulated elements as such in patterns of communication and habits of social interaction is, in the first place, presupposed to critical activity. For, as we have seen, until such coding is introduced into the world which is objective as Umwelt, there is not yet *culture* in its distinction from and difference respecting (a purely perceptual) Umwelt, a *social* world (yet not a socio-*cultural* world) such as can be found in many nonhuman species of animal. In the most general sense, criticism begins at that unique moment when a sign, experienced as *stipulable* and seized upon as such, is further deployed under a communicative intention which transforms, or attempts to transform (for the outcome of the effort is by no means certain), that sign into a vehicle such as it would not otherwise be. At that moment, something arbitrary is made to function in a prospectively natural way, by serving as ground for a relationship transporting a subjective idea into a conception intersubjectively shared with a conspecific and thereby *codified* as a node of public access to an objective world no longer tied to the perceptual level as such of biological heritage.

194. Also at that moment, the Lebenswelt in its difference from Umwelt originates. The code—the idea objectified relationally beyond the psychic subjectivity of participants in an interaction and, as such, in principle rendered *customary* under some perceptible aspect of physical being with which it is *identified* but not *identical*—carries the difference, elaborates it, and transforms the whole of experience into an intertext. At that moment also *critick* is born, the possibilities of criticism as the irreducibly human dimension of anthroposemiosis whereby the arbitrary is made to serve the communicative intention.

195. Like textuality itself, therefore, language in the root sense is coextensive with the possibility of human experience. As Baer remarks (1981: 202), "The human *Lebensform*—that is, *Lebensform* considered from the point of view of anthroposemiotics—is language, and language is always a form of life" (Baer speaks of "The Envelope of Language" [1988: 185-186], a curious inversion of Plant's metaphor [1950]). Criticism in the most general sense, consequently, is an expression of the inner side whence the coded objectivities accumulated in human experience survive as something more than a deadweight of the past on present discourse (ibid.: 203):

> The moment one intuits that all taxonomies involved in our descriptions of the world are directly or indirectly connected with language, then it is only appropriate for us to reverse the dialectical relation and investigate the nonlinguistic (understood even now as a linguistic construction) on its own terms.[31]

The error comes in drawing from this situation a corollary which in fact does not follow (ibid.):

> The thesis of the linguistic mediation of the world does not entail acceptance of the position that the linguistic model should dominate semiotic analysis. On the contrary, in order to show the mutual containment of verbal and nonverbal sign systems, the models and rules for their analysis must be generated in a way which is internal to each system at hand. . . . [T]he reciprocal preconditions of anthroposemiotics and zoösemiotics [along with the several other semiotic levels identifiable from within experience] presuppose, like Thom's catastrophes, an interplay of autonomy and correlative heteronomy.

196. Seen in this light, criticism is a pervasive and necessary activity of the intelligence in dealing with the inevitable accumulation of past conceptions in the public experience of the world and in the aspectual assimilation of that accumulation—often fragmented and unrealized as such, to be sure—to communicative discourse at every level. In this sense, criticism is the intelligent activity most distinctive of anthroposemiosis. But criticism is at the same time the least independent of intelligent activities, for it depends in every case, for the matter upon which it is exercised, on the arbitrary elements made intelligible through the choices of others in communicative efforts insofar as the efforts were successful and became part of the objective content of experience on its publicly accessible side.

197. Nor do these arbitrary elements stand alone within experience, but rather as integrated into the peculiar pattern of objectivity accessible only through language. The codes demarcating culture in its proper being incorporate, while at the same time contrasting with, the physical side of natural things and the objective "things" comprising together the Umwelts (the experience and structure of experience) of the various species interacting within the objective human world, or (outside our awareness perhaps—but vitally and biologically in contrast with "culturally") within the organismic population comprising the human species as a biological entity. As such, these codes define a zone of the "already understood"—that is, of a way of conceiving the realm of experience. This zone constitutes, in itself, a possible world which, even insofar as it includes the actual state of society and culture at a given time, remains "at loose ends" with itself. The reason for this situation is that this zone of the "presumed understood" is not only objective in contrast to (as well as partially incorporative of) the physical, but also "arbitrary" in its resting on communitized individual choices ("conventions"). These communitized choices impose themselves inevitably but often as otherwise than what *this* individual "here and now" would have the structure of experience be were it reducible to choices guided by immediate individual preferences of interaction, whether primarily communicative (discursive) or primarily modificative (in the realm of secondness).

198. We see in this contrast to physical and psychic subjectivity of the objective as further differentiated from within by codes the reason why "conceptual models of society are necessarily models of equilibrium systems" whereas "real societies can never be in equilibrium" (Leach 1954: 4). The enculturated dimension transforming human-Umwelt-as-biological-expression into Lebenswelt-no-longer-strictly-proportioned-to-biological-heritage (and hence to subjectivity in its dual dimension) is accessible, moreover, in its proper being, only through language (with all the conflicting codification of choices we have seen this accumulates). Hence this dimension is imperceptible in principle even when, as is always the case, it involves and rests upon perceptible aspects of the environment. The result is a "model world" which indeed implies that (Leach 1964: xii) "the facts under observation at any one time will appear to belong to several quite different 'systems'."

199. But the underlying reason for this polyvalency is emphatically not that the "equilibrium assumptions" are of a "fictional (idealist) nature" derived from an evaluation of verbal categories which "is, in the final analysis, illusory" (ibid.: xi-xii). Systematic ordering in historical events involving human experience as such has an elusive but hardly illusory dimension vis-à-vis the so-called "empirical facts" (the aspects of the events reducible to what can be directly observed within a perceptual field) precisely because of their objective character in the semiotic sense we have established. The political systems of Highland Burma are no different in this regard from the political systems of middle America or Renaissance Sicily. It is the anthroposemiosic nature of human experience in its difference from the zoösemiosic nature of the Umwelt in its biological provenance that creates the difficulty, the relative "autonomy of meaning and irreducibility of experience" to physical world, in Toews' expression (1987).

200. This "loose-endedness" of the world experienced as understood (as Lebenswelt) is exacerbated by the cumulative residuality of the codes whereby they are, for any given individual, only incompletely actualized (within consciousness especially), while remaining operative virtually as a totality at cross purposes with itself (in the residual oppositions of perspective encoded into the objective world through past discourse and social interaction). Hence, for example (Eco 1977: 31; cf. Compton-Carlton 1649: Sec. 6): "From one speaker to another there can be differences in the complexity of semantic analysis of a term: these differences produce *sub-codes* on the basis of which one speaker could assign meanings to the terms which other speakers would not assign to them; the different mastery of such sub-codes reveals class differences in social interaction". We glimpse here the

PART III. CRITICK   87

general rationale for what Herzfeld calls the "semiotic sensitivity" (1985: 47-48) to gesture and dress as well as to linguistic behavior and lexicological etymology discernable within an ethnic group.

201. A further general point that bears on the "loose-endedness" of the objectivity of the human world is this: The mind-dependent relations constitutive of language as such are, one and all, formal aspects of intelligibility introduced into the material unities and diversities of perception without any necessary regard for the divisions among objects in their aspects as things. Hence not only can "one and the same thing be considered in different respects", but one and the same sign-vehicle can be used to convey different or even opposed significations. The fact that the relations are mind-dependent, therefore, is enough to ensure that there is and can be no external guarantee that the same divisions will be made by any two "speakers" using the perceptibly same sign-vehicle, nor, more importantly, that the number of divisions made using the same basis can be limited over time. This synechistic consequence of the nature of species-specifically human discourse can be nicely expressed using a formula worked out by Ketner and Putnam to grasp Peirce's notion of the continuum as he expressed it in his 1898 Cambridge Conferences. As soon as we have an objective world in which some discursive possibilities are realized, "we immediately see that there is a possible world in which still *more* divisions can be made", and hence there is no possible world in which "*non-exclusive* possibilities are *all* actualized" (Ketner and Putnam 1992: 53).[32] Keeping in mind that anthropic experience draws on the psychological subjectivity of psyches and the physical subjectivity of things alike in the semiosic preocess of textualizing the objective world as a species-specific public zone of communicative interactions, we find in Eco (1992b: 88) a splendid statement of the relative autonomy of the objective sphere vis-à-vis the twin subjectivities feeding into it: "Between the mysterious history of a textual production and the uncontrollable drift of its future readings, the text qua text still represents a comfortable presence, the point to which we can stick".

202. Consequently, as the method proper to the human sciences (insofar as they can be placed under a common denominator and contrasted to the empirical research methods required for natural science), criticism, especially if it takes a deconstructive turn, finds itself provided with the possible illusion of a universe all on its own, which can be explored ad infinitum without excessive regard for the crass concerns or requirements of field research or laboratory techniques. Taking experience from the side of its objective transcendence of psychic and physical subjectivity alike and in terms of the nodes irreducibly arbitrary from the standpoint of individuals living at later stages of or taking alternate stances in an historically constituted community (such as is now and early became the case for every individual without exception in the evolution of the human species), the mind can, with a little cleverness, turn every element of experience and discourse into a plaything ad infinitum. It is, alas, all too easy to become "bored by the facts which his anthropological colleagues present" (Firth 1954: vii, recounting Leach's usual circumstance).

203. The exaptation of language to speech consists in *stipulating* a variously *stipulatable* objectivity in order to make of it a sign-vehicle functioning under a measure of critical control but at the same time one that is *arbitrary* in being, however stipulated, both further stipulable and able to have been otherwise stipulated. There results a contrast between the free play of understanding and the requirements of understanding subordinating choices to the goal of some discernible measure of success in communicating or in achieving some ascertainable measure of correspondence with the prejacent and here-and-now mind-independent physical factors operative environmentally within experience in the establishment of a "factual" element.

204. In the history of these questions, this further contrast between the goal of communicating according to a correspondence with the physical as such versus simply according to an objective content to be shared regardless of any physical correspondence or lack thereof within it was early recognized in the philosophical tradition as defining a general difference between logos and mythos. But the possibility within this difference of extending logos to the understanding of mythos itself and objectivity generally in its contrast with physical existence and being was underestimated and, indeed, ill-understood.

205. In the original conception of scientifically logical thought, correspondence with the physical was treated as eo ipso the criterion for distinguishing scientific inquiry. Already in Aristotle's time we find the distinction between, on the one hand, the understanding operating in the line of assigning a prospective reason for a defined state or condition of being experienced as irreducible to the experience of it, and, on the other hand, understanding operating in the line of wishful conjecture free of the restraints imposed by the aim of coinciding discursively in a determinate (if partial) way with structures of experience which represent accurately prejacent dimensions and elements of physical being as they stand in their independence of our experience of them.

206. Among the Latin scholastics, appreciation of this difference was enshrined in an adage or maxim: "Processus ad infinitum absolute repugnat". The point of this maxim for scientific understanding was quite specific: a given condition or state of physical being always requires a specific cause for its coming to be (an initiating cause) and a specific series of here and now interdependent causes which enable it to continue in existence. It is only respecting this here and now series of causes essentially subordinated to the maintenance of the effect as determined by its initiating cause that an infinite process of causes is ruled out, by the fact that the state or condition in question (the effect) is a determinate state or condition, whereas a series of antecedent causes and conditions required here and now to sustain this determinate state or condition posited as infinite is, precisely, not determinate.

207. The point is neither easy to grasp nor generally well understood, so let us dwell on it for awhile.

208. To begin with, the denial of an infinite process in explanation through causes is specific, not generic. That is, not every form of infinite process is denied, but only an infinite process within the series of essentially subordinated causes which, *as essentially subordinated*, here and now sustain a determinate state or condition of being.[33] For example, the parents of a child at the moment of conception are the proper causes of the child's existence. As a proper effect, the being of the child is essentially subordinated to the procreative action of the parents, but the procreative action of the parents is only incidentally, not essentially, subordinated to the being of the child. Relative to the series of causes required to maintain and develop the conceived child, the procreative action of the parents is only a temporary link which, in its own being, that is to say, outside the series of essentially subordinated causes required to maintain the effect once produced, may well be a link in an infinite series of accidentally chained causes which were required in order for the procreative action in question to be posited in the first place.

209. Thus so-called "historical causation" (Roe and Simpson 1958: 21ff.) such as is required to explain evolution, both in the universe at large (the development of galactic and intergalactic phenomena, especially star systems and stars with subordinate planetary systems) and in the biosphere of earth, was not traditionally thought to be inconsistent with an infinite process among causes for at least two reasons. There is, in the first place, no way of knowing that the cosmos as a whole is not eternal. Behind the "Big Bang" may simply lie a previously imploding universe out of which our—for now—expanding universe has emerged as the proper effect of an initiating cause. Besides this, there is nothing to prevent a present condition or state of being from depending for its existence on antecedent intersections of mutually independently determinate causal actions or series—that is to say, on *tychisms* or *chances*.

210. The infinite process which is incompatible with causal determinism is only that process which bears on the here and now *maintenance* of a specific state or condition of being, not that which bears on the antecedent factors which made the state or condition a proximate possibility in the first place.[34]

211. Thus, among causes, it is necessary to distinguish between those which are productive but not preservative of their effects and those which are preservative as well as "present at the production". Among the former causes, considered outside the order to *this* effect to be preserved, an infinite process does not repugn. Among the latter causes, an infinite process removes the very possibility of the effect in question, or, looked at from the "standpoint of the observer", renders the effect in question an unintelligible prospect. Any effect is a determinate outcome of an action or series of actions. Insofar as it survives the action producing it, it requires the operation of further determinate causes, upon the cessation of which the effect itself would pass. It is among *these* causes as such, that is, as the determinate causes of the being of the effect in question in its here and now duration, that an infinite process is precluded. By contrast, nothing precludes infinite process within the past series of occurrences indirectly and, as it happens (*tychistically*), involved in the present possibility of the effect in question. Nor is an infinite process precluded within the future series of occurrences which may bear traces of the present effect after it has passed away (i.e., the occurrences respecting which the present effect, through its present being, exercises a causal influence that becomes, perforce, indirect not only once the source of the causal influence has ceased to exist but also even when the source exercises its causal influence not in a context of essential subordination to the outcome but vicariously through some *other* being which is an "effect of the effect" only accidentally as far its here and now continuance in existence is concerned, whether or not its initiating cause in this aspect of its continuing being has passed away). The sustaining causes of any given effect, in contrast to the initiating causes, cannot as such be involved directly in a causal regress to infinity: that is the primary import of the maxim we have been examining.

212. From the standpoint of experience, the maxim affirms the finite and temporal reality of individual existence as such and bears on the physical factors as such responsible for anything existing here and now as circumscribed recognizably within the sphere of experience being in this rather than that way.

213. An example should help to grasp the point. "If we know from the start that the sun suffers eclipse", Aristotle remarks (c.348-347BC: *Posterior Analytics*, Book II, Chap. 1, 89b27ff.), "we do not inquire whether it does so or not". Aristotle of course did not have the advantage of seeing how a deconstructionist could show, starting with elements of the above character strings that are from the start conventional and involved with irreducibly arbitrary factors, that the notion of eclipse might be reduced to a purely linguistic and thoroughly unclear play of language. Aristotle considered the situation on a more straightforward level: "When we know that the sun is being eclipsed and that an earthquake is in progress, it is the reason of eclipse or earthquake into which we inquire"; and he well understood that the means whereby answers even to environmental questions must be reached are thoroughly semiotic, thoroughly dependent on criticism—but not on a criticism detached from the integrity of the experience of which it criticizes the linguistic formulation.

214. This brings us to yet another meaning of the adage "processus ad infinitum absolute repugnat" which was also understood among the Latins, but perhaps not as well as it needs to be as far as it has a special bearing on the development of semiotic consciousness. Where the phenomenon in question involves the protrusion of a relatively closed physical system in its own right within the sphere of experience, involvement of an explanation in such a process is an infallible sign that the understanding has disengaged from the *phaenomenon explanandum* as such in favor of essential entanglement with a construct of its own making, indeed. But it is also the case that such a slippage is possible in the first place because there is a form of infinite process unique to the objective order, a form which is directly rooted in semiosis itself and hence, to a certain extent, unavoidable.

215. As the case of phlogiston in the history of understanding combustion or of ether in the history of modern physics or any of a thousand other cases swept under the rug in the record rooms of science amply manifest, substituting an objective creature of its own making in the place of proper causes and mistaking this relative nonbeing for being is an error to which positive science is always liable and against which it must constantly be on guard, especially through methodological precautions. Here the brute force of secondness is of the greatest assistance, and the understanding's main ally in working out the thirdness of environmental sciences. Indeed, just this is the whole point of experimentation, and what experimentation is all about.

216. But the sciences of culture face a more difficult problem, to which the multiplication of reflexive methodologies in anthropology and the social sciences provides as much a clue to the problem as a measure of its solution. For culture is not just an objective puzzle alongside the physical environment; it is a puzzle respecting which the physical aspects of environmental being, including artifacts, are external, even when, as in the case of artifacts, they are also externalizations of the objectivity proper to culture.

217. The objectivity proper to culture, nonetheless, consists entirely of relations. Its "internal being", so to speak, is nothing but relations patterned in specific ways. And these patterns, though physical nature collaborates in them and is incorporated— sometimes coerced—into them, do not exist as such apart from the human mind. They are, thus, the objective phenomenon par excellence, a pure thirdness, comparatively speaking, in which secondness has, exactly, a secondary part, not, as in the realm of "hard science", a primary role in revealing the being of things. The firstness of culture has not the finite-mind-independent depth of physical nature in which an anchor can be cast in processes of explanation. Here semiosis comes fully into its own and is, so to speak, "on its own" when it comes to achieving genuine understanding and progress in the life of the mind.

218. Relations, which in nature are based only on individuals and physical aspects of individuals (units in a system, such as the planets and other bodies of our solar system), in culture are both units of the systems and the systems themselves. Here the infinite process knows not the check of essentially subordinated efficient or material causes, for the causality at work is purely objective, as we have seen, and external to whatever formal embodiment it may have been given in rituals, artifacts, or whatever other "patterns of culture". As a result (Culler 1992: 121), "describable semiotic mechanisms function in recursive ways, the limits of which cannot be identified in advance".

219. When it comes to understanding the foundations of culture, anthroposemiosis confronts itself, and especially its distinctive objective offspring, in a nearly pure—were the mind infinite, it would no doubt be truly pure—play of thirdness. Since the process is finite, it has limits. But since the process has no intrinsic repugnancy to infinite regress among objective causes, finding those limits is often problematic and ad hoc.

220. The problem comes to a nub in language, as a symbolic system freed to serve whatever practical function through its fundamental exaptation first of all to be at the disposal of the communicative function as detached from, as we have seen, a limiting strict proportion to biological constitution, and hence to here and now zoösemiotic modalities of social interaction.

221. The critical control of objectivity, aided in science by the play of brute force in secondness, is thrown back in language upon its own resources. "Criticism" in the most general sense as the attempt to acquire consciousness *in actu signato* in the use of codes is the response to this dilemma, just as the recent development of reflexive methodologies in anthropology is a specific response in the realm of critick. "If our interest is not so much in the receiving of intended messages but in understanding, say, the mechanisms of linguistic and social interaction," Culler suggests (1992: 113), we shall have to practice "asking precisely those questions which are *not* necessary for normal communication but which enable us to reflect on its functioning." For example (ibid.):

> it is useful from time to time to stand back and ask why someone said some perfectly straightforward thing such as, 'Lovely day, isn't it?' What does it mean that *this* should be

a casual form of greeting? What does that tell us about this culture as opposed to others that might have different phatic forms or habits?

222. The thirdness of anthroposemiosis finds its principal life in hunches and guesses, formulating and following abductive hypotheses down every path they lead. It is a world of could bes and could have beens much more than it is an actual world. The actual world repugns the infinite process in its essential regional structures, as we have seen, allowing it only in the accidents of history and the accidental subordination of events to time backwards into the immeasurably distant past and beyond the foreseeable future. But the objective world is constituted in its proper being by, and thrives at each point on, the syncategorematicity of infinite regress as a process in time.

223. To place the point with a strength appropriate to its importance, we can say that just as the finite structure of physical being precludes an infinite regress within any given series of essentially subordinated sustenative causes, so the finite structure of objective being and human discourse requires an infinite progress wherever it is a question of thirdness within semiosis as such. In the specific case of anthroposemiosis, the conjectural nature of judgment specifically assures that the approach to truth must be communitarian and asymptotic overall. "A sign is objectively *vague*, in so far as, leaving its interpretation more or less indeterminate, it reserves for some other possible sign or experience the function of completing the determination", Peirce tells us (5.505; cf. 5.447). And Almeder (1979: 331) makes an observation which enables us to tie the situation of vagueness directly to the shifting boundary between objects and things, which again is an immediate consequence of the finiteness of human consciousness:

> Since no object in the universe can ever be fully determinate with respect to its having or not having every known property, it follows that any proposition about the universe is vague in the sense that it cannot hope to fully specify a determinate set of properties.

224. From this situation we can read off directly the dynamic and infinite character of semiosis, as Peirce best showed in his definition of the sign (1901: 2.303) as "anything which determines

something else (its *interpretant*) to refer to an object to which it itself refers (its *object*) in the same way, the interpretant becoming in turn a sign, and so on *ad infinitum*". Corrington, in his excellent synoptic presentation of Peirce's thought (1993: 86-87), has shown more specifically what this infinity means, both for semiosis in general and for anthroposemiosis in particular:

> Any given sign will push outward into a relational network in which it will become more and more efficacious. Initially, a sign points to an emerging thought that is its interpretation. By the same token, and at the same time (since these are not temporally distinct stages), the sign will point to an object, even though that object may remain partially veiled from view. Finally, the sign will refer to its object in particular finite ways. Signs may be somewhat vague, but they will always have some value or quality in terms of which they support the predication of a trait to an object. When we apply this threefold analysis of the sign to the self, we get the first glimpse of the sophistications found in a semiotic anthropology.
> We appear to ourselves as a sign, or, more precisely, as an intersection of various sign series. Each given sign helps to establish the contour of the self through its threefold structure. First, the sign generates a subsequent thought/sign that is an enhanced expression of the outward involvements of the self (dimension of the future). Second, that same sign points toward the object that is the self in its previous state (dimension of the past). Finally, the sign points to a quality of the previous self that is still pertinent in the present (dimension of the present). The self is an asymmetrical sign series that is continually being built up and, in different respects, torn down and reconfigured. This process is fully temporal and involves, as noted in the first chapter, a kind of internal dialogue. The present self is constituted by signs of the past self, which in turn point toward an emergent future self. The self and its signs are temporally extended. No natural beginning nor ending can be seen for this extended process of signification.[35]

Except, of course, for the individual. For each individual the spiral of semiosis begins at conception and ends at death, as I have diagrammed elsewhere in terms of the interlocking wheelings of abduction, deduction, and induction which weave the fabric of experience and individual life (Deely 1985a: 321, where "A" = abduction, "B" = deduction, and "C" induction):

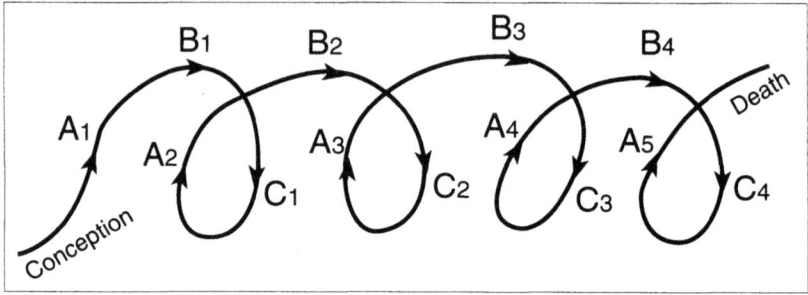

Figure 9. The Abductive Spiral of Experiences

225. We arrive thus at a perfectly general formula: while interpretation, if well done, increases the definiteness of a sign or sign-system, where an interpretation, however excellent, leaves off, there the signs on which it depends and by which it achieved itself are left imperfect in the transition to objects manifested.

226. Yet the fact that an interpretation is always incomplete in some respect does not mean that there are no limits whatever to semiosis in its mode as criticism, whether in general or in any specific regard. Semiosis as such is an infinite progression, yes, but it is not an actual infinity of significations simultaneously given as such. Semiosis proceeds rather through a succession of significations only some of which are simultaneously achieved, while others are achieved successively and with many duplications, lapses, and overlaps. The infinity of semiosis, in other words, is a *syncategorematic* infinity, in Poinsot's apt expression— a prospective and virtual one, not one actually achieved at any given moment or in any given sign sequence or sign system.

227. Here we need to repeat and extend Ransdell's explanation briefly cited in ¶ 87 above (Ransdell 1986: 676):

> The key to understanding the apparently puzzling infinities involved . . . is [to understand] that they pertain to the object-sign-interpretant relation considered *in abstracto*, whereas in the concrete application of semiotic conceptions there will always be legitimating reasons for regarding certain signs as the first signs of the object and certain interpretants as the last interpretants. The infinities involved

in the theoretical conception function in practice only as a theoretical reminder and a logical guarantee that there can never be an absolutely definitive and minute semiotic analysis or account of anything, but only an analysis or account that satisfies whatever intellectual motives instigate the concrete inquiry or specific line of inquiry.

Insofar as the limits of a cultural semiosis in particular are ad hoc, their recognition analytically may be said to depend upon a certain integrity of the individual performing a criticism in any given case. In this light, it can almost be said that Aristotle anticipated an answer to the thoroughgoing deconstructionist. The contingency of the linguistic sign is infinitely exploitable, but only if we insist on its externality vis-à-vis an actual situation at hand (c.348-347BC: Book I, Chap. 10, 76b23-27):

> All syllogism, and a fortiori demonstration, is addressed not to the spoken word, but to the discourse within the soul, and though we can always raise objections to the spoken word, to the inward discourse we cannot always object.[36]

228. And of course it is not just a question of *semiotic analysis* but, more fundamentally, of the *semiosis itself* that such an analysis presupposes as its subject matter or "object"; and here it is not a question of the integrity of the inquirer but rather of the integrity of the pattern of significations into which inquiry is made. It is, after all, integrity on the side of the object that the inquirer needs integrity (subjective integrity, integrity as a "virtue") to handle in intellectually just ways. Eco generalizes this point in terms of the historical situation of language itself as a finite system of subordinated objective causality (1990: 36):

> If it is true that a notion of literal meaning is highly problematic, it cannot be denied that in order to explore all the possibilities of a text, even those that its author did not conceive of, the interpreter must first of all take for granted a zero-degree meaning, the one authorized by the state of a given language in a given historical moment, the one that every member of a community of healthy native speakers cannot deny. Every sentence can be interpreted metaphorically: even the assertion *John eats an apple every morning* can be interpreted as "John repeats Adam's sin every day". But in order to support such an interpretation, everybody must take for granted that *apple* means a given fruit, that *Adam*

is intended as the first man, and that, according to our biblical competence, Adam ate a forbidden fruit.

Eco is right to conclude (1992: 23) that, even in the realm of culture and of texts in the most narrow sense, just as in the realm of experience and textuality in its most encompassing sense, "the notion of unlimited semiosis does not lead to the conclusion that interpretation has no criteria".

229. Thus, within the specifically cultural dimension of anthroposemiosis, that is, under the species-specific aspect as such of anthroposemiosis in its involvement, as we have seen, with the many other shared—zoösemiotic, phytosemiotic, physiosemiotic, etc.—aspects of semiosis at work upon and within the anthropos, even the practical limits have a theoretical importance in distinguishing semiosis from drift of whatever variety. Yet the theoretical importance of any given practical limits is never so great as to close down in principle the possibility of a further semiosis, if only one not now possible to the participants in an interpretive dialogue that has "run out of steam"—or to the members as such of a culture that has run up against phenomena that must be assimilated under the pressures of secondness but cannot be assimilated given the pattern of thirdness defining the culture in question. Cultural collisions often result in a breakdown of thirdness before forces of virtual secondness, such as occurred between the European settlers and many of the indigenous Indian tribes, and continues to happen wherever today technological pressures are brought to bear on heretofore non-technological (or "primitively technological", to coin a forbidden, more accurate phrase) human groupings. The actual world at any given moment, respecting semiosis, is more like a residue or a precipitate than it is of the ongoing essence of the process, especially the process of anthroposemiosis in its prospective infinity and syncategorematic character as it realizes itself even in the most well-defined and determinedly closed ("xenophobic") culture. Here, the nature of semiosis defeats the will of rulers, as happened in fourteenth-century China, to take a particularly dramatic example, but as also happens every day in families where parents are determined to channel their children's career and the like, in a thousand homely, local examples that have no grand bearing.

230. Unlike the actual world at any given moment, the world of could bes and could have beens admits of the infinite process, synchronically as well as diachronically. The question is twofold: on one hand of the boundary line between the physical universe and the universe of discourse not in their objective overlaps but in their respective constitution as different, and on the other hand of consistency of thought vs. the application of consistent thought to the content of experience in order to show, so far as we are able, why the world—be our explanatory emphasis on nature or culture in a given case—is the way it is in this or that respect. Hence what overlaps there are between objective world and physical environment within experience partake of the contingent, and this contingency finds maximum embodiment in the linguistic sign—i.e., in the exaptation of language to communicate by the systematization of stipulable signs respecting speech acts.

231. Criticism as a method moves precisely in this zone of contingent exaptation (the domain of critick), which is why there are as many authentic roles for criticism as there are ways of bringing into the objective sphere with greater explicitness and formalizing the roles played or playable by the traces left in experience of the workings of intelligence over these many generations present through the past. Such traces are especially apparent in the linguistic sign, "the ideological phenomenon par excellence", as Volosinov remarked (1929: 13), but also in general in that surplus of semiosis we have come to call "textuality" or "culture" in the sense of postlinguistic structures (Deely 1982: 198 n. 1, after Morris 1946).

232. Given this purview, the semiological systems of Roland Barthes and Jacques Derrida find in spite of themselves a theoretical ground within what Sebeok calls (1977: 81) the "major tradition" of semiotic development. So also do the systems which, inspired (or perhaps, as Eco rather suggests [1992: 23], overinspired) by Eco's *Opera aperata* (1962), without calling themselves semiological, yet share the ideology of equating semiosis with the tracings and workings of codes within culture precisely as conventional (in the base sense of standing in part on that irreducible element of the arbitrary which is inseparable from the stipulability of signs seized upon by the understanding and actualized unavoidably in the very attempt to share—that is, regardless of the degree of success or failure of the attempt). The ideology in question of itself lucubrates absorption of the indexical and iconic as such to the symbolic. But I think this requires ignoring the fact that the conventional codes involve more than what convention itself accounts for, which is but to say again that anthroposemiosis is not an autonomous process *tout court*, but involves, besides its species-specific linguistic and cultural dimension, the further surrounding and sustaining dimensions of zoösemiosis, phytosemiosis, and physiosemiosis (for "the human being is generated by man and the sun as well").

233. The indexical dimension of signs is a matter of brute secondness in order to be a thirdness. It will not do to absorb, even theoretically, secondness into thirdness except as an ideological move vitiated by its own pretensions. The matter of iconicity is more problematic, for what is "similar" can be stylized to a very high degree within a culture, perhaps asymptotically, and so become a matter of convention in its own right. Yet here, I think, the biological heritage of the anthropos particularly asserts itself, and no matter how stylized a resemblance convention may become, the underlying mechanisms for perceiving a resemblance are perceptual and zoösemiotic more than conceptual and species-specifically anthroposemiosic.[37] This is enough, it seems to me, to guarantee that the iconic as well as the indexical will always retain in general, even if not in every specific case, a rootedness beyond the boundaries of the symbolic as such. Particularly is this so where it is a question of the symbolic in anthroposemiosis where, insofar as it is a species-specific symbolicity, the fundamental ground is stipulative rather than associative (as happens in zoösemiosis and, in general, in "teaching language to apes").

234. Beyond being a rhetorical ploy, the label "major tradition" is a way of referring to a strategy within semiotics today for encouraging a view of semiotic not as a theory in either the traditional critical sense or in the traditional scientific sense, but as a *doctrine* of signs which transcends the opposition of culture to nature. As a doctrine, semiotics attains this transcendence by having for its unifying object the action of signs, *semiosis*, an action rooted in the indifference of relation in its distinctive formality as an entitative mode of being to physical or psychical realization (being suprasubjective in either case) and explicitly recognized as an activity or process constructive not only of human experience but of all organismic experience and of the physical environment itself as tending to give rise to and supportive of the existence of the plethora of Umwelts (including the species-specifically human one) precisely in their contrast, as objec-

tive worlds, to the physical realm of the environment which the objective worlds not only rest upon, but indirectly modify, partially include, and restructure in the inclusion.

235. What is at issue simply is the intent and scope of the term "semiotic" as Locke introduced it, and of the notion of "reality" as the perspective Locke labeled opens unto it. The "major and minor traditions", rightly understood, are no more opposed than are *"ens reale* and *ens rationis"* in the perspective proper to a doctrine of signs (Deely 1986a): It is not a relation of exclusion that obtains, but of part to whole—and of a *pars pro toto* fallacy that prevails when proponents of the part mistake it or try to set it in opposition to the whole of which it forms a part.[38] The contours of the totum, of course, being themselves established semiosically, can never be drawn fully and finally but come into focus rather only asymptotically as a function both of the future and of the community.

236. On such a view, criticism as a method is a part or activity within anthroposemiosis at once privileged and necessary, but incommensurate with anthroposemiosis *tout court*. Like deduction, criticism has a limited validity, but, further like deduction, it has a tendency in the hands of many practitioners to create an illusion of autonomous adequacy through an excess of cleverness in raising questions about "whatever has been said" (or "observed"), or in constructing alternative considerations within discourse on the order of Ptolemaic epicycles.

237. The decisive shift in the strategy to move semiotics away from a one-sided subjection to the linguistic model, then, not surprisingly, turns on our conception of *language* itself. We saw above, in line with our view of language as the species-specifically human Innenwelt, that the essence of language is arguably equatable with the reconstitution of objects (and objects experienced as signs) as *stipulable*. As such reconstitution takes place within the Umwelt consequent upon the discovery of the relation of signification, perhaps rather we should say that the essence of language is arguably equatable with the subsequent use of any sign in the light of an apprehended difference between, on the one hand, whatever object signified as such, and, on the other hand, whatever sign-vehicle (or *signifier*) as such, in the mutual difference of signifier and signified from the *linkage itself* between the two as able to be abstracted and codified for purposes of communication. Apprehension of this difference alone

constitutes the linkage itself as susceptible of being made available within the Umwelt for affecting the experience of conspecifics able similarly to abstract the connection from the connecteds in favor of alternative embodiments in communicative channels restructuring the objective precisely as understood and hence as subsequently experienced and experiencable.

238. "By the same stroke", notes Maritain (1957: 54), "a field of infinite possibilities would have opened"—the field of unlimited semiosis; for, as Merrell nicely puts it (1988: 257), "if a dog and the idea of a dog were separate, then there would be a relation between them, and therefore an idea of this relation, and so on, ad infinitum."

239. Precisely this objective difference between *idea* and *ideatum* not only linked by a relation but further by an idea of this relation, we saw, provides the basis for the development of the *codes* as such of cultural semiosis (along with the prospective infinity for the actualization of which, as Peirce noted [1901: 2.303], "intelligent consciousness must enter into the series"). Once developed, the codes, correlated with some sense-accessible *moyen* or channel of the physical surroundings (some material element of the "environment" in that part of its natural being which is also objectified for the species in question—in this case, our own species), stand in contrast with the "idea" itself conceived fundamentally (that is to say, subjectively) as the intraorganismic factor on the basis of which the object signified is rendered present within the experience—the objective field or Umwelt—of an utterer or an interpreter.

240. The code as such of cultural semiosis is, accordingly, that which establishes and provides the basis of the difference between objectivity in its bare difference from physical being or surroundings and objectivity as susceptible of some degree of critical control aimed at bringing out discursively for understanding the *differences within experience* between this and that (whatever be this and whatever that: any *contrast* as such viewed as important by a prospective utterer). Textuality, as the name for the objective order so modified by the stipulable realized (seized *ut significata* and implemented *ad placitum*), thus, constitutes the Lebenswelt or human Umwelt in its difference "as an intersection of textual surfaces" (Kristeva 1967: 65) from a biological Umwelt, which owes its objective structure to a strict correlation with a biological heritage.

241. Every Umwelt, every objective world, is species-specific and stands in contrast to the physical surroundings as a superordinate objective structure of relationships according to which the experienced unities and groupings owe their being as experienced. But the human Umwelt differs in that the Innenwelt with which it stands in correlation for its proper being as objective is one in which the users of signs use the signs used with an awareness of and play upon the signs' difference in their proper being—as relations—from both the perceptible vehicles of their signification and the objects of their signification.

242. Through this awareness, the communicative interactions of human animals results in a unique encoding whereby the element of stipulability comes to be actualized not just on the side of the Innenwelt, but in the objective structures themselves of experience, making for an objective world that is Lamarckian as well as Darwinian in its provenance. What is unique about the encoding, of course, is that the awareness on which it is based occurs regardless of the status of the objects signified vis-à-vis the physical elements of the surroundings.

243. For example, it makes no difference whether the putative physical elements of the objects of discourse—the objective elements posited or presupposed by the disourse to be also physical—are identified with perceptual items (such as sounds or colors), or with items de facto eluding our particular biological channels of sense (because they are too remote, as in the case of the surface features of planets and stars; or too tiny, as in the case of elements such as quarks and photons, molecules and atoms), or even with items de jure precluded from access by any biological channel of sense as such (the pure spirits, the God of later monotheism in general, Allah specifically, etc.). The point is that the relations of the human objective world as originally Umwelt come to be communicatively elaborated upon, restructured, and—above all—multiplied through the human use of signs so as to give rise to constantly new objects and aspects of objects which would never become known absent the dimension of stipulability experienced and grasped within perceived objects. Stipulability becomes a source in its own right for the creation of new relations, or more precisely, new sign-vehicles, which are shuttlecocks for weaving together natural perceptions and abductions in the fabric of hypotheses grasped as such and verified or modified (normally both in different respects) over the course of further experience as now including discourse in the species-specifically human sense.

244. This partial element of discursive critical control of objectification, introduced within the objective world by successful stipulations resulting in codes, is what makes of the objective world itself as dwelt in by human animals a text to be rewritten as well as merely interpreted through perceptual relations as such established through social interaction as such together with biological heritage. The human animal not only makes use of signs, but knows that the signs it makes use of are signs, not merely extensions of objects to be sought, avoided, or safely ignored. Whence, for the anthropos, "every picture of the world (be it a scientific law or a novel) is a book in its own right, open to further interpretation" (Eco 1992c: 150).

245. Textuality thus is objectivity marked by experienced differences in understanding, beginning from a difference in understanding rendered public through a having been transferred into the very objects experienced by the modality of sensible elements, whether unwittingly encoded or (the paradigm case) consciously picked for what seems promising in the circumstance to the one seeking to convey the difference (*signum ad placitum: deliberately coded objectivity*). In giving in this way a place to textuality as the objectivity proper to human beings, we saw also that what is required at the foundation of humanly species-specific objectivity is a notion of language larger and more fundamental than the network of differences conveyed through the employment of the arbitrary array we call "linguistic signs" in relation to the network of conventions and contrasts constituting them formally.

246. This larger and more fundamental notion required for language, indeed, appears to be something like what we have seen distinguishes anthroposemiosis *from* zoösemiosis and *within* biosemiosis generally, something like what Bakhtin asserts (as cited by Danow 1985: 139): "The human act is a text *in potentia*". Maritain observes of this larger notion, this surplus creating an admixture whereby the whole of experience is textualized through culture (c.1964: 91):

> The term *language* does not relate only to the words which we use, it covers also all that which serves us to make ourselves understood, and therefore the whole imagery which

we use and which is that of the men to whom we speak, at such and such a moment of time and in such and such a place on earth. (Supposing that through some telephone through duration we could tell a contemporary of Julius Caesar something which concerns our epoch, could we speak to him of airplanes and of electronic machines, of the British Parliament, or of the Praesidium of the Communist Party? The other person would not understand anything; it would indeed be necessary to use the imagery furnished by his own type of culture, as well as his own words and his own syntax.)

247. Given the coextensiveness, then, of textuality with the objective world of human experience, it is all a question not only of how one is to construe the "linguistic admixture" demonstrable within every semiological system—i.e., within the totality of human experience, including the experience of "nature" so-called—but also of how one accounts for the *semiological surplus*. This accounting brings us to the heart of the question of what semiotics finally is and what it has to contribute to the study of either branch or any subdivision of the accepted division of university studies today into the "sciences" on the one hand and the "humanities" on the other, including literature and anthropology (linked today in the recent realization that ethnographic writing itself knows its fashions and constitutes a distinct "literary genre" with several varieties).

248. Contrary to the popular consciousness which thinks of semiotics as pertaining to the humanities side of the traditional division, and to literary and structuralist concerns in particular, semiotics introduces a point of view which encompasses both sides of the division and assimilates to itself the very foundations which the traditional division of sciences into human and natural presupposes.

249. Thure von Uexküll (1981: 148) puts the matter in a nutshell:

A science which embraces the natural sign systems alongside and before the human sign systems we call "language" must at the same time break down the traditional division between the human sciences and the natural sciences.

Thus semiotics pertains to a renewal of the foundations of our understanding of knowledge and experience and a transformation of the disciplinary superstructures culturally distributing that understanding (the traditional disciplines as currently founded), more than it pertains to the renewal of any single currently established discipline within the humanities.

250. It is not just a question of new foundations for the human sciences, and a putting aside of the ill-advised or—as Culler more mordantly muses (1981: 20)—"futile attempt to distinguish the humanities from the social sciences". It is a question rather of the understanding—that is, of the interpretation *secundum ideam et consuetudines subsumptas ad placitum* or the *encoding* of objectivity *hic et nunc*; and of a message "in living speech" for which ultimately "there is no code" except the prospective one of the dialogical moment carried here and now by this sensory *moyen* from among the many possible (such as braille, to cite a local example of "this-planetary" semiosis).

251. The question of understanding posed in this way requires that understanding itself be viewed in the totality of its actual situation as the pattern or rather network of patterns which give to experience its human hue. Even the natural sciences, no less than and in their very contrast with the human sciences, appear as specified derivatives from the larger process of semiosis which englobes the whole of knowledge and belief as a construct developed from experienced relations in their aspect of "renvoi" (Jakobson 1979). Without exception, the very work by which a given object is defined and investigated becomes itself part of the object's constitution within experience as a node of an intertextual whole. Even the putative "natural signs", which are experienced precisely as involving relations independent of the interpretation whereby they enjoy "renvoi", are subordinate also to historical contexts of anthroposemiosis whereby they exist as interpreted in this or that way—as we see in the distinctive medical and scientific practices, as well as in the literary traditions, genres, and styles of distinct cultural Umwelts. In just this way, "the fact that our knowledge is relational and that we cannot separate facts from the language by means of which we expresss (and construct) them, encourages interpretation" (Eco 1992c: 143).

252. Semiotics appears thus not as a discipline or science among other disciplines and sciences, whether human or natural, but as a *perspective* concerned with *the matrix of all the disci-*

plines inasmuch as the action of signs gives the texture and pattern to experience. In this way, through the action of signs, nature becomes ever more fully aware of itself and achieves something of totality in the transcendence over physical being of the historical Umwelts as species-specific objective worlds. This transcendence achieves a critical threshold in the reflexivity of the Lebenswelt. Here the action of signs makes of each object a prospective text and of each text an intertext incorporating not only life and fiction but the whole of nature as well through unlimited semiosis. And, from within anthroposemiosis itself, the grasp of the actions of signs *in actu signato* thematized for study in its own right is what semiotics finally is.

253. The action of signs as responsible for objectivity in the first place and throughout, thus, is at the bottom of semiotics' so-called "imperialism". It is not a question of imperialism, however, but of a study of the action of signs, which soon enough forces the investigator to recognize the role of experience as the ground of understanding at all points (Deely 1992a), and the centrality of history in making of that ground a rich and fertile soil for the growth of experience (Williams and Pencak 1991). It is more a question of *recovering from* the imperialism of the natural sciences, physics in particular, as the distinct heritage of positivism, and of seeing the subsets of semiosis within anthroposemiosis for what they are in relation to the whole. Floyd Merrell makes the point nicely (1988: 262 n. 12):

> In general the hermeneutical movement has been beneficial insofar as it has directed attention to the role of interpretation and understanding in the humanities. However, Stephen Toulmin observes, and rightly so [1982: 99-100], that this movement 'has done us a disservice also because it does not recognize any comparable role for interpretation in the natural sciences and in this way sharply separates the two fields of scholarship and experience. Consequently, . . . the central truths and virtues of hermeneutics have become encumbered with a whole string of false inferences and misleading dichotomies.

254. A truly "radical hermeneutics", such as Caputo calls for (1987), must first of all come round to the semiotic point of view. That point of view, that standpoint, achieved its first systematic expression (Poinsot 1632a) precisely by realizing and thematizing the point that interpretive activity or "hermeneutics" (the privi-

leged term for the notion in Latin times was "perihermenias", as I noted in *Introducing Semiotic*, p. 188ff., note 16) is subextensive with the life of the mind and subtensive of nature itself as engendering life. This is the governing insight of the semiotic enterprise integrally conceived in all its phases and periods. Semiotics provides a perspective on the whole of experience in what is proper to it as experience, and is thus "first" among the sciences not as one among the others, such as traditional metaphysics envisaged, but as *doctrina* contrasts to *scientia* (Deely 1982: 127-130, 1986c; Williams 1985a; Anderson et al. 1984; Sebeok 1976: ix). Semiotics addresses what is first in the understanding, in contrast with what is derivative therefrom (Deely 1987).

255. It is thus a question of realizing what is proper to the semiotic point of view, and of distinguishing what is foundational from what is consequent thereto and partial thereof.

256. From the beginning, both from outside (e.g., Ricoeur 1981 and after) and from within (e.g., Barthes 1964; Bakhtin 1971[39]), the semiotics movement has suffered from practitioners who mistook some part of semiosis for the whole of semiotics and who systematically strove to reduce the perspective of semiotic to the perspective of that part with which they identified it.

257. From within, the problem has been more serious. The European influence after Saussure has created in the popular consciousness, even within anthropology, a de facto equation of semiotics with structuralist and literary concerns. This influence is only now beginning to be absorbed in the broader American influence emanating from Peirce (whose writings from at least 1867 [see Peirce's comment in c.1909: 6.322] until his death are subtended by the arc of semiotics in its foundational concerns and prospective totality as the perspective of experience itself engendering and nurturing throughout specialized inquiries into nature and culture as nature's human part).

258. To this day, in much of the literature sociologically defining the contemporary development of semiotics, a naive assumption remains transparently at work equating the semiotic point of view with literary preoccupations. This assumption, in tending toward the explicit extreme of equating semiosis with "the product of encoding signs" (Morgan 1985: 8), has begotten a bizarre intertextuality through which Peirce is, as it were, stood on a Barthian head: "linguistics is not a part of the general science of signs, even a privileged part, it is semiology which is a part of linguistics" (Roland Barthes 1964: 11). Thus, as prominent an author as Robert Scholes is able to assert that, "usually defined as the study of signs (from a Greek root meaning *sign*), semiotics has in fact become the study of codes" (1982: ix).

259. To all such views—the gamut of writings more or less dominated by the tendency within semiotics toward the explicitly glottocentric extreme—apply Sebeok's blunt rejoinder to Hawkes' assertion (1977: 124) that the boundaries of semiotics "are coterminous with structuralism" and that "the interests of the two spheres are not fundamentally separate":

> Nothing could be a more deluded misconstrual of the facts of the matter, but the speciousness of this and associated historical deformations are due to our own inertia in having hitherto neglected the serious exploration of our true lineage [Sebeok 1984: 2].

260. It is a question of ignorance, not only in the historical sense (a negation of knowledge), but also in the sense defined by Aristotle in his treatise on scientific proof (c.348-347BC: Book I, Chap. 16, 79b23-24) as "a positive state of mind"—to wit, "error produced by inference", the erroneous inference that the linguistic texture of anthroposemiosis justifies a linguistic model as the paradigm for semiotic analysis. The semiological tendency to treat intertextuality as a self-contained whole, centered on the literary sign and closed in upon itself through an unlimited (but autistic) semiosis, is fundamentally misguided because of the compartmentalization of nature from culture that results from importing the presuppositions of idealistic philosophy into the perspective opened by the sign. This imposition amounts to an attempt to find a way around facing the task of developing the perspective of semiotics from within, according to the requirements of its own object—semiosis (as we have said). But the attempt fails, leading only to a *cul de sac*.

261. Developed from within, the perspective opened by the sign is as removed from idealism as it is from realism, precisely because it constitutes a thirdness in the place of their binary opposition. What was for Peirce a mere sop to Cerberus—i.e., the insertion of "upon a person" in one of his definitions of the interpretant as the effect proper to the sign as such (1908: 80-81)—becomes in this way an artificial boundary (as in Riffaterre 1985: 52), a *pars pro toto* fallacy, as has been said (¶ 235 above, Glosses 38 and 39). The study of sign action cannot properly be confined to the boundaries of the artifactual nor measured by the paradigm of linguistic exchanges. When it is artificially so confined and measured, it is cut off from the context required ultimately even for the intelligibility of the literary, as Johansen demonstrated in his masterful "Prolegomena to a semiotic theory of text interpretation" (1985).

262. A perspective which, while striving to be semiotic, takes for its object specifically literary textuality as constituted terminatively, that is, as itself objectified and scrutinized as known—much as if it were the "given" for semiotics comparable to the stones of the geologist or the reptilian bones of paleontology—has yet to achieve the standpoint proper to the sign. The perspective proper to semiotic arises, exactly as in Locke's anomalous conclusion (1690: 361-362), with the idea of the idea as a nexus of relationships which carry the cognizant subject beyond itself and constitute at the same time an Umwelt, a cognitive map of the environment which is strictly irreducible to the prejacent physical and species-specific for every life form, including the human one. In the human case, however, as we have seen, the Umwelt or "Lebenswelt" contrasts with the Umwelts of purely zoösemiotic life forms in being yet transformable into an asymptotic number of variant models through the unique *moyen* of language in its proper essence as distinct from communication (for which language is only exapted).

263. Thus, within experience, the experience of alterity taken as such, linguistically marked, and not necessarily extinguished, first gives rise to the human Umwelt in its difference from the experience structures which are purely zoösemiotically developed. When Heidegger asks "Why does Being get 'conceived' 'proximally' in terms of the present-at-hand *and not* in terms of the ready-to-hand, which indeed lies *closer* to us?" (1927: 487), the answer is to be found in the difference between zoösemiosis as common to animals and anthroposemiosis as unique to linguistic animals, a claim we will examine more in detail in Part IV. Aspects of the physical surroundings are objectified within the Umwelt as ready-to-hand and are thus closer to us zoösemiotically as **animal linguisticum**, but these same aspects are further objectified within the Lebenswelt as also ("in themselves",

i.e., in their environmentality) present-at-hand and are thus closer to us anthroposemiotically as *animal linguisticum*. This is the origin not only of the reductive idea of "reality" (as we saw in ¶ 134 above, text and Gloss 24), but also of the very idea and possibility of code as a system of contrastive relations such as Saussure's *langue*. The semiotic self of the Innenwelt, as finely brought out by Danow (1984, 1984a, 1991), is already dialogical and hence capable of constituting Bourdieu's (claimed) fact (1977: 20, more accurately "Bourdieu's counterfactual"): "coherently and appropriately using an infinite number of sentences in an infinite number of situations".

264. In the end, it is the idea of reality as the species-specific objective world that gives intelligibility to critick and place to the activity of criticism in the human world. For the relationship of Innenwelt to Umwelt is such that we finally understand that what has been called "fiction" is not an imitation of something else so much as an expression of a semiosis which makes of the something else just as easily an imitation of what began as fiction.

265. In this way, as Culler puts it (1981: 38), "one of the effects of semiotics is to question the distinction between literary and nonliterary discourse". It is a question of remodeling the world—the objective world, but as it includes in its proper being something also of physical surroundings. It is not so much that "realism is in essence deeply mythic" (Con Davis 1985: 56) as that reality—the reality of human experience, wherein the line between what is dependent upon and independent of interpretive activity can never be finally drawn because that very line itself shifts with each new achievement of understanding—is in essence thoroughly semiosic. The consequences of this for mimetic theory have only begun to be explored. In this context, one can appreciate Culler's reasons (1981: 35) for deeming literature—if not "the" at least "a"—"most interesting case of semiosis":

> Though [literature] is clearly a form of communication, it is cut off from the immediate pragmatic purposes which simplify other sign situations. The potential complexities of signifying processes work freely in literature. Moreover, the difficulty of saying precisely what is communicated is here accompanied by the fact that signification is indubitably taking place. One cannot argue, as one might when dealing

with physical objects or events of various kinds, that the phenomena in question are meaningless. Literature forces one to face the problem of the indeterminacy of meaning, which is a central if paradoxical property of semiotic systems.[40] Finally, unlike so many other systems which are devoted to ends external to themselves and their own processes, literature is itself a continual exploration of and reflection upon signification in all its forms: an interpretation of experience; a commentary on the validity of various ways of interpreting experience; an exploration of the creative, revelatory, and deceptive powers of language; a critique of the codes and interpretive processes manifested in our languages and in previous literature. In so far as literature turns back on itself and examines, parodies, or treats ironically its own signifying procedures, it becomes the most complex account of signification we possess.

266. It is difficult to see how the word "account" is used here, where some synonym of "example" or "token" seems to be demanded by the context. Also, the concluding "we possess" is essential here, for our creation of literature is only an extension of the larger semiosis of nature itself within which anthroposemiosis constitutes a local field. It surely cannot be soberly claimed that literature is more complex than the semiosis which possesses us rather than we it.

267. What should perhaps be said is that literature, as the most presuppositioned phase of anthroposemiosis able to deal directly with the object as nonexistent (instead of discovering its nonexistence by chagrin, as happens in natural science), requires the most complete account of signification, for the reason Johansen states (1985: 261-262; cf. King 1987): while a literary "text itself need not refer to any past experiences", nonetheless, "experience of objects, actions, or events, similar to what is referred to in a given text is a prerequisite to the understanding of it".

268. That and how the universe of discourse—any discourse, including literary—"is bound with the experience of the parties" to the discourse is exactly what Johansen has shown in his essay bringing literary theory into the mainstream of Sebeok's "major tradition". Johansen gives three reasons for his original introduction of the diagrammatic model of the "pyramid of [anthropo] semiosis" examined in ¶ 180 above (1985: 265):

on the one hand, it is intended as a heuristic device which should make it possible to recognize the multiple relationships of each element; on the other, it should further the inquiry into the nature of the signifying process by calling attention to the interrelations between certain aspects of meaning production and interpretation, and, of course, by provoking objections.

269. For these very same reasons, we can here fruitfully redistribute Johansen's model according to the ten interdependent triangular planes comprising the model—six radiating from the sign-pole, four from the organismic poles of utterer and interpreter—in order to underscore how presuppositioned and farthest removed from autonomy ("the myth of intertextuality and intersemioticity", as we might say) a literary semiotics is in the scheme of experience. Reflecting our idea that it is more a question of semiotic surplus than of linguistic admixture that ought to guide our understanding of textuality, Johansen remarks flatly (1985: 286), as the reason for "the point made in [his] article", that "without taking into consideration the role played by nonverbal semiosis in the generation and interpretation of text meaning, the very fact that meaning is possible becomes a mystery". And he dismisses as a "fiction" the idea that "verbal knowledge" can be derived or operate independently of the knower's experience, as word meaning itself is already an abduction.

270. In effect, Johansen's pyramid can be made to serve as an interpretant for Bakhtin's remark (1975: 48) that the language of a novel "is a system of intersecting planes", as can be seen (on the following page) by the dissection to which Johansen's pyramid lends itself.

271. Dr. Raymond Wilson of the Loras College literature faculty observed that, of the ten planes, only the propositional plane is divorced from contact with both the pole of the semiotic self (the addresser, author or "utterer") and the pole of the semiotic other (the addressee, reader or "interpreter"). This radical detachment of course explains the impersonal quality of "validity" as a logical property of arguments. But Johansen points out that it by no means follows that "propositional content" (dicisignificative utterance, I would rather say) is unrelated to the historicity of the speech community, as logicians (e.g., Quine 1965: 6) ritually pretend in their own version of literature. The content of

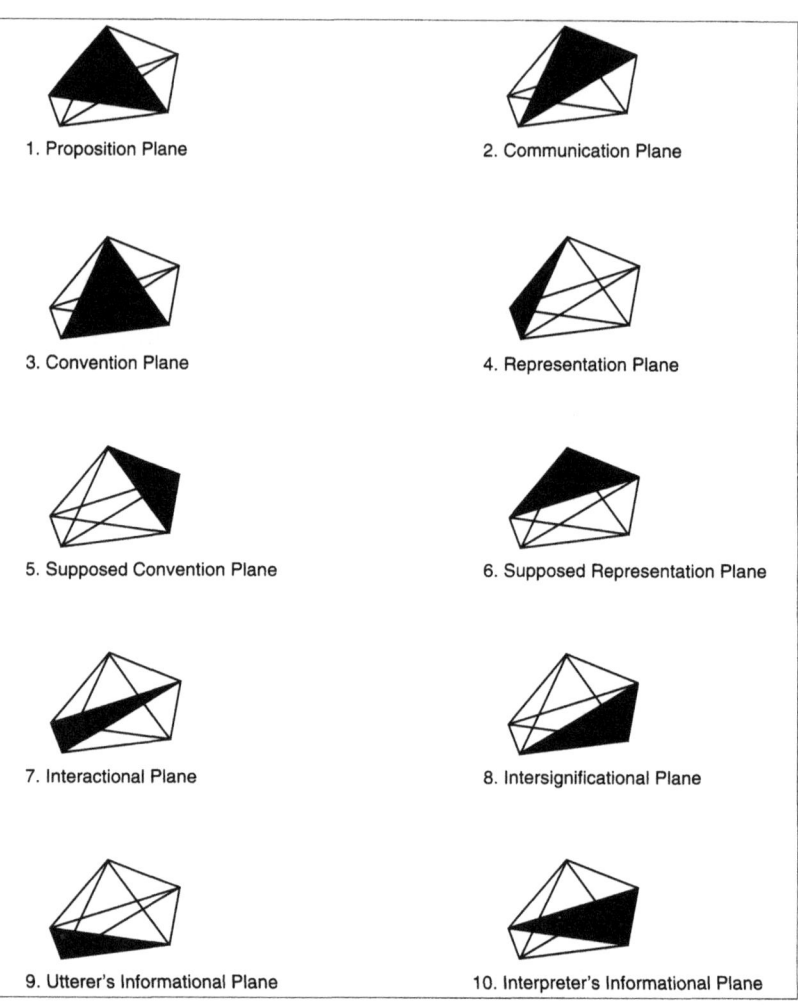

Figure 10. The Planes of Semiosis within Discourse

natural language is inevitably presupposed to logical symbolizations, in the quite strong sense that any further stipulative system is an abstraction whose explanation requires eventual recursion to a natural language matrix. And here, in Johansen's words (1985: 286): "just as the building up of the propositional aspect of language is related to the informational semiosis and its dependence upon a historical environment, so is the actional aspect of language embedded in other semiotic interactional systems which historically are dependent on the group, class, and culture to which the parties belong".

272. But, beyond the anthroposemiotic peculiarities of the plane of dicisigns, one enters seriously into Johansen's argument when one realizes that the semiotics of texts, if pursued integrally rather than according to faddish abstractions, involves one with all these planes simultaneously according to emphases that can be varied for the purposes of the analysis at hand. But one realizes as well that semiotics begins to be constituted in the full scope of its proper possibilities precisely when its foundational inquiries are made commensurate with the full scope of semiosis as a process subtending the whole of nature so far as nature involves a development in time along lines that transcend the physically established patterns of any given moment in the cosmic evolution (Deely 1990: Chapter 6; 1991). (Small wonder that Peirce occasionally despaired—as in 1908: 80-81—"of making my own broader conception understood".[41]) And as that constitution makes itself visible in the diverse works contributing more and more consciously to its edification, we see that the "place marked out in advance" for semiotics and giving it "a right to existence", in Saussure's curious expression (i.1906-1911: 33; cf. Russell 1982, Gloss 30 on ¶ 190 above), is something that cannot be defined in a way exclusive of any activity of interpretation, but rather can be defined only inclusive thereof.

273. To study the sign is to uncover semiosis, and therewith a web as vast as nature itself. Within this comprehensive web, that "miniscule segment" which we try to compartmentalize as culture appears rather as a part to be synthesized in the destructive distillation of the single insight-without-parts,[42] namely, the insight that the speculative and the practical achievements of human understanding—the scientific and the literary, let us say—are themselves alike mobile interpretive structures. These structures, as *interpretive* structures, succeed only as long as they maintain the renvoi whereby they are constantly carried beyond what can be reduced to physically given and sensibly accessible elements, even though it is precisely by containing those elements and supporting them as nodes in the whole network of renvoi that the interpretations of language can be shared and developed throughout the species and, to some extent, along interspecific lines as well.

274. The highest achievement of semiosis in the physical environment is life and the concomitant transformation of the physical surroundings to sustain and develop life. But life itself finds

its highest achievement first in the species-specific Umwelts and then, through the exaptation of language in communication of alternative models, in the Lebenswelt specific to the anthroposemiosis whence our interpretations always arise and to which they inevitably recur—even if only further to transform that objective world by new understandings and arrangements of old possibilities which, in the rearrangement, themselves become transformed in ways not merely unexpected, but previously unforeseeable. It is the arrangement, the web of renvoi sustaining the environmental and sensible elements at each moment according to patterns which are not themselves sensible nor reducible to what is sensible, that constitutes the semiotic object in its full possibilities for understanding.

275. The web of renvoi constituting experience and providing all access to objects of whatever type is a "reality" quite different from that conceived by the ancients, medievals, and early moderns alike—a prejacent given in which the mind had no part and to which the observer contributed hopefully nothing. Nor is it a reality wholly reducible to the mind's own workings on the basis of a hidden outer realm and a hidden inner mechanism of understanding linked only by the phenomena constituted by the mind itself, as the late moderns came to fancy as a kind of forced conclusion (from the equation of objects with ideas with which modernity in philosophy mistakenly began). The reality in question is something much richer than either reduction, something more collusive even than the rapport between fly trap and fly in the realm of insects and flowers. It is, in a phrase, semiotic reality, the true reality of direct and immediate experience, wherein the distinction between what is dependent upon and what is independent of interpretive activity can never be finally drawn because the very basis itself of the distinction is reconstituted by the shift occasioned by each new achievement of understanding, whether "speculative" or "practical", "scientific" or "literary".

276. In cases where the object of inquiry is in important respects given in fully determinate ways in advance of the investigation, as well as "alongside it" (as it were—it is a question here of the "physical lining" requisite to experience), such as occurs when the study is to be of some natural science, the difficulty of understanding the perspective within which the object appears, as Heidegger noted (1927: 10), though present, is not so great as to be overwhelming.

277. Consider the case of the human sciences, especially from such a perspective as that provided by semiotics, which seeks to understand the appearing of any object whatsoever within experience, and within which even the natural sciences themselves appear as specified derivatives from the larger process of semiosis which englobes the whole of knowledge and belief as a construct from experienced relations in their aspect of "renvoi". In this case the very work by which the objectification of semiosis is defined and investigated becomes itself part of the object's constitution. This aspect of "renvoi" that experienced relations acquire occurs only in and through experience, as Poinsot notes (1632a: Book I, Question 2, 137/4, note 4): hence the fact (noted in ¶ 231 above) remains that even the putative "natural signs", which involve relations independently of the interpretation whereby they enjoy "renvoi", become subordinate to historical contexts of semiosis, wherein they exist as interpreted in this or that way. This fact, as we have observed, is notably illustrated in the medical practices (acupuncture, anesthesia, circumcision, etc.) of distinct cultural Umwelts.

278. In short, like all the human sciences for which it provides the matrix, "semiotics is not only a field of different approaches to a unique object but also a field of sometimes conflicting philosophical definitions of this unique object" (Eco 1979: 77). Indeed, semiotics is a field whereby alone its object is constituted in its full actuality not just as a process in nature but also as the *prise de conscience* whereby nature becomes fully aware of itself and achieves its final totality in the transcendence over physical being of the historical Umwelts as realized through the reflexivity of the Lebenswelt.

279. Among the human sciences, semiotics is unique in being a study concerned with the matrix of all the sciences—not only the disciplines of the humanities but of the natural sciences as well—and in revealing the centrality of history to the enterprise of understanding in its totality. This centrality is revealed through the codes of culture which alone sustain, beyond the individual insight, the *commens*, or shared mentality, which defines a language (such as English), a discipline (such as physics or literary criticism), a subculture, a nation, and, ultimately, civilization itself. The centrality of history for large-scale human understanding, we may observe, is evidenced in all of civilization's conflicting strands of temporally embedded interpre-

tations giving structure to the everyday experience of the conspecifics capable of language in the larger sense sketched by Maritain and insisted upon by Bakhtin (1971: 214, as cited in Todorov 1981: 56): "in living speech, messages are, strictly speaking, created for the first time in the process of transmission, and ultimately [i.e., prejacent to and independent of the anthroposemiosis itself] there is no code".[43] (Hence "Bourdieu's fact", as we saw in ¶ 263 above.)

280. In this perspective, criticism—reflexive methodologies in general explorative of the domain of critick—need not be a parasitic function of terminal cleverness, a tiresome exercise in ideological harassment, or an exercise in empty formalisms making of living discourse an idler's puzzle. Criticism can contribute in its own right to bringing into explicit objectivity contributions of the understanding which have been left in a virtual state of exercise rather than expressly signified and recognized as such. This function, in whatever specific genre and modality, would be criticism at its best, criticism displaying the rich art of evaluating and analyzing with knowledge and propriety the works of civilization, especially art, music, and literature, wherein the free play of intellect and the full contrast of the objective to the biological and physical orders come into prominence. It would also be a criticism not equated with semiotics but participating in the development of semiotics, a development drawing into its network of renvoi the whole of previous thought, present science, and future civilization.

281. Anthroposemiosis thus reveals itself as the fulfillment of human "nature" in the creations of "culture", scientific and literary alike, and as inseparable from the zoösemiotic achievements with which human nature is continuous and on which it depends.

282. Zoösemiosis not only defines an objective structure whereby the human species is inserted into the general biosemiotic interplay of Umwelts, but also in its turn rests upon the phytosemiotic and endosemiotic lines of thirdness whereby the secondness of physical nature itself is bound up with biosemiosis as the "common universe of action". This universe is, as Johansen so well put it (1985: 261), the "necessary precondition of understanding" and the final redoubt of thirdness through the abstract governance (in physiosemiosis) of physical laws.

283. In this vast development of emergent levels, novel on their own plane but semiotically interdependent with what has gone before and what might come after, anthropsemiosis develops through a modeling system which not only transcends the physical (in its zoösemiotic phases) but also achieves (in its anthroposemiotic phases), both in science and fiction, an independence of the prejacent physical unparalleled in semiosis elsewhere, zoösemiosis in particular. Here, in the freedom of the intellect, anthroposemiosis comes into its final responsibility for what kind of world semiosis shall have wrought in this planetary situation. Here, anthroposemiosis is responsible not just for our conspecifics, but for that whole plethora of sign systems which have made and continue to make our conspecifics able to thrive and indulge in the fantasies whereby codes of domination and institutions of servitude are revealed as increasingly intolerable and improper to the condition of a being able to play with the line between what is and what could be by way of human design. Humans are able (whence follows the obligation) constantly to redraw that line in favor of the possibilities which enhance the quality, let us say, not of the biosphere, but of the semiosphere. For "we move in signs as bodies move in space and time, we think and feel in signs, and we ourselves, along with our analyses of signs, are produced by signs" (Baer 1981: 197).

284. In attempting to model anthroposemiosis, we are attempting to thematize this realization of "man's glassy essence" (Peirce 1892; Singer 1984; Corrington 1992a; Deely 1992b) and to see how appear through that glassy essence all those other achievements of nature in "the common universe of action" which fiction presupposes and anthroposemiosis constitutes insofar as such a universe is grasped from within human experience and known in any particular—that is to say, objectively.

Part IV. Otherness

285. If our preceding analysis is anywhere near the mark, discovery of "the other" is far from anything unique to anthropology. Anthropology's object of investigation is unique only in that the "otherness" it brings within our purview as demanding to be understood is on the same essential level as that of the investigator. The problem is less one of passing an "acid test" of including our own perceptions under the 'ethno-' rubric (Herzfeld 1987: 199) than it is one of thematically realizing and critically controlling the consequences of such inclusion. The risk of "tumbling back into a second barbarism" (ibid.) is much reduced once it is well understood that the inevitable and irreducible ethnocentricity of our own perceptions as such need never be given the last word in the development of an interpretation, for the reason that, as we shall shortly see, the primordial horizon of interpretation, insofar as interpretation is an anthroposemiotic phenomenon inclusive of but differentiating zoösemiosis from within, *begins* with the other.

286. Naive ethnocentrism (Eurocentrism) as the first barbarism arose from the failure to understand, within anthropology, that every Lebenswelt, including a researcher's, is experienced from within as an Umwelt first of all: the objective world of the human animal is the human animal's reality. Researchers who fail to understand that the Lebenswelt in its difference from Umwelt is yet never separated therefrom, never completely removed from the virtualities of zoösemiotic influence as such, create the risk of the second barbarism (cf. Briggs 1986: esp. 112-125), the barbarism of the standpoint supposed to have transcended all perspectivization. Ethnocentrism need not be naive, but neither is it completely eliminable. We are required to subject it reflexively and in a thematic way to critical control, so as to keep track of the changing aspects in which perceptions of superiority may or may not be justified in the nature of given situations.

287. In this sense, we cannot avoid including our own perceptions under the "ethno" rubric. For however diverse the patterns of culture and modes of socialization separating the anthropologist from the individuals whom the anthropologist observes, discourses with, and learns to interact with socially through gradually but increasingly (even if asymptotically) common categories (objective modalities) of encounter, the otherness is bound up with the underlying common measure of conspecificity (discursive conspecificity, as we have said in ¶s 154 and 167, not biological conspecificity as happens to obtain among linguistic animals on this planet). The assimilation of other to self and self to other at this level depends in principle on the reliance of anthropology from the outset directly on grasping the relations as such bound up with all artifacts, but especially with artifacts and patterns of behavior as observable which are dependent on language for their proper intelligibility. Postlinguistic symbols, structures, and behaviors alone provide the adequate object of anthropology. Yet these, as we have seen, are totally inaccessible to the understanding except through the vehicle of species-specifically human discourse. (Whence Ardener's puzzlement [1977: 173]: "The practice of anthropology cannot be quite analogous to literary translation, although the differences are not easy to express.")

288. Otherness created through semiosis within conspecificity, however, while transparently a function of the networking of objective relations superordinate to the elements of the physical environment as such, requires to be seen as an instance of a much more general phenomenon. What our analysis has suggested is that the idea of reality itself is the original idea of otherness, and that this idea occurs at, or very near to, the awakening of human intelligence itself in its contrast as a mode of awareness with perception.

289. The contrast of "sense" with "intellect" is an ancient one in philosophy, often overdrawn[44] and, in modern times, generally denied.[45] But there is a difference within experience between what is sensed and what is understood regardless of whether or not it can also be sensed. We examined this difference in the discussion above of textuality, especially with reference to objects whose very understanding essentially excludes a proper sensory instantiation, either because the object in question has never existed in the physical environment, or, more radically, because the manner of existence postulated for the object is *ex hypothesi* of its nature inaccessible to any sensory modality.

290. There is, accordingly, something which can be expressed through linguistic means that cannot be communicated in any other way, something that differentiates human awareness as species-specifically as the exaptation of language species-specifically differentiates human communication, and does so more primordially, since the apprehension in question antecedes the exaptation of language and, moreover, seems to be of a piece with it. There is, to borrow Thomas Aquinas's characterization of the situation, something which is to understanding (or "intellection") as sound is to hearing (c.1266: I. q. 5. art. 2, p. 191) and color is to seeing (c.1254-1256: In 1. sent. dist. 19. q. 5. ad 7., p. 55). There is, in short, a *primum intelligibile*, just as there is a *primum visibile* and a *primum audibile*.

291. This is not a question often posed or easily faced. When we look at things, it is the diversity of shapes and colors, not the omnipresent fact of color as enabling seeing at all, that interests us. So too when we listen: it is the particular sounds and combinations of sounds that interest us, not the general fact that sound as such enables the particular hearings. So too in investigating what anything is, it is the particulars of the case, the reasons for this feature and that characteristic, that interest us, not the fact that were things not intelligible in general, the particulars of the case would both forever elude us and could not be inquired into in the first place.

292. The first of all species-specifically human conceptions, therefore, is not a starting point for intellectual knowledge in a temporal sense. That is to say, it is not a question of a linear beginning which is left behind as understanding progresses. The question concerns what must be present throughout intellectual awareness whenever and as long as understanding occurs. Other particularized moments of understanding may proceed out of it, but it itself can proceed from nothing else, precisely because, respecting this object (this aspect or dimension of objectivity, let us say), there is no other preceding cognition as basis of its formation. The eye works together with the ear and with touch and taste, and so forth, in forming our perception of an object as sensible. Yet the contribution of each channel is distinct and irreducible. So also with the understanding, which contributes precisely intelligibility to what is directly perceived and sensed. What this intelligibility consists in is the objective world presented in perception apprehended in relation to itself.

293. The relation of an object to itself is a mind-dependent relation. Even if the object is in one or another aspect also a thing, i.e., a mind-independent element of the physical environment, as is always in part the case with an Umwelt, any given thing "in itself" simply is what it is—it is not *related to* itself, it *is* itself. For a thing to be *related* to itself cognition must intervene, and cognition of a specifically intellectual type, able to construct and grasp relations independent of the related terms which, in the present case, are not even mind-independently distinct. Here, however, at the level of *primum intelligibile*, it is not a question of any given object of perception being cognized under a relation to itself. It is rather a question of the objective world as such, the Umwelt as the totality of objectification at any given moment, being grasped in relation to itself.[46] Peirce calls this "Firstness", "the Idea of that which is such as it is regardless of anything else" (1903d: CP 5.66); "the positive internal characters of the subject in itself" (c.1906: CP 5.469); "the conception of being or existing independent of anything else" (1891: CP 6.32); "the present, in general", or "IT" (1867: CP 1.547):

> This is a conception, because it is universal. But as the act of *attention* has no connotation at all, but is the pure denotative power of the mind, that is to say, the power which directs the mind to an object, in contradistinction to the power of thinking any predicate of that object,—so the conception of *what is present in general*, which is nothing but the general recognition of what is contained in attention, has no connotation, and therefore no proper unity. . . . Before any comparison or discrimination can be made between what is present, what is present must have been recognized as such, as *it*, and subsequently the metaphysical parts which are recognized by abstraction are attributed to this *it*, but the *it* cannot itself be made a predicate.

Peirce goes on to identify this "it", the objective world as the here and now present in general, with one of the meanings of the philosophical term substance, and to exclude from "it" the conception of *being* as a predicative notion bound up with the copula. But his remarks show an ignorance of a main Latin tradition in one of its little explored particulars, the very one we are attempting to explore now, namely, the determination of the species-specifically human contribution to cognition from which language and the postlinguistic symbols of culture in general arise. Being in the sense Peirce rejects as inapplicable to the IT, the being wherein the junction of predicate to subject occurs, is only one of more than a dozen or so *derivative* senses Aquinas assigns to "being" as the *"primum cognitum"* of intellection.[47]

294. The term "being" is one of those most bandied about in the history of philosophy. Whence it has been assigned a number of determinate meanings, including substance, which Peirce also assigns "in one of its meanings" to Firstness or the IT (ibid.). But in making this assignment Peirce is violating the Third as well as the Sixth Rule of the "Ethics of Terminology". Even the one sense of substance which partially fits the IT—Aristotle's "first substance", which is neither predicated of a subject nor in a subject—does not justify the identification of the two notions, for two reasons. First, that which is first known by understanding in its difference from sense perception does not fail to be a predicate because it is identified with, or includes in itself, the notion of first substance. It fails because "in the first intellectual cognition of all things neither can the understanding apply itself nor the will the understanding, since there will not have been another cognition by virtue of which such application could be made, and therefore there is only at work in the case the immediate proportion of object known with power knowing".[48] Second, that which is first known by understanding is the prospectively definable structure or essence of perceptible objects, not by any means as restricted to "substance" as the being proper to individuals existing as such, but as including equally "whatever can be conceived in the manner of some nature and essence, including characteristics of individuals and modes, and indeed singularity itself can be understood after the manner of an essence".[49] The understanding investigates the properties of perceived objects through the concept of a definable unifying structure or principle having an order and dependence on the perception as on the point of departure from which the sought for principle of unification can be derived.[50]

295. We can say, then, that that which is first apprehended intellectually, insofar as intellection differs from perception, is the objective world in relation to itself. In this apprehension the imperceptible "relation to itself" is the sole contribution of understanding. Yet this contribution is sufficient both to elevate the perceptible elements of the Umwelt to the level of intelligibility and, by the same stroke, to transform the Umwelt into a Lebenswelt, that is to say, an objective world perfused with stipulable signs apprehended as such in the heart of otherwise naturally determined significations.

296. It was a very important and insufficiently understood insight of Latin scholasticism that the physical environment, insofar as it enters into the cognitive structure constituting an Umwelt, is of itself sensible but not of itself intelligible. Understanding itself, taking the materials of sensation and perception as its base, has to make that material actually intelligible. This it does by first seeing the whole material of perception—the objective world or Umwelt in all its parts—in relation to itself, over and above the relations to biological needs and interests which are already factored into the structure of the Umwelt by virtue of the biological heritage of the cognitive organism.[51] Hence the objective world, seen in relation to itself, already consists of a mixture of mind-independent and mind-dependent relations structuring particular objects but undistinguished as such in the apprehension constitutive of Lebenswelt.[52] Thus the first action of the understanding is to apprehend its objects in such a way that they *can eventually* be understood critically, and this is to apprehend the objective world under that mind-dependent relation which allows its contents to appear, truly or falsely, as present-at-hand and not merely ready-to-hand (as they appear to the animals which are not human). *Ens ut primum cognitum*, "Firstness", does no more than establish the foundation for the eventual arising of questions of the form "What is that?"

> The idea of the absolutely first must be entirely separated from all conception of or reference to anything else; for what involves a second is itself a second to that second. The first must therefore be present and immediate, so as not to be a second to a representation. It must be fresh and new, for if old it is second to its former state. It must be initiative, original, spontaneous, and free; otherwise it is second to a determining cause. It is also something vivid and conscious;

so only it avoids being the object of some sensation. It precedes all synthesis and all differentiation; it has no unity and no parts. It cannot be articulately thought: assert it, and it has already lost its characteristic innocence; for assertion always implies a denial of something else. Stop to think of it, and it has flown! What the world was to Adam on the day he opened his eyes to it, before he had drawn any distinctions, or had become conscious of his own existence—that is first, present, immediate, fresh, new, initiative, original, spontaneous, free, vivid, conscious, evanescent. Only, remember that every description of it must be false to it [Peirce c.1890: CP 1.357, emphasis added].

297. The animal aware of its objective world in such a fashion is alone positioned to form the conception, along with reality, and of a piece with it, of *otherness*. This notion arises precisely within experience through "brute actions of one subject or substance on another, regardless of law or of any third subject" (c.1906: CP 5.469). It is "the conception of being relative to, the conception of reaction with, something else" (1891: CP 6.32). It is, in a word, the conception of something other, of one thing different from another thing within the play of objects of awareness. The experience of otherness within firstness is the motivation of every question of the form "What is that?"[53]

298. We have already seen that the ground of this question is established by the mind itself in presenting the objective world intellectually as relative to itself and, insofar, intelligible. "The formal rationale of knowing of the understanding," the Latins argued, "in which understanding is distinguished from perception, is not the singularity itself of sensations, but the very definable structure of which singularity is a mode."[54] Sense perception and understanding work together as contraries within the genus of knowing, the former primarily and essentially ordered to manifesting the individuating sensible characteristics of objects signified, the latter primarily and essentially ordered to manifesting the relative structure which gives to the sensible properties their pattern of intelligibility as manifesting the underlying relations which give to the world as perceived its definable structures, both "natural" and "cultural".[55] We see, then, that the so-called "essences of material things" actually consist, so far as understanding is concerned, in *patterns of relationships* instantiated or verified in perceptible objectivities, but that the *relationships themselves*, in contrast to the elements of the system related, are never as such perceptible, though they can be understood. Thus the grasping of the relationships themselves, in their distinction from the perceptible aspects of the objective world which manifest them, is precluded for an animal which has only sensation and perception to rely on, in their contrast with understanding.

299. Especially important to grasp at this juncture is a point made in passing by Thomas Aquinas quite early in his career (c.1254-1256: In I sent. dist. 19. q. 5. art. 1. ad 7) in reflecting on the medieval doctrine that the intellect (in its difference from sense) is ordered to grasping "the definable structures of material being" ("quidditates rerum sensibilium"): *"even the being of an essence is a kind of being of reason"* ("etiam quidditatis esse est quoddam esse rationis"). This is so in the sense that the pattern of relations constituting what any given phenomenon—natural or cultural—is, so far as the understanding grasps that structure, is constructed by the understanding on the pattern of relations it has experienced as physically given and obtaining within the objective world.

300. Thus the sensations elaborated within perception give us a structured world of embodied objects, and those aspects of the objects sensible as such coincide further with the physical surroundings as an environment common—as physical—to all the life forms. On the basis of things as presented through the senses, the mind is provided with materials for the imagination to construct worlds which are not presented as such within perception, but "only imagined". Within these materials provided through perception, the understanding finds relations as well as related things, where perception finds only related things; and understanding constructs also relations of its own devising. The relations constructed by the mind on the pattern of physical relations given in experience have this in common with the physical relations at their modular base: both the constructed relations and the physically given relations are truly relations and are experienced as such within the world of society, language, and culture. In contrast to these objective constructs are the objective constructs which are made on the basis of our experience of individuals and their characteristics, which are decidedly not themselves relations though they are involved in relations and are experienced, as we have seen, through these relations. Thus we see not merely colors, shapes, and movements, but college presidents, diplomats, and policemen. The latter are, from the standpoint of the physical environment as such, mixtures of mind-dependent and mind-independent relations, both of which—the mind-dependent and the mind-independent, the relatively "unreal" and the relatively "real", relations—constitute the object of experience as such in its proper being and as "first intentions" thereof.[56]

301. When we "invent" a character, such as Sherlock Holmes or Hamlet, in contrast to "real" characters such as Detective Tom Schaefer of the Dubuque Police Department or Cleopatra, the invented character is nothing beside a pattern of characteristics. Some of these—the relations in which the character is involved, such as social roles, kinship, legal adversary, paternity—are themselves, as relations, just what that after which they are patterned are. Other of the characteristics, the size, weight, gender, and physiognomy of the character, say, consist in a being patterned after—consist in mind-dependent relations imitating—that which they themselves are not, namely, subjective characteristics of being given in our experience of objects as coincident with physical things.

302. Yet *the whole* of the invented creature is a pattern of relationships, both those of its features which are presented as if they were not mere relationships ("beings patterned after") and those of its features which are presented just as if they were physical relationships, even though all of its features are "in reality" only objective relations. For this reason Poinsot, here following Aquinas and other major Latin authors, divided being into natural and mind-dependent being. Natural being is further subdivided into individuals with their characteristics and relations. Mind-dependent being is divided into relations formed on the pattern of natural relations and relations formed on the pattern of individuals with their subjective characteristics. This last class of mind-dependent relations the Latins called "negations", because—being relations—they were *not*, as relations, what their exemplars in nature *are*, namely, subjects (individuals) with their subjective characteristics. Negations and relations, thus, constitute the entire inventory of mind-dependent being. In a word, *relations* constitute the entire inventory of mind-dependent being, both that part of it which diverges from the physical reality of the environment and that part of it which coincides with aspects and features of the physical surroundings.

303. From this we see that *objective* relations as such are neither physical (mind-independent) nor psychical (mind-dependent), but, although always determinately one or the other in a given case, are capable of being either, depending on changing circumstances. Two lovers traveling to meet one another at 1900 hours are involved in a whole network of physical and objective relations, and some of the physical relations in which they are involved are as such objective, i.e., physical relations of which the parties are well aware. At precisely 1845 (i.e., 6:45PM), unbeknownst to the young man who continues toward his appointed and agreed rendezvous, the young woman is struck by a meteor and instantly killed. At that moment, whatever physical relations she was involved in as such ceased, for physical relations require the existence of both terms in order to exist. The objective relations, of course, being sustained not by the dynamics of physical being as such but by semiosis, are, as objective, unaffected by the dramatic change in circumstances—except in this important particular: those of the objective relations which were *also* physical became, at 1845, *only* objective, though, for want of knowledge of the changed circumstances, the young man continued to rush on at 1850 hours just as he had been rushing at 1840 hours, so as not to keep his love waiting.

304. This example makes a quintessential point: the entitative character of a relation in its rationale as a relation is unaffected by the difference between being mind-dependent or mind-independent. One and the same relation, under different circumstances, can be one time only physical, one time both physical and objective, and another time only objective, in each case owing wholly to surrounding circumstances extrinsic to the being of the relation as such.

305. This crucial point bears directly on the matter of supposed essences or "quiddities" of things insofar as they are *known* essences, that is to say, objective.

306. There is no doubt that physical structures of the environment are internally determined and structured in their parts and in their relations to other physical structures.[57] Let us take the bone of a dinosaur already mentioned in ¶ 113 above. It is a physical structure. That structure can come to be known and, if respected, can even be made to tell us whether it is the bone of a brontosaurus, a pterodactyl, or indeed of some other of the great reptiles. But in order to yield up its secrets of the physical world and the past, the bone must first of all be perceived.

307. The one perceiving the bone may be an ignorant human animal, or indeed an animal other than human. As a key to the past and to some scientific knowledge, it is in this case wasted, though it may be excellent to chew on or to use as a club. However, with luck, the one perceiving the bone, the one for whom the bone is objectified, may happen to be a paleontologist. In this circumstance the bone becomes a sign, not of a chew toy or of warfare, but of the age of the dinosaurs, and of some individual and type of individual dinosaur as well. A relation which was once physical between the bone and the dinosaur whose bone it was now has a chance of being reconstructed by the scientific mind. Should that happen, a relation once only physical comes to exist again, unchanged as a relation—that is to say, in its essential rationale and structure as a relation—but now as purely objective. The bone is not the bone of a shark. It is, and was all along, the bone of a dinosaur. But for its *relation* to be realized, either the dinosaur had still to exist *or* a sufficiently knowledgeable observer had to objectify the bone. Either circumstance gives rise to the relation "of a dinosaur", whereas in the absence of both circumstances the *relation* as such, but not indeed *the bone* as such (the bone as a physical structure of calcium, etc.), wants for existence.

308. Now since mind-dependent and mind-independent relations are univocal in their being as *objective* relations, just this circumstance arises: we can be deceived and cannot always tell when a relationship we have posited for the purpose of understanding some physical structure, or, indeed, some cultural structure, is real or unreal. We perforce rely on models in order to answer the question what something is, and models are systems of objective relations which may or may not be duplications of a system of *physical* relations as well. Insofar as the model is an accurate model, that is, insofar as it actually models the physical structure we seek to understand, it provides us with the essence, the "quiddity", of the structure in question, whether that structure be natural or cultural. This need for models is nicely conveyed in a text Aquinas penned quite late in his lifelong series of reflections on *ens ut primum cognitum* (c.1266: I. q. 84. art. 7c):

It is impossible for the human mind . . . to actually understand anything except by the use of models in the imagination. . . . This is something that anyone can experience for themselves, namely, the fact that when one tries to understand something, one forms for the purpose some imaginary model to provide examples in which one can, as it were, inspect that which one desires to understand. And thence it is that even when we wish to make someone else understand something, we propose for that person examples on the basis of which he or she can form a model for understanding. This is the reason why it is necessary for this, that the human intelligence actually understand its own proper object, that it rely on imagined models—in order to inspect the universal nature existing in a particular.[58]

These models, Aquinas explains, in which our knowledge of "essences" physical or cultural principally, though not exclusively, consists, are not in themselves true or false, though such a model can be said to be "true" insofar as it adequates the "reality" it has been constructed to explain.[59]

309. The task of anthropology, in this light, appears as no different than the task of any science which must construct its object on the basis of observations and hypotheses, beginning with the discovery of otherness which lies at, or just next to, the very base of human understanding.[60] The only difference is that, uniquely in the case of anthropology (though it shares this singularity to some extent also with history, sociology and psychology), the otherness it seeks to bring into its orbit of explanation and understanding is the otherness of discursive conspecifics (be they aliens of this or other worlds). Conspecifics in this discursive sense are such precisely as they have made a part of themselves—invested as their unique intelligibility—a distinctive network of objective relations which alone convey their history and idea of themselves as a people, their aspirations, beliefs and other socially structured ways of coming to terms with human existence in its various requirements, achievements, and disappointments. The coding of the objective world made Lebenswelt thus gives anthropology endlessly new keys for understanding the subjectivity—the actual existence—of the anthropos through its objectification in time.

310. So far as this task involves *purely* cultural and linguistic aspects, a Saussurean semiology provides indispensable analytical tools. But the task, of its nature, as we have seen, can never be reduced to purely cultural and linguistic aspects. Anthropology must be physical besides being cultural, and, in both cases, above all *objective*, where nature and culture together weave that historical being we call anthropos and partially know as ourselves. How this is possible is best explained through Poinsot's account of the being proper to signs as relations as such indifferent to their subjective source or occasional ground, now in nature, now in culture.[61] What Peirce has contributed to the overall task is an understanding of its dynamic nature. Though he was well anticipated in his categories of firstness and secondness by the Latins with their uniquely rich development of the firstness of *ens ut primum cognitum* and of *ens praedicamentale* as the home of secondness, it was left for Peirce unambiguously to declare the nature of thirdness. Through the action of signs, firstness and secondness are brought together in a spiral of interactions whereby not only knowledge and human consciousness but mayhap the universe itself evolves in the direction of a community centered on truth as an achievement in time, the essential complement of otherness, especially in objective being.

311. It remains that the anthropologist, of all the scientists, has as scientific object the richest of the objects of science. While far from all the objects science investigates are, *in what the scientist seeks to know of them*, products of anthroposemiosis, nonetheless, in the case of anthropology, both the object and what the scientist seeks to know of it is precisely the product of anthroposemiosis in its most inclusive sense; and, unlike literature, of which such anthropological writing as ethnology is a subset, anthroposemiosis itself, which anthropology studies, cannot even pretend to autonomy in that wider universe embracing the universe of existent *anthropos* as a part. With anthropology we recover the microcosm, wherein the whole of nature is reflected and, at the same moment, transcended in the direction of a development of understanding over time.

Paragraphal Glosses

1. *Gloss on* ¶ 4. Peter Caruso, on reading this text, challenged the existence of the word "dimanate" on the ground that it could not be found in his dictionary. I explained to him that this was probably because he did not use the Oxford, only to discover to my chagrin that the Oxford did not contain the term, but only a feeble cognate, "dimane" ("dimaine" or "dimayne", from 1657, 1642, and 1620, respectively): "to flow forth from; to spring, originate, or derive its origin from". I am forced to conclude that dimanation as a technical term represents one of the several concepts of Latin philosophy which did not survive the transition to the national language traditions of modern times, and I am accordingly, on reintroducing it here, obliged by the Third Rule of the ethics of terminology to explain its proper sense.

Dimanation is the resultance of something from an action which is not the proper effect of the action but accompanies that effect as a necessary concomitant. Thus in the case of dimanant properties, no action intervenes between the effect and its accompaniment, but the very action of producing which was immediately terminated at the nature of the effect produced is mediately terminated also at the dimanation accompanying the effect as a property thereof. The effect results from the action as that by which the dimanation results. Thus, regarded entitatively (or in the order of physical being), dimanation is the action of the agent producing an effect, whether formally or virtually. But with respect to the nature of the effect from which, for example, a relation is said to emanate, dimanation is not an action, but the connection or dependency of the relation upon the effect as its foundation or ground which is such that, when the action generating the effect is posited, by that very action the properties which accompany the effect are also attained. Thus (Poinsot 1632: 456a17-21) dimanation "properly is not an efficient causality, that is, it is not that which acts through an action, but it participates in the effective productive" ("dicimus dimanationem proprie non esse causalitatem effectivam, id est quae per actionem agat, sed habet modum efficientiae").

Imagine a unique entity of which a copy is made: as soon as the copy is completed, the originally unique entity ceases to be singular by becoming now similar to its copy. That relation of similarity is not the copy produced, but accompanies the production of the copy. This manner of accompaniment is what is called dimanation.

Poinsot explains this concept (which he traces back through most of the main figures of Latin tradition) at a number of places; but see in particular his "Appendix De Dimanatione" following Q. 12 of his Phil. nat. 1. p. (1633: 267b26-270b19), and also the discussion in his Phil. nat. 4. p. q. 2. art. 1 (1635: 61a33-74a3, esp. 65b26-67b42), from which I take the following summary (67b10-18):

> Dimanation entitatively is properly called an action. But because it has two principles, one from which it primarily issues (namely, the efficient or generating cause), another by which it attains the proper effect by reason of being connected thereto, therefore, in respect of the first principle a dimanation is called an action or operation, in respect of the second an emanation or resultance.

In other words, dimanation is a triadic dimension that arises from a dyadic interaction, and has as such considerable import for understanding how semiosis can be at work virtually in inorganic nature—how, that is, there can be such a thing as physiosemiosis properly so-called: see especially ¶ 93 in this text.

2. *Gloss on* ¶ 9. The argument of this work as a whole will be that the combined notions of objectivity (understood in contrast with but also as able to exhibit and aspectually include in a labile way as part of its own order the subjectivity of physical and psychic events or states alike) and code (as the objective correlate varying independently of idea in the psychological sense) provide the central focus for understanding the action of signs relative to the phenomena of culture as such. This argument in

an abbreviated form first appeared in 1990 as an article (Deely 1990b) and as Chapter 5 of *Basics of Semiotics*. Concerning the latter version Parmentier (1991: 966) wrote: the "reorientation of philosophical terminology about the 'object' will disorient even the philosophically trained anthropologist".

Yet no reorientation is more important to anthropology for getting clear about the nature of culture within the human social system and understanding the nature of code at the basis of cultural phenomena as such. Accordingly, it does not seem too much to say that readers may judge their success in reading this book by the clarity they achieve in grasping the twin notions of objectivity (as it pertains equally to zoösemiosis and anthroposemiosis within nature) and code (as code differentiates the objective order from within to constitute the human Umwelt in its difference from the Umwelt of animals whose system of communication and Innenwelt does not include language—as code constitutes the biologically human Umwelt, that is to say, as, additionally, an enculturated Umwelt, or Lebenswelt). Similarly, readers may judge the success of the book itself, eventually, by the degree to which it succeeds in having the concept of the objective understood in the sense of the content of awareness as including aspects and changing aspects of physical and psychic subjectivities without being reducible to either.

This notion of objectivity, I think, is strictly required to describe the action of signs within experience, and required, hence, within semiotics. It is imposed by semiosis as the action of signs. The reader will find helpful pointers toward the notion in K. R. Popper's discussion of a "third world" (Popper 1972; Popper and Eccles 1977), but the same notion strictly speaking I do not believe is to be found fully realized anywhere outside contemporary semiotics. The "tilt of culture theory to semiotics" (Singer 1978: 203) is best explicable, ultimately, at least on theoretical grounds, through this notion. Such at least is the present argument.

3. *Gloss on* ¶ 13. Joseph and Joseph (1987: 2) make this point well: "Man is, of course, a codifying animal. We get nowhere without having some sort of schemata for understanding our particular universes. Yet this truism in itself is banal. What excites our theoretical attention is a set of interlocking questions about the nature of codifying signs and the purposes such signs serve. We know that we do not go about randomly thinking about external realities. Rather, our world is modeled". The question

is, how does the specifically human modeling process come about? As we will see, the modification of objectivity that comes about through intelligence is what reconstitutes the sign within experience as stipulable, and hence codifiable in the manner required to account for the postlinguistic patterns of objectivity, which constitute culture as the species-specifically distinct dimension of human social interaction.

4. *Gloss on ¶ 77.* An earlier section of this same essay (Peirce c.1906: 5.473) clarifies this contrast between dynamical interaction and semiosis considerably:

> But now when a microscopist is in doubt whether a motion of an animalcule is guided by intelligence, of however low an order, the test he always used to apply when I went to school, and I suppose he does so still, is to ascertain whether event, A, produces a second event, B, as a means to the production of a third event, C, or not. That is, he asks whether B will be produced if it will produce or is likely to produce C in its turn, but will not be produced if it will not produce C in its turn nor is likely to do so. Suppose, for example, an officer of a squad or company of infantry gives the word of command, "Ground arms!" This order is, of course, a sign. That thing which causes a sign as such is called the object (according to the usage of speech, the "real", but more accurately, the existent object) represented by the sign: the sign is determined to some species of correspondence with that object. In the present case, the object the command represents is the will of the officer that the butts of the muskets be brought down to the ground. Nevertheless, the action of his will upon the sign is not simply dyadic; for if he thought the soldiers were deaf mutes, or did not know a word of English, or were raw recruits utterly undrilled, or were indisposed to obedience, his will probably would not produce the word of command. However, although this condition is most usually fulfilled, it is not essential to the action of a sign. For the acceleration of the pulse is a probable symptom of fever and the rise of the mercury in an ordinary thermometer or the bending of the double strip of metal in a metallic thermometer is an indication, or, to use the technical term, an index, of an increase of atmospheric temperature, which, nevertheless, acts upon it in a purely brute and dyadic way. In these cases,

however, a mental representation of the index is produced, which mental representation is called the immediate object of the sign; and this object does triadically produce the intended, or proper, effect of the sign strictly by means of another mental sign; and that this triadic character of the action is regarded as essential is shown by the fact that if the thermometer is dynamically connected with the heating and cooling apparatus, so as to check either effect, we do not, in ordinary parlance speak of there being any semeiosy, or action of a sign, but, on the contrary, say that there is an "automatic regulation", an idea opposed, in our minds, to that of semeiosy. For the proper significate outcome of a sign, I propose the name, the interpretant of the sign. . . . it need not be of a mental mode of being . . . but it seems to me convenient to make the triadic production of the interpretant essential to a "sign". . . . On these terms, it is very easy to see what the interpretant of a sign is: it is all that is explicit in the sign itself apart from its context and circumstances of utterance.

For commentary, see *Basics of Semiotics* (Deely 1990 Chapter 3, esp. pp. 23-27).

A comparison with Poinsot 1632: 195/9-17, 196/21 etc., is instructive regarding the point that the object presented in semiosis, in sharp contrast to an object of dyadic action as such, need not be existent: see Gloss 22 below.

5. *First Gloss on ¶ 86.* "In structuralistic terms," says Eco (1990: 28), "one could say that for Peirce semiosis is potentially unlimited from the point of view of the system but is not unlimited from the point of view of the process. In the course of a semiosic process we want to know only what is relevant according to a given universe of discourse."

Eco is speaking of a robust semiosis, to be sure, but I am not sure that associative drifts or even leaps do not have a subsidiary role in the process. To reduce semiosis to such associations, however, is quite another thing, as Eco has well shown with his distinction of semiosis as such from the various forms of cancerous drift that have tried to claim the name for their own vagary. "A passage from similarity to semiosis," Eco notes (1992a: 47), "is not automatic."

6. *Second Gloss on ¶ 86.* Eco continues (1990: 40): "It is true that even the practical effect must then be spelled out by and through

language, and that the very agreement among the members of the community cannot but take the form of a new chain of signs. Nevertheless, the agreement concerns something—be it a practical effect or the possibility of a practical effect—that is produced outside semiosis".

7. *Gloss on ¶ 87.* "If perception is—as it is for Peirce—semiosis, then even at the original moment of our perceptive acquaintance with the external world the external world becomes understandable to us only under the form of an Immediate Object. For Peirce, when the sign is produced the Dynamic Object is no more there (and before the sign was produced it was not an object at all [it was, I should say, a bare physical entity or element in the environment]). What is present to our mind and to the semiosic discourse is only the Immediate Object to be interpreted by other signs. But the presence of the representamen as well as the presence (in the mind or elsewhere) of the Immediate Object means that in some way the Dynamic Object, which is not there, was somewhere. Being not present, or not-being-there, the object of an act of interpretation has been" (Eco 1990: 39)—and, I would add, might be still. I would also add that Eco's analysis of perception needs to be refined by the analysis of the sensory element within perception as such. Such a refinement would reveal that the dynamic object not only was somewhere but, in fragmented and partial modes, is present within the immediate object as providing a common measure for disagreements about what is perceived. See the analyses of Johansen 1993, 1993a.

8. *Gloss on ¶ 96.* Exploiting the mechanisms of Hermetic drift ever present in human language as an inevitable consequence of semiosis, in itself, is a matter of tracing out patterns of extrinsic formal causality operative in a text beyond authorial control of the text. Hence the "will of the interpreter" as interpretant of any given deconstruction need not be a malign narcissism determined to reveal nihilistic possibilities within the most positive of texts, but can just as well be a benign and laudable effort to open up a text to its own possibilities for supporting further understandings. In either case, the deconstruction presupposes semiosis without constituting it as such. To mistake deconstruction, an in-itself neutral method among many others needed to exploit the perspective of the sign, for semiotics is therefore to beg the question of what semiosis is.

9. *First Gloss on ¶ 102.* "Partes dicuntur causare totum causalitate intrinseca et constituente ipsum totum, non extrinsece se habente,

sicut etiam praedicata essentialia dicuntur constituere quidditatem. Causae autem intrinsecae non distinguuntur a causato entitative, quia non causant per emissionem alterius entitatis a se, sed per communicationem sui in entitate, quam constituunt, sicut forma materiam informant communicando se illi. Et iste est effectus formalis formae, communicatio sui passiva, quae entitative non distinguitur a forma se communicante, et sic est effectus realis, quatenus est realis communicatio sui. Vel etiam dicitur, quod in ista causatione totius etiam intercedit realis et propria causatio ipsarum partium inter se. Materia enim et forma ad invicem sunt causae, . . . et distinguuntur inter se, et ex ista causatione reali resultat totum indistinctum realiter ab ipsis partibus, non tamquam immediate causatum, sed ut ex illa priori causatione partium inter se resultans; et hoc sufficit ad salvandam causationem realem, scilicet mediate" (Poinsot 1633: 107b35-108a15).

10. Second Gloss on ¶ 102. Nonetheless, from another standpoint, the final cause is intrinsic to a natural effect, in the case of organisms, as an embodied tendency, and, in the case of an artifact, is identical with the embodied form as that which makes the artifact suitable for this or that function, regardless of whether it is actually so used or not.

11. Third Gloss on ¶ 102. A principle of natural being, Poinsot writes (1633: 41a38-b11), "solum importat ea, a quibus res essentialiter pendet, sive in facto esse sive in fieri, ut a componentibus vel inchoantibus, eo quod principium et principiatum ita se habent, quod principiatum resolvitur in principium. Principium autem in quantum tale non resolvitur in aliud, nisi etiam sit principiatum; et ita in quantum principium, non est ex alio. Causa autem efficiens et quaecumque alia extrinseca non includitur in definitione ista principiorum naturalium. . . . Nec enim causae extrinsecae sunt principia, ex quibus natura ipsa rerum constat sive in fieri sive in facto esse, sed efficiens dicitur 'id, a quo incipit motus', finis, propter quem incipit, exemplar, ad cuius imitationem fit, nulla vero causa extrinseca dicitur, ex quo aliquid fit".

12. Gloss on ¶ 106. And I would note in this etymological context the remark of Sebeok (1991: 2): "In my view, the midmost target of semiotics is indeed, as Rey so persuasively argued [1984], epistemology, understood in the broad sense of the cognitive constitution of living entities, comprehending the physiological and psychological make-up of each in their interaction. In semiotics, we must in any case think of ourselves as both working within a tradition that changes over time and trying to grasp things as they 'really are'".

13. *First Gloss on ¶ 107*. For a synoptic summary of the Latin discussions on efficient, material, intrinsic formal, and extrinsic exemplary formal causality, see Poinsot 1633: Questions 10-13, 197a11-287b43, where, however, extrinsic *specificative* formal causality ("objective causality") is mentioned only in response to an objection confusing it with exemplary causality (245a24-43, 247a7-14).

The discussion of formal causality as extrinsic specification is to be found rather in Poinsot 1632: Q. 17, Arts. 5-7, 595b25-608b7, Q. 21, Arts. 4 and 5, 670a11-693a31, Q. 22, Arts. 1-4, 693a34-715a21; and Poinsot 1635—i.e., in the context of his discussion of cognitive organisms in the biological treatises—Q. 6., Arts. 2-4, 177b1-198a16, Q. 8, Art. 4, 265b1-271b20, Q. 10, Arts. 1-5, 295b1-339a45, Q. 11, Arts. 1 and 2, 344b1-366b34.

Notice, therefore, the generally biological and epistemological contexts in which these questions mainly arise, not to mention the specifically semiotic ones (Poinsot 1632a: Book I, Questions 4 and 5; Book II, Questions 1-4), where it is not too much to say that some of the most difficult and extended passages in Poinsot's attempt to systematize the foundations of semiotic inquiry arise from the need to make this heretofore peripheral topic of natural inquiry central to the establishment of semiotic.

14. *Second Gloss on ¶ 107*. Peirce's reflections on the ethical obligations incumbent on philosophers in their use of terms is an extraordinary document, summarizing thoughts that had preoccupied him, as Ketner demonstrates (1981: 334-341), over his entire career. Superficially similar earlier formulations can be found in Bacon 1620 and Locke 1690: Book III, Ch. X, and applications of such ideas were explicitly made in modern times particularly in the development of biology and chemistry (Ketner 1981: 328-334). To this extent, it can be said (ibid.: 327) that Peirce's reflections on this question were "a culmination of scientific traditions antedating him by at least two centuries".

Corrington notes in regard to Peirce's view (1993: 51) that the philosopher "must always be careful to shape a term so that its integrity and scope are truly commensurate with its subject matter", and "must always probe into the full connotation and denotation of any technical term". But these observations, while true, do not go to the heart of Peirce's ethical claims in this matter.

Otiose is the analogy Putnam strives to draw (in Ketner 1992: 93) between Peirce's "charming section on the ethics of terminology" and Quine's "Mathematosis" (1987: 127-129). This is ritual symbolism in the contemporary politics of academe carried to the point of farce.

What needs to be specially attended to in Peirce's strictures is his pointing out that care in choice of terms presupposes most fundamentally a *historical* obligation in *intellectual justice* to keep a kind of running account of the *decisive achievements of our predecessors*, with an eye "to keep the *essence* of every scientific term unchanged and exact", with the duty of supplying new terms and families of cognate terms (as in the case of semiotics) falling "upon the persons who introduce the new conception", a duty "not to be undertaken without a thorough knowledge of the principles and a large acquaintance with the details and history of the special terminology in which it is to take place, nor without a sufficient comprehension of the principles of word-formation of the national language, nor without a proper study of the laws of symbols in general" (Peirce 1903: 2.222). In other words, ethics in the use of terminology is of a piece with the communitarian nature of anthropic progress in the pursuit of truth.

This historical dimension of the growth of symbols in the species-specifically human communication system (*langue* as opposed to *parole*) Peirce saw as providing our main—and perhaps only—safeguard against "arbitrary dictation in scientific matters", the sort of short-sighted present-mindedness introduced into twentieth-century philosophy by the early pretensions of Wittgenstein and Russell to have solved or dissolved all the problems of philosophical tradition.

In the case of philosophy, which here means simply any foundational inquiry such as the present one in anthropology, there is both "positive need of popular words in popular senses . . . as objects of its study", such as the subjective-objective dichotomy of modern parlance, and a "peculiar need of a language distinct and detached from the common speech . . . so outlandish that loose thinkers will not be tempted to borrow its words" (Peirce 1903: 2.223). With respect to this latter language, though it may indeed eventually influence the popular speech and in some measure become in turn part thereof (just as disastrously happened with Kant's use of 'subjective' and 'objective'), in the interim, "if a reader does not know the meaning of the words, it is infinitely better that he should know that he does not know" (ibid.), which holds equally for the female reader.

In any event, Peirce's strictures on terminology are so important in their implications for thinkers concerned with matters of intellectual justice and integrity that I have annexed Peirce's codification of his reflections on terminology at the end of these Paragraphal Glosses, where the reader can find stated in full the ethical rules for employment of terms.

15. Gloss on ¶ 116. It should be sufficiently clear from the previous paragraphs that "the being proper to signs", the "soul of the sign", in Peirce's metaphor, is that being which must be theirs in order for signs to function as constructive through experience of a world precisely objective throughout, even at those points of intersection where what is objective coincides with what is physical or what is psychical. Such coincidences are like the case of an iceberg revealed through its tip, protruding into experience as a sign and sometimes a warning of what is there and at work beyond the merely objective segment experienced as object here and now. Thus Peirce remarks (c.1902: 35-36): ". . . it is easy to see that the object of a sign, that to which it virtually at least professes to be applicable, can itself only be a sign. For example, the object of an ordinary proposition is a generalization from a group of perceptual facts. It represents those facts. These perceptual facts are themselves abstract representatives, through we know not precisely what intermediaries, of the percepts themselves, and these are themselves viewed as, and are—if the judgment has any truth—representations, primarily impressions of sense, ultimately of a dark underlying something, which cannot be specified without its manifesting itself as a sign of something below. There is, we think, and reasonably think, a limit to this, an ultimate reality, like a zero of temperature. But in the nature of things, it can only be approached; it can only be represented. The immediate object which any sign seeks to represent is itself a sign", even when, as objectifying some thing, it is also more than a sign, as in cases where signification also involves the self-representation proper to the object in its distinction from sign (Poinsot 1632: 26/39-27/6, 117/22-17, etc.), particularly in the sensory core of perceptual and conceptual activity (Deely 1992a). We can see in this way that "to try to peel off signs & get down to the real thing is like trying to peel an onion and get down to onion itself" (Peirce 1905b).

16. *Gloss on ¶ 121.* It is in this way, I suggest, that is best met the "need to explain in what way alterity is able to infiltrate the very sphere of the symbolic" (Ponzio 1990: 197).

17. *Gloss on ¶ 129.* In the German and Kantian context, as in the modern context generally, the opposition of the terms "subjective" and "objective" is a firmly established dichotomy whose transparency is deemed self-evident. Within this context, von Uexküll himself, who, as his son notes (T. von Uexküll 1981: 148), did not think of his work thematically under the rubric of semiotic, had no choice but to see the Umwelt in opposition to the objective, and as belonging to the phenomenal realm in Kant's sense—on the side of the "subjective", that is, dichotomically conceived in opposition to the supposed "objective". This prejacent context of German philosophy has been the occasion for much misunderstanding of von Uexküll's work in general (through misplaced associations with "vitalism"), and, notoriously, for difficulties in interpreting (or "translating") the key term, "Umwelt". These difficulties are already a clue to the real problem: himself immersed in the Kantian philosophy—i.e., the most classical of the classical modern idealism—Jakob von Uexküll yet was creating a notion which belonged to another context entirely, a context which had yet to catalyze thematically and receive general acceptance under its own proper name, to wit, the context of semiotic as the doctrine of signs. A formula applied to Heidegger (Deely 1986: 56), mutatis mutandis (i.e., substituting "biologist" for "philosopher"), applies equally to von Uexküll: among modern biologists he is the one who struggled most against the coils of German idealism and in the direction of a semiotic.

This aspect of his father's work Thure von Uexküll seems unwilling to develop at the level of fundamental terminology and as regards the elder von Uexküll's reliance on the Kantian scheme for philosophy of mind generally. The son seems to be insufficiently abraded by the inconsistency latent in his own account of his father's theory, according to which (I choose an example where the inconsistency running throughout is illustrated within the same short paragraph, T. von Uexküll 1981: 161), on the one hand, "A schema is a strictly private program" for the formation of complex signs "in our subjective universe", and, on the other hand, "The schemata which we have formed during our life are intersubjectively identical" at least "in the most general outlines". But, of course, to speak of the intersubjective save as a pure appearance, in a Kantian context, is as internally inconsistent as to speak of a grasping of the ding-an-sich in that same context.

Nonetheless, once it is understood that the subject-object dichotomy is rendered nugatory within the perspective of a doctrine of signs, and that, within this context, the term "objective" functions precisely to mean the prospectively intersubjective, in opposition—this is the whole point (Deely 1986a: 265-271, esp. 268-269)—to both terms of the classical subject-object dichotomy, new possibilities of understanding are opened up. These possibilities are more in line with what is at the center of, and original to, von Uexküll's work than could be seen through the filter of Kantian idealism. It was not, as the father thought and the son is content to repeat (T. von Uexküll 1981: 171), a question of "further adapting Kant's initiative to the field of biology", so much as a question of introducing into the field of biology a radically new initiative cloaked (and so disguised, even to itself) in the only language then available to a scientist of philosophical bent, the language of German idealism.

I referred above to the clue provided by the difficulty of rendering von Uexküll's key terms outside the German—especially Umwelt but also the related terms "by which von Uexküll seeks to represent the relations between the objective world and the world as it appears to the animal" (Schiller 1957: xiii, where "objective" retains its modern sense of physical environment). Fortunately, Schiller decided to retain Umwelt, allowing the new English context to give it a new sense beyond the explicit choices of a translator. Perhaps she was sufficiently warned by MacKinnon's "translation" of von Uexküll 1920, which left everything in the dark: better at least to bring one term, the central one, into the light of day.

But the clue here can also be viewed in reverse: if J. von Uexküll's key terms within the German context of his original work have the explicitly Kantian sense T. von Uexküll tries to insist upon, why have they been so widely misunderstood also by German speakers who know quite well the Kantian philosophy? Our reappropriation from the modern context of the term "object" and "objective", we will see, is necessary to make sense of the very title von Uexküll gives to a main section in one of his key essays (1934: 73), "The Same Subject as an Object in Different Umwelts". In reality, the problem is not linguistic: von Uexküll's terms are also original in German, although their novelty there is hidden behind the pre-existing verbal forms (Heidegger's *Dasein* presented a similar problem). The problem, as I have recently had occasion to argue at length (Deely 1988, 1990), is more radical and also systematic. The problem is one of perspective: the perspective of semiotic is not assimilable to the previous perspective of an idealism any more than to the perspective of a realism. In the case before us, as Peirce so trenchantly remarked (1903: 223), "Kant's adjectives 'objective' and 'subjective' proved not to be barbarous enough, by half, long to retain their usefulness in philosophy, even if [as is far from the case] there had been no other objection to them". See the discussion in Gloss 14 above.

18. *First Gloss on* ¶ *130.* Poinsot's remark (1632: 159/16-22) is worth citing here: "Much less does being known or apprehended in a sign (which some call proximate apprehensibility) found or complete the rationale of the sign, because being known does not pertain to the rationale of a sign, but to its exercise (for when a sign represents in act, it is cognized in act), not as it is something which might be a representative". This last suffices to complete the rationale of sign wherever the relation so founded is among physical aspects of the environment. Cf. 124/42-134/10. See Deely 1989, and 1990 Chapter 6; and see also ¶ 108 within.

19. *Second Gloss on* ¶ *130.* By way of obviating needless misunderstanding here, it should be noted that Peirce sometimes (e.g., 1904: 20-21) defined the percept in just this sense, as "the direct object apprehended", "the very existing thing itself, independent of and exterior to mind". But, in speaking this way, he had also to say that the percept in this sense "does not possess fully developed reality", for the reason that when a material structure of the environment (the physical surroundings) becomes an object directly apprehended in experience, it becomes so aspectually and not in the totality of its being as irreducible to experience. This objectified aspect (the "immediate object"), along with, but in contrast to, the physical being therewith aspectually accessed (the "dynamic object"), has its proper being as part of the Umwelt, correlative to the Innenwelt of the experiencing organism. The physical being accessed possesses fully developed reality in its environmental existence, but in its objective existence it possesses rather an aspectual and correlative existence, a developing existence, objectively speaking. This existence, the existence proper to the percept in Peirce's sense, is simultaneously grounded in the environmental structure experienced and in the cognitional structure of the experiencing, but in different ways, and it is an element of the experience as such only as terminating a relation grounded in (dimanating from) the one experiencing, i.e., as cor-

relative to an element of an Innenwelt. Peirce, in the definition under discussion, is regarding the percept in terms of the environmental structure experienced, that is, as it belongs to the Umwelt in its partial coincidence with physical environment, whereas I am regarding the percept in the present discussion in terms of the cognitional structure of the experiencing. Our definitions are complementary, not contradictory (more precisely, they relate logically as subcontraries), the one—Peirce's—regarding a relation in experience from the side of its objective terminus, the other—mine—regarding that same relation but from the side of its fundamentum, its subjective ground. See Santaella Braga 1993.

20. *Gloss on ¶ 134.* According to the dictionary at my disposal (the record of, from my standpoint on this particular, prejacent codes—codes secundum me entia realia et secundum se entia rationis), "stipulatable".

21. *Gloss on ¶ 139.* Baer (1992: 355) has grasped the point perfectly: "Once signs are recognized as imperceptible ontological relations which correlate objects and/or things, we are at the threshold of what for Deely is specifically anthroposemiotic, the ability to introduce into objects the dimension of stipulability. This ability underlies the capacity for language and renders semiosis in principle unlimited. The stipulable sign is the characteristic trait of what Deely calls 'text'. And it is the capacity to produce texts that distinguishes anthroposemiosis from zoösemiosis. It is species-specific for human semiosis".

22. *Gloss on ¶ 145.* In making this point Johansen cites the following text from Peirce (c.1903: 2.261): "A Replica of the word 'camel' is likewise a Rhematic Indexical Sinsign being really affected, through the knowledge of camels, common to the speaker and auditor, by the real camel it denotes, even if this one is not individually known to the auditor; and it is through such real connecting that the word 'camel' calls up the idea of a camel. The same thing is true of the word 'phoenix'. For although no phoenix really exists, real descriptions of the phoenix are well known to the speaker and his auditor; and the word is really affected by the Object denoted". This is the very point made by Poinsot in the passage cited in Section I, ¶ 60 above (1632: 195/3-9, 18-29) concerning the difference between the action of signs and the productive causality exercised by physical entities as such. In the case of camels in their difference from phoenixes,

namely, comparative nonexistence, Poinsot comments as follows (1632: 195/9-17, 196/21-24): "In cases [such as the camel] where the very object possesses also an effective force for applying itself to a cognitive power, this active capacity functions materially and incidentally relative to the object as an extrinsic specificative [the object as object, or in its being as objective], just as in the case of natural beings a form manifests its presence in matter, but precisely as derived from the form that presence does not exist effectively—that is, productively—by the agent applying and uniting the form to its matter". To excite effectively (i.e., to directly stimulate) does not pertain to the rationale of an object "because in an excitation the object is that which is applied to a power, but it is not required that it be itself the thing effectively producing the application", whence it need not exist physically in order to be something signified.

23. *First Gloss on ¶ 146.* French and Kennedy (1985: 302) cite Bohr's observation that ". . . 'reality' is also a word, a word which we must learn to use correctly". See Deely 1992a.

24. *Second Gloss on ¶ 146.* With mild understatement, Corrington notes (1987: 48) that "not all communities need be scientific", and "semiotic convergence . . . can prevail in a wide variety of communal structures and can often flower in contexts that Peirce and Royce would be forced to reject as inappropriate to the life of the interpreter". Indeed, how else could one take into account the radically diverse notions of reality held from within opposed fundamentalist religious sects, to take an extreme example, although such oppositions occur everywhere in ethnic groupings, as amply demonstrated by ethnographic studies within anthropology—or the dramatic dissolution of Yugoslavia through violence almost immediately upon the collapse of the Soviet Union in 1991.

25. *Gloss on ¶ 154.* This notion of the prejacent physical environment is a paradigmatic meaning of "reality" since the most ancient of times—or at least since our earliest records of the notion (cf. Peirce 1913: 38-39, cited in Johansen 1985: 232-233; Deely 1986a: 265-267).

In this regard, the difference between the action of signs as realized within anthroposemiosis and zoösemiosis provides the grounds for Heidegger's observation (1927: 246) that "the Real is essentially accessible only as entities within-the-world", while also explaining why (ibid.) "all access to such entities is founded ontologically upon the basic state of Dasein, Being-in-the-World", where "Being-in-the-World" is tantamount to existing within an Umwelt codified linguistically, as our analysis is making clear.

26. *Gloss on ¶ 165.* "The invasion of codes", Eco remarks (1977: 27), "means that we are not gods: we are moved by rules. But we ought to decide (and here the epistemologies of code are in disagreement) whether we are not gods because we are motivated on the basis of rules which historically we give ourselves, or if we are not gods because divinity is precisely the Rule (the Code of Codes) which stands behind us." The choice, as Eco sees it (similar to Sahlins 1976: 55), is between the historical and the mechanistic. But this seems to overstate the situation.

The question is whether codes are not a finite mediating ground between nature and culture, wherein the "Code of Codes" is neither immutable nor wholly culturally freely chosen. The choice, then, is not between a frame of reference either historical or mechanistic, but between seeing culture as a semiotic phenomenon cut off from nature by linguistic coding or seeing culture as founded in, while transforming at its own level (that is to say, through the semiotic modalities characteristic of anthroposemiosis), the "natural" Umwelt.

27. *Gloss on ¶ 171.* The process is also clear in Bakhtin, e.g. 1963: 202: "For the word is not a material thing but rather the eternally mobile, eternally fickle medium of dialogic interaction. It never gravitates toward a single consciousness or a single voice. The life of the word is contained in its transfer from one mouth to another, from one context to another context, from one social collective to another, from one generation to another generation. In this process the word does not forget its own path and cannot completely free itself from the power of these concrete contexts into which it has entered.

"When a member of a speaking collective comes upon a word, it is not as a neutral word of language, not as a word free from the aspirations and evaluations of others, uninhabited by others' voices. No, he receives the word from another's voice and filled with that other voice. The word enters his context from another context, permeated with the interpretations of others. His own thought finds the word already inhabited. Therefore the orientation of a word among words, the varying perception of another's word and the various means for reacting to it, are perhaps the most fundamental problems for the metalinguistic study of any kind of discourse, including the artistic." (In Petrilli's curious categorization [1990: 391], the "materiality of signifying otherness . . . is strongest when mulitvoicedness is greatest".)

Barthes (1970) speaks similarly of code as "so many fragments of something that has always been already read, seen, done, experienced; the code is the wake of that already". But the code is more than a wake of the past: it is at the same time a wave of the future as it is taken up, modified, and given life anew by the individual appropriating an old understanding or forging a new one within the Lebenswelt. The code provides not a prisonhouse (Jameson 1972) but a clearinghouse, wherein the most prominent item is not the past but the colorful "fact that words have a capacity for learning" (Johansen 1985: 240) and an orientation towards the future. Bakhtin (1963: 166) has a beautiful answer to Peirce's inquiry (c.1902: 24) "whether meaning does not always refer to the future":

Nothing conclusive has yet taken place in the world, the ultimate word of the world and about the world has not yet been spoken, the world is open and free, everything is still in the future and will always be in the future.

We see then the penetration of Crick's observation (1976: 97) that "we cannot think of language, mind and meaning in an individual context, and then try to fit others into the scheme: they all three exist in a shared context". Like truth and reality itself, language and the objective understandings it conveys are the work of an anthroposemiosic community. And the semiotic objectivity constituted by and achieved only within such a community, embodying, as it does, aspects of both psychic and physical subjectivity, explains the possibility of the "familiar situation for someone else to know one's mind better than one knows it oneself, as for example happens when one accepts another person's account of one's action which conflicts with the explanation one had originally given oneself" (ibid.: 97).

28. Gloss on ¶ 179. In this way, Johansen's model helps to answer Parmentier's objection (conveyed to me by a letter of 19 August 1987) that "there simply is no room in Peirce for the differential mediation by and through semiotic codes—namely, a concept of 'culture'". Nonetheless, Parmentier's insistence that "cultural semiotics needs both Peirce's notion of indexicality and

Saussure's notion of code" was my main stimulus for thinking through the notion of textuality outlined above, and I think it has been a useful stimulus, as was his essay (Parmentier 1986) which occasioned our correspondence.

29. *Gloss on ¶ 181.* The question, however, is perhaps poorly put. The point is that, when it comes to semiosis at any level and in any form, a triadic diagram provides the indispensable minimum with which it is possible profitably to begin, as was already explained in Poinsot (1632: Book I, Question 3), and as Volosinov neatly summarizes for the more restricted context of anthroposemiosis (1976: 105): "any locution actually said aloud or written down for intelligible communication . . . is the expression and product of the social interaction of three participants: the speaker (author), the listener (reader), and the topic (the who or the what) of speech . . . ".

30. *Gloss on ¶ 190.* Peirce (e.g., 1903c: 1.606) was fond of drawing the parallel between logic and ethics as the two forms of self-control in human affairs, the one governing thought and the other action. A startling application of such an idea to semiotics itself, by way of inferring a moral obligation from Saussure's original formula for semiology, is ingeniously developed by A. Russell in his remarkable essay on "The Semiosis Linking the Human World and Physical Reality" (Russell 1982).

31. *Gloss on ¶ 195.* Hence what Parmentier rightly calls (1986: 72) "the privileged place of language with respect to other semiotic systems".

32. *Gloss on ¶ 201.* Ketner and Putnam "take Peirce's daring metaphysical hypothesis to be" that "what answers to our conception of a continuum is a possibility of repeated divisions which can never be exhausted in any possible world, not even in a possible world in which one can complete abnumerably infinite processes" (1992: 51). I would see the proposition in question to be an immediate consequence of the mind-dependent status of the continuum as an intelligible unity of objectification.

33. *Gloss on ¶ 208.* "Cum causae sint subordinatae essentialiter, non potest una incipere et causare quin ab alia priori, cui subordinatur, mota sit; et idem dicemus de illa si supponit aliam priorem cui subordinetur. Unde infinitus processus in causis est

idem atque indeterminata causalitas et motio: infinitas enim in ipsa dependentia et subordinatione obstat determinationi: siquidem quocumque dato, ut aliquid incipiat, requiritur aliud prius a quo dependet: et sic numquam finiuntur dependentiae de novo; quod est non finiri condiciones requisitas, at aliquid operetur. Ex quo intelligiur, quod quando dicitur infinitum esse impertransibile, . . . intelligitur . . . etiam quod [infinitum] non est pertransibile quantum ad dependentias et condiciones de novo requisitas ad causandum. Licet enim possimus imaginari, quod infinitae causae simul operentur, seu simul concurrant in eumdem effectum: tamen intelligi non potest quod una causa ex subordinatione et motione alterius incipiat aliquid deternubate et de novo, si requiruntur ad id infinitae dependentiae et condiciones: nulla enim erit inceptio determinata, si ad quamlibet requiruntur infinitae: quia hoc ipso quod sunt infinitae, sunt indeterminatae; cum enim quaelibet debeat incipere operationem ab alia prius movente et causante, et haec non possit causare nisi ab alia priori moveatur, et illa ab alia, et in hoc non est ponere terminum: restat ut numquam illa causa ultima determinetur, quia numquam finiuntur condiciones et motiones, seu subordinationes ad illam requisitae: quia quâlibet datâ, alia restat praerequisita; et sine omnibus non potest operari: quamdiu enim omnes dependentiae et condiciones requisitae non exhauriuntur et ponuntur, causa non manet determinata ad operandum. Nec simul possunt concurrere et ex aequo poni infinitae illae motiones: siquidem licet essent omnes in eodem instanti temporis (quod tamen non est verum, quia multa operantur successive, ut videmus), tamen una subordinatur essentialiter alteri, et praerequirit alteram ad operandum tamquam moventem et determinantem se; ergo non potest ista operari, nisi praesupponantur infinitae causalitates; et illa quae movet istam, etiam praesupponit infinitas causalitates, et illa alia alias infinitas; ergo numquam est causa quae praesupponat finitas condiciones seu motiones, aut nullam; ergo non est finis praesupponendi requisita ad operandum in nulla causarum; ergo neque est initium operandi, quia antequam omnes praesupponantur, non incipit operatio. . . . ubi non ex infinitate durationis, sed ex infinitate causalitatum, quae indeterminationem facit, sequitur non dari processum in infinitum. Quare non reducitur hoc ad opinativam sententiam, quae negat dari infinitum: quia licet sit opinio an possint dari infinita per modum effectûs, non tamen infinita per modum causalitatis requisitae ad unumquemque effectum; sic enim numquam esset determinatus et novus effectus, si non esset finis in his quae requiruntur ad causandum: et de hoc non est opinio" (Poinsot 1637: 424-425, para. 19).

Up to the last decades of the Latin age, the heavens were regarded as an essentially subordinated and essentially unchanging series of proper causes, a system of spheres and epicycles from the Primum Mobile, or outermost sphere, to the lowest sphere, or Sphere of the Moon, transmitting the sequence of influences specifically (but not individually) regulating all generations and corruptions of terrestrial individuals. At the bottom of this vertical series the interactions of the individuals themselves, including the reproductive interactions, formed rather a horizontal series of accidentally subordinated causes, which Aristotle explicitly regarded as infinite in retrospect and prospect. (See Konkle 1992 for a full discussion. Konkle's treatment has the essential merit of clearly understanding the difference for Aristotle between properly physical arguments concerning the infinite and arguments which improperly transfer mathematical considerations to the context of natural science inquiry.) The essential series constituted by the system of spheres, by contrast, was viewed as immediately requiring for its completion the existence of an "Unmoved Mover", a being which, as the Latins best explicated, acts without undergoing a transition from potency to act.

Modern cosmology complicates this view considerably, presenting us not with a single series of essentially subordinated causes constituting a single cosmos but with an array of star systems and other galactic and intergalactic phenomena which do not seem to constitute any single whole but a plethora of relatively independent wholes (such as our own Milky Way). Each of these, moreover, both relates to the other macrophenomena through a prospectively infinite series of accidentally subordinated causes and generates within itself other such series, among which is the evolutionary causal chain responsible for the earthly biosphere (see Deely 1969). This cosmological picture is almost the inverse of what the ancients opined. Instead of a single totalizing celestial series of essentially subordinated causes as the vertical framework for a horizontal infinite series of accidentally subordinated causal interactions at the terrestrial level, the modern picture is of an infinite series of accidentally subordinated causal interactions. With respect to these interactions, the notions of vertical and horizontal make only metaphorical sense. And within these interactions, systems of essentially subordinated causes develop as regional and local phenomena which are themselves, first, but nodes in a much larger picture of accidentally subordinated causes, and, second, themselves accidental considered *ad extra* against the backdrop, both diachronic and synchronic, of the infinite series within which essentially subordinated systems appear as regions and localities (species and individuals, within the biosphere), endure for awhile, and pass away. The picture, which is quite astounding and astoundingly different from anything envisaged in the ancient cosmology of celestial spheres, is of a situation nicely symbolized in the appropriation of the term "chaos" to express the theoretical requirements of a contemporary cosmology (see Gleick 1987, Waldrop 1992, etc.).

Hence the application of the infinite process argument to the question of the existence of God in the contemporary context requires a different interpretation from the one simply found in the classical Latin commentators. What seems to be required is a shift from the notion of essentially subordinated series, which, as such, is today perfectly explicable as a side-effect of a series of otherwise accidentally subordinated causes "syncategorematically infinite", as Poinsot said (that is, infinite respecting past and future time), to the notion of a cause which, in causing change or motion, itself undergoes transition from potency to act. All of the causes known to science are precisely of this kind. Hence each requires in turn an explanation of its causality, i.e., its transition from potency to act in causing, and so on ad infinitum. An infinite series of this kind, indifferently horizontal or vertical, as it were, is precisely one in which the explanation is never complete, no matter how far it extends. So we must postulate, as simultaneous with the action of the moved mover (the cause which in causing undergoes transition from potency to act), an action which bears equally on mover and moved but has as its source a being purely actual so as to undergo in acting no transition from a potential state; and the postulation is made not so much to *complete* any given series or series of series as to *sustain the universal interactions at each moment here and now* (and so infinitely backwards and forwards in time, as long as the series has lasted or will last).

But this is another story. Here we are concerned only with the physical sense in which, as Sebeok put it (1991: 82), "semiosis is by no means unlimited". This is the exact sense in which the Latins postulated that a "processus ad infinitum absolute repugnat", namely, with respect to any given essentially subordinated causal series constituting a determinate effect for a temporary duration (such an effect as are each one of us, along with our planetary system, etc.)—before and after which, however, the larger complex of processes continues along its infinitely merry way.

34. Gloss on ¶ 210. "A human being is begotten by other human beings and by the sun as well" was the medievals' way of expressing the fact that a human life depends on a whole environment of co-operating causes and not simply on the parents, following Aristotle's famous remark in Book II of his Physics (Aquinas c.1266: I. q. 115. art. 3. ad 2, p. 349: "secundum quod dicitur in ii. physic., quod homo generat hominem, et sol"). Indeed, the being of the offspring is not even essentially subordinated to the causality of the parents, for it continues when that causality—and mayhap the being of the parents as well—has passed away. But were the sun to cease, so would all life on this planet, respecting which the sun is a sustaining cause involved also in the production of earthly life, not indirectly, but equivocally, in the medievals' sense.

And what was involved in the production of the sun? An infinity of causes, to be sure, just as an infinity of causes along with tychistic events went indirectly into the parents being there to beget that offspring. But given their presence, through whatever causes: as determinately being these parents of that offspring, it was not the infinity of causes at work that produced the offspring, but the finite complex directly operative there and then as sustaining the parents' being in their production the offspring.

35. Gloss on ¶ 224. Cf. Peirce 1868a: 5.283-286: "283. The third principle whose consequences we have to deduce is, that, whenever we think, we have present to the consciousness some feeling, image, conception, or other representation, which serves as a sign. But it follows from our own existence (which is proved by the occurrence of ignorance and error [cf. 1868: 5.233]) that everything which is present to us is a phenomenal manifestation of ourselves. This does not prevent its being a phenomenon of something without us, just as a rainbow is at once a manifestation both of the sun and of the rain. When we think, then, we ourselves, as we are at that moment, appear as a sign. Now a sign has, as such, three references: first, it is a sign to some thought which interprets it; second, it is a sign for some object to which in that thought it is equivalent; third, it is a sign, in some respect or quality, which brings it into connection with its object. Let us ask what the three correlates are to which a thought-sign refers.

"284. (1) When we think, to what thought does that thought-sign which is ourself address itself? It may, through the medium of outward expression, which it reaches perhaps only after considerable internal development, come to address itself to thought of another person. But whether this happens or not, it is always interpreted by a subsequent thought of our own. If, after any thought, the current of ideas flows on freely, it follows the law of mental association. In that case, each former thought suggests something to the thought which follows it, i.e., is the sign of something to this latter. Our train of thought may, it is true, be interrupted. But we must remember that, in addition to the principal element of thought at any moment, there are a hundred things in our mind to which but a small fraction of attention or consciousness is conceded. It does not, therefore, follow, because a new constituent of thought gets the uppermost that the train of thought which it displaces is broken off altogether. On the contrary, from our second principle, that there is no intuition or cognition not determined by previous cognitions, it follows that the striking in of a new experience is never an instantaneous affair, but is an event occupying time, and coming to pass by a continuous process. Its prominence in consciousness, therefore must probably be the consummation of a growing process; and if so, there is no sufficient cause for the thought which had been the leading one just before, to cease abruptly and instantaneously. But if a train of thought ceases by gradually dying out, it freely follows its own law of association as long as it lasts, and there is no moment at which there is a thought belonging to this series, subsequently to which there is not a thought which interprets or repeats it. There is no exception, therefore, to the law that every thought-sign is translated or interpreted in a subsequent one, unless it be that all thought comes to an abrupt and final end in death.

"285. (2) The next question is: For what does the thought-sign stand—what does it name—what is its suppositum? The outward thing, undoubtedly, when a real outward thing is thought of. But still, as the thought is determined by a previous thought of the same object, it only refers to the thing through denoting this previous thought. Let us suppose, for example, that Toussaint is thought of, and first thought of as a negro, but not distinctly as a man. If this distinctness is afterwards added, it is through the thought that a negro is a man; that is to say, the subsequent thought, man, refers to the outward thing by being predicated of that previous thought, negro, which has been had of that thing. If we afterwards think of Toussaint as a general, then we think that this negro, this man, was a general. And so in every case the subsequent thought denotes what was thought in the previous thought.

"286. (3) The thought-sign stands for its object in the respect which is thought; that is to say, this respect is the immediate object of consciousness in the thought, or, in other words, it is the thought itself, or at least what the thought is thought to be in the subsequent thought to which it is a sign."

36. *Gloss on ¶ 227.* Aquinas gives the following concrete example (c.1268: In 4 met. lect. 6. n. 6, p. 421): "impossibile enim est quemcumque suscipere, sive opinari, quod idem sit simul et non sit: quamvis quidam arbitrentur Heraclitum hoc opinatum fuisse. Verum est autem, quod Heraclitus hoc dixit, non tamen hoc potuit opinari. Non enim necessarium est, quod quicquid aliquis dicit, haec mente sucsipiat vel opinetur".

37. *Gloss on ¶ 233.* Peirce 1905a 4.539 (bearing in mind Gloss 19 above): "The Immediate Object of all knowledge and all thought is, in the last analysis, the Percept. This doctrine in no wise conflicts with Pragmaticism, which holds that the Immediate Interpretant of all thought proper is Conduct. Nothing is more indispensable to a sound epistemology than a crystal-clear discrimination between the Object and the Interpretant of knowledge; . . . and the one discrimination is not more rudimentary than the other. That we are conscious of our Percepts is a theory that seems to be to be beyond dispute; but it is not a fact of Immediate Perception. A fact of Immediate Perception is not a Percept, nor any part of a Percept; a Percept is a Seme, while a fact of Immediate Perception or rather the Perceptual Judgment of which such fact is the Immediate Interpretant, is a Pheme that is the direct Dynamical Interpretant of the Percept, and of which the Percept is the Dynamical Object, and is with some considerable difficulty (as the history of psychology shows), distinguished from the Immediate Object, though the distinction is highly significant [CP note: i.e., the perceptual judgment is a proposition of existence determined by the percept, which it interprets]. But not to interrupt our train of thought, let us go on to note that while the Immediate Object of a Percept is excessively vague, yet natural thought makes up for that lack (as it almost amounts to), as follows. A late Dynamical Interpretant of the whole complex of Percepts is the Seme of a Perceptual Universe that is represented in instinctive thought as determining the original Immediate Object of every Percept. [CP note: A complex of percepts yields a picture of a perceptual universe. Without reflection, that universe is taken to be the cause of such objects as are represented in a percept. Though each percept is vague, as it is

recognized that its object is the result of the action of the universe on the perceiver, it is so far clear.] [Cf. Deely 1992a.] Of course, I must be understood as talking not psychology, but the logic of mental operations. Subsequent Interpretants furnish new Semes of Universes resulting from various adjunctions to the Perceptual Universe. They are, however, all of them, Interpretants of Percepts.

"Finally, and in particular, we get a Seme of that highest of all Universes, which is regarded as the Object of every true Proposition, and which, if we name it [at] all, we call by the somewhat misleading title of 'The Truth'." But by that time, of course, we are into anthroposemiosis proper and therefore in the zone where even perceptual similarity can be stylized and transferred, as it were (at least to some degree), to a conventional base.

38. Gloss on ¶ 235. The "Editor's Preface" to Deely et al. 1986: viii-xvii, takes its title "Pars Pro Toto" from the theme of identifying this fallacy, which is there fully exposed. New light has been shed on this matter by Baer (1992: 354-356), who applies to the point the logical distinction between comprehension (or "intension") and extension: "Extensionally, regarding what I have called the denotational range of semiotics, the major tradition includes of course the minor ones. But intensionally, by which I mean, insofar as our concepts excavate the possibility of what we ultimately can experience as objects, the minor traditions, understood as discourse analysis with philosophical implications, may include the major one". I take Baer's point here to be the same as, or closely analogous to, that made by Heidegger with regard to the manner in which positive investigation is dependent on the manner in which the foundations for the sciences are laid: see Heidegger 1927: 30-31.

39. Gloss on ¶ 256. No doubt the most startling example of mistaking semiotics from within is provided by the late notes of Bakhtin, who seems never to have recovered from his youthful conception of semiotics as of a piece with Russian Formalism (Bakhtin 1971: 147): "Semiotics deals primarily with the transmission of ready-made communication using a ready-made code. But in live speech, strictly speaking, communication is first created in the process of transmission, and there is, in essence no code", which I interpret to say "prejacent to and independent of the anthroposemiosis itself" (unfortunately, this fragment concludes by ending in the middle of a tantalizing sentence posing "The problem of changing the code in inner speech . . ."). In setting his own work, unmistakably and centrally semiotic in our terms, over against semiotics thus, Bakhtin himself illustrates the prevalence, as well as the seriousness, of the misunderstanding behind the pars pro toto fallacy discussed above.

40. Gloss on ¶ 265. Actually, as we have seen in our discussion of the meaning and aspects of adages concerning "infinite process", anyone who studies the foundations of the action of signs, quite apart from literature, is required to face this problem, which is actually a general one by no means specific to literature (Peirce 1905-1906: 5.448n.1): "It seems a strange thing, when one comes to ponder over it, that a sign should leave its interpreter to supply a part of its meaning; but the explanation of the phenomenon lies in the fact that the entire universe—not merely the universe of existents, but all that wider universe, embracing the universe of existents as a part, the universe which we are all accustomed to refer to as 'the truth'—that all this universe is perfused with signs, if it is not composed exclusively of signs. Let us note this in passing as having a bearing on the question of pragmaticism".

41. Gloss on ¶ 272. The difficulties and theoretical requirements of this "broader conception" are discussed at length in Deely 1989: "The Grand Vision".

42. Gloss on ¶ 273. The insight, that is to say, that the sign lies at the base and heart of any object given as such in experience, construed along the lines suggested by Peirce in making his "Guess at the Riddle" (c.1890: 1.384):

> Kant gives the erroneous view that ideas are presented separated and then thought together by the mind. This is his doctrine that a mental synthesis precedes every analysis. What really happens is that something is presented which in itself has no parts, but which nevertheless is analyzed by the mind, that is to say, its having parts consists in this, that the mind afterward recognizes those parts in it. Those partial ideas are really not in the first idea, in itself, though they are separated out from it. It is a case of destructive distillation. When, having thus separated them, we think over them, we are carried in spite of ourselves from one thought to another, and therein lies the first real synthesis.

An application of this idea to the derivation of semiotic from Locke's Essay of 1690 is worked out in Deely 1986b.

43. *Gloss on* ¶ 279. "The individual's act is not just one of communication: each individual analyzes nature, takes in or rejects types of relationships and phenomena, channels the process of reasoning, and builds the house of consciousness" (Santaella Braga 1992: 309). "The constant tension between individual experience and the collective means for expressing and interpreting that experience is the dynamic relationship by which culture comes to be and through which it is constantly changing" (Dougherty and Fernandez 1981: 413).

44. *First Gloss on* ¶ 289. Among neoscholastic authors in particular, the bad habit took root of comparing "universal intellectual concepts" with "singulars as given in external sensation" in order to "establish" the distinction between sense and intellect. But such a procedure is completely question-begging, because the difference between sense and intellect requires to be established at the level of perception, not the level of sensation. This practice of the neoscholastics is all the more baffling when one considers that they have at their disposal much more sophisticated and ample theoretical resources for placing the question at its proper level, as I have shown in the scholastic analysis of "Animal Intelligence and Concept-Formation" (Deely 1971: esp. 55-83).

45. *Second Gloss on* ¶ 289. After Darwin particularly, the view whose foundations were laid in the empiricist development of early modern philosophy came to be popularly entertained. This view was baldly stated by Hobbes (1651: 27): "The imagination that is raised in man, or any other creature endued with the faculty of imagining, by words, or other voluntary signs, is what we generally call understanding; and is common to man and beast". Recent decades of "ape language experiments" hardly made sense on any other supposition.

46. *First Gloss on* ¶ 293. Poinsot 1635: 315b6-13, 315b30-40: "in intellectu aliud est capacitas, aliud virtus. Capacitas correspondet intellectui possibili, ut est sub statu purae potentiae seu capacitatis, virtus vero intellectui ut formato specie sibi connaturali seu modo habendi species connaturales . . . .".

". . . Caietanus recte advertit [1507: In I p. q. 79. art. 7] potentiam intellectivam non adaequari a suo obiecto motivo, sed solum a terminativo. Excedit ergo capacitas specificationem, quae a motivo sumitur, et ita, ut dicit S. Thomas, respicit pro obiecto omne ens, nec in ista amplitudine diversificatur intellectus aliqua differentia entium, sed omnes amplectitur."

This text is difficult to convey. In the index to the present work ("Intellect, capacity contrasted to situation of vital response"), "virtus" is rendered as "situation of vital response", a rendering that, to say the least, raises a number of questions (while at least addressing the difficulty). The point that Poinsot, Cajetan, and Aquinas before them struggle to make is perhaps clarified in the contemporary formulation of Corrington (1992: 41): on the one hand, "embodiment radically limits the reach of the self and binds it to the fragmentary conditions of origin": this is the *virtus intellectus*; on the other hand, "the human process is not confined to its sheer embodiment but moves outward through its products and utterances": this is the *capacitas intellectus*, the asymptotic (or syncategorematic) "full reach of the human process" beyond its condition of emobdiment—a reach doomed to fall short, to be sure, if actual achievement of infinity is the measure, but a reaching nonetheless ever-more infinite in prospect and succession in time, according to the Peircean idea that the truth to which mankind has devotion ought not to be merely the "truth as we understand it", but precisely truths we do not yet understand.

47. Second Gloss on ¶ 293. Aquinas made the point as clearly as one could wish (De veritate, c.1256-1259: q. 1. art. 1c): "oportet fieri reductionem in aliqua principia per se intellectui nota . . . investigando quid est unumquodque; alias . . . in infinitum iretur, et sic periret omnino scientia et cognitio rerum. Illud autem quod primo intellectus concipit quasi notissimum, et in quod conceptiones omnes resolvit, est ens, ut Avicenna dicit in principio suae metaphysicae. Unde oportet quod omnes aliae conceptiones intellectus accipiantur ex additione ad ens. Sed enti non possunt addi aliqua quasi extranea per modum quo differentia additur generi, vel accidens subiecto, quia quaelibet natura est essentialiter ens; unde probat etiam philosophus in iii metaphys. quod 'ens non potest esse genus, sed secundum hoc aliqua dicuntur addere super ens, in quantum exprimunt modum ipsius entis qui nomine entis non exprimitur'. Quod dupliciter contingit: uno modo ut modus expressus sit aliquis specialis modus entis. Sunt enim diversi gradus entitatis, secundum quos accipiuntur diversi modi essendi, et iuxta hos modos accipiuntur diversa rerum genera. Substantia enim non addit super ens aliquam differentiam, quae designet aliquam naturam superadditam enti, sed nomine substantiae exprimitur specialis quidam modus essendi, scilicet per se ens; et ita est in aliis generibus. Alio modo ita quod modus expressus sit modus generalis consequens omne ens; et hic modus dupliciter accipi potest: uno modo secundum quod consequitur unumquodque ens in se; alio modo secundum quod consequitur unum ens in ordine ad aliud. Si primo modo, hoc est dupliciter. Quia vel exprimitur in ente aliquid affirmative vel negative. Non autem invenitur aliquid affirmative dictum absolute quod possit accipi in omni ente, nisi essentia eius, secundum quam esse dicitur; et sic imponitur hoc nomen res, quod in hoc differt ab ente, secundum Avicennam in principio metaphys., 'quod ens sumitur ab actu essendi, sed nomen rei exprimit quidditatem vel essentiam entis'. Negatio autem consequens omne ens absolute, est indivisio; et hanc exprimit hoc nomen unum: hihil aliud enim est unum quam ens indivisum. Si autem modus entis accipiatur secundo modo, scilicet secundum ordinem unius ad alterum, hoc potest esse dupliciter. Uno modo secundum divisionem unius ab altero; et hoc exprimit hoc nomen aliquid: dicitur enim aliquid quasi aliud quid; unde sicut ens dicitur unum, in quantum est individum in se, ita dicitur aliquid, in quantum est ab aliis divisum. Alio modo secundum convenientiam unius entis ad aliud; et hoc quidem non potest esse nisi accipiatur aliquid quod natum sit convenire cum omni ente: hoc autem est anima, quae 'quodammodo est omnia', ut dicitur in iii de anima. In anima autem est vis cognitiva et appetitiva, convenientiam ergo entis ad appetitum exprimit hoc nomen bonum, ut in principio ethic. dicitur quod bonum est quod omnia appetunt. Convenientiam vero entis ad intellectum exprimit hoc nomen verum. Omnis autem cognitio perficitur per assimilationem cognoscentis ad rem cognitam, ita quod assimilatio dicta est causa cognitionis: sicut visus per hoc quod disponitur secundum speciem coloris, cog-noscit colorem. Prima ergo comparatio entis ad intellectum est ut ens intellectui concordet: quae quidem concordia adaequatio intellectus et rei dicitur; in hoc formaliter ratio veri perficitur. Hoc est ergo quod addit verum super ens, scilicet conformitatem, sive adaequationem rei et intellectus; ad quam conformitatem, ut dictum est, sequitur cognitio rei. Sic ergo entitas rei praecedit rationem veritatis, sed cognitio est quidam veritatis effectus. Secundum hoc ergo veritas sive verum tripliciter invenitur diffiniri. Uno modo secundum illud quod praecedit rationem veritatis, in quo verum fundatur; et sic Augustinus definit in lib. solil.: verum est id quod est; et avicenna in sua metaphysic.: veritas cuiusque rei est proprietas sui esse quod stabilitum est ei; et quidam sic: verum est indivisio esse, et quod est. Alio modo definitur secundum id in quo formaliter ratio veri perficitur; et sic dicit Isaac quod veritas est adaequatio rei et intellectus; et anselmus in lib. de veritate: veritas est rectitudo sola mente perseptibilis. 'Rectitudo' enim ista secundum adaequationem quamdam dicitur, et philosophus dicit in iv metaphysic., quod 'definientes verum dicimus cum dicitur esse quod est, aut non esse quod non est'. Tertio modo definitur verum, secundum effectum consequentem; et sic dicit Hilarius, quod verum est declarativum et manifestativum esse; et Augustinus in lib. de vera relig.: veritas est qua ostenditur id quod est; et in eodem libro: veritas est secundum quam de inferioribus iudicamus."

The argument can be reduced to a diagram:

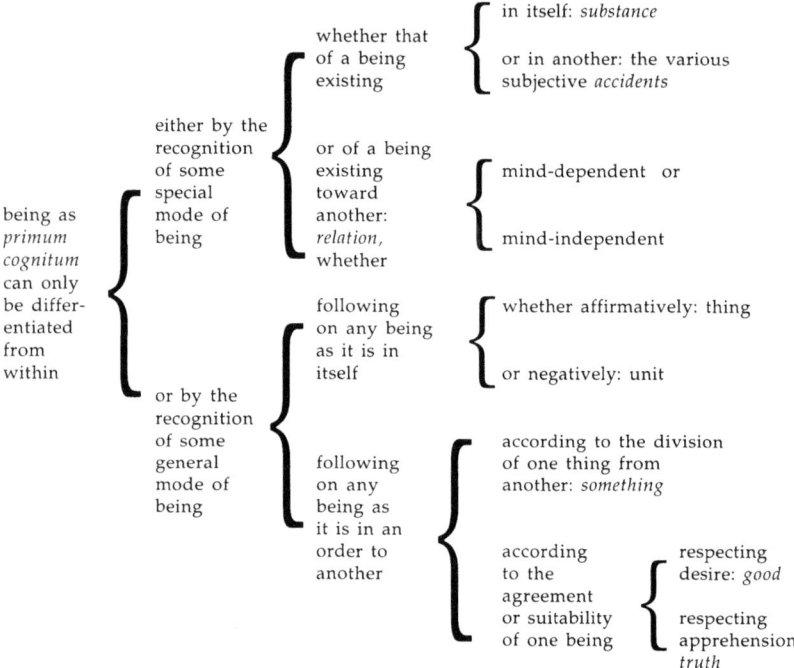

Figure 11. Aquinas's Derivation of Properties and Types of Being *from within* Being as *Primum Cognitum*

48. First Gloss on ¶ 294. Poinsot 1633: 26b34-27a28: "Quodsi inquiras, an sicut cognoscitur ens tamquam primum cognitum ab intellectu, ita necessario debeat intellectus procedendo de potentia ad actum prius attingere praedicata universaliora, quae sequuntur post ens, eo quod confusiora sunt, quam praedicata minus communia: respondetur (quod et advertit Caietanus quaestione illa prima de Ente et Essentia concl. 2. [but see also Gloss 52 below]) non esse ordinem essentialem inter ens, quod est primo cognitum, et reliqua praedicata inferiora in cognoscendo quantum ad applicationem et exercitium cognoscendi, licet ex parte rei cognitae maior proportio sit in praedicatis communioribus ad intellectum imperfecte cognoscentem. Ratio est, quia in prima omnium cognitione neque intellectus se potest applicare neque voluntas intellectum, cum non praecesserit alia cognition, virtute cuius se applicet, et ideo tantum operatur ibi proportio immediata obiecti cum potentia. Et cum potentia sit tunc in statu purae potentialitatis, non proportionatur illi obiectum secundum rationem magis actualem et distinctam, sed secundum potentialem et confusam, et ab illa movetur tunc intellectus. Ceterum post illam primam cognitionem potest intellectus se movere vel per voluntatem applicari ad id, quod voluerit, sicque relictis intermediis generibus ad praedicatum infimae speciei se applicare, unde contingit cognoscere aliquando praedicatum specificum ignorato genere intermedio, imperfecte tamen propter ignorantiam praedicati intermedii, quod ex parte rei cognitae praecise magis proportionatum est potentiae procedenti de imperfecto ad perfectum".

49. Second Gloss on ¶ 294. Poinsot 1635: 318b7-19: "Obiectum autem proprotionatum nostri intellectus . . . est quidditas rei sensibilis et quidquid per connotationem ad illam cognoscibile est. . . . Et nomine quidditatis non solam substantiam praedicamentalem intelligimus, sed quidquid per modum naturae alicuius et essentiae concipi potest, etiam accidentia et modi, imo et singularitas ipsa ad instar essentiae alicuius accipi potest".

50. Third Gloss on ¶ 294. Poinsot 1633: 33b5-17: "quae sunt propria phantasmatum, investigat intellectus per conceptum quidditatis ut habentis ordinem et dependentiam a phantasmate ut a termino a quo est extracta. Et haec est cognitio reflexa seu indirecta, qua cognoscitur singulare, quia scilicet cognoscitur quidditas attendendo etiam ad connotationem et ordinem, quem habet ad phantasmata, a quibus extracta est, et propterea dicitur reflecti super illa".

51. First Gloss on ¶ 296. Poinsot 1635: 318b25-319a5, emphasis added: ". . . anima . . . ab obiectis sensibilibus accipit cognitionem suam nec alio modo intelligit quam ex sensibilibus et convertendo se ad phantasmata, ut experientia ipsa testatur et ipsa natura animae postulat, quae cum sit infima in toto ordine intelligibili, maxime conformatur intelligibil infimo et imperfecto, *quale est intelligibile in potentia. Hoc autem debet esse aliqua quidditas non spiritualis et immaterialis in actu, sed immaterialis in poten-*

tia et per abstractionem facta intelligibilis in actu, et ita vocatur quidditas rei sensibilis. [But this is to be some definable structure not imperceptible and objective in act, but objective in potency and made actually intelligible through an abstraction, and is called in this sense the definable structure of a sensible thing.] Ex eo enim, quod ad modum quidditatis et substantiae accipitur, modo intelligibili res illa concipitur, modo intelligibili res illa concipitur et ut abstrahens a conditionibus materialibus, v.g., a loco et tempore aliisque sensibilibus, a quibus abstrahunt res spirituales. Tale enim intelligibile connaturale debet esse alicui intellectui, et non alteri quam nostro, qui coniungitur sensibus, ut ab ipsis siensibilibus possit cognitionem suam haurire per modum quidditatis ea intelligendo et abstracte".

Notice that "abstraction" spoken of here is not a scientific procedure, but the simple negative process whereby a cognitive power—in this case, understanding or intellect—fastens on its proper object (i.e., the object which correlatively defines the power in its difference from what other channels of apprehension present or manifest) to the exclusion of all else that falls outside that formality (Poinsot 1633: 31a5-28): "cum dicitur ens esse primo cognitum et praedicata universaliora esse notiora, non sumitur ens, ut subest abstractioni positivae, sive formali sive totali, sicut de illo tractat Metaphysica, sed ut concipitur secundum se et sub abstractione negativa, qualis etiam potest contingere in sensu, qui accipit unim omisso alio, v.g. colorem in pomo omisso sapore, et in ipso colore possumus videre a longe rationem colorati singularis, non discernendo propriam differentiam talis coloris. Sic in prima cognitione intellectus accipit ens ut concretum quidditati sensibili, non quia abstractionem positivam eius formet, nec quia propriam et determinatam rationem praedicate inferioris accipiat, sed quia in ipsa quidditate sensibili solum accipit rationem confusiorem vel communiorem secundum se, quae est magis imperfecta et potentialis". Compare this with Peirce's discussion of abstraction or "prescission" in his "New List of Categories" (1867: W 2.50 § 5; cf. CP1.549).

Thus the ens ut primum cognitum, contrary to common assumptions of the neoscholastics, is irreducible to ens as it is studied in any of the special sciences—ens reale or ens mobile which is studied in physics, ens quantitativum which is studied in mathematics, ens commune or ens ut sic or even ens transcendentale such as is studied in Aristotelian or Thomistic metaphysics. Ens ut primum cognitum is a notion sui generis, prior to all predication as that which makes predication possible, from which all other notions of being, logical, scientific, or metaphysical, are derived ab intra (see Gloss 47 above), and on which all other specifically intellectual notions depend.

52. *Second Gloss on ¶ 296.* Aquinas, c.1265: de pot. q. 9. art. 7. ad 6: "inter ista quatuor prima [ens, unum, verum, et bonum], maxime primum est ens: et ideo oportet quod positive praedicetur; negatio enim vel privatio non potest esse primum quod intellectu concipitur, cum semper quod negatur vel privatur sit de intellectu negationis vel privationis. Oportet autem quod alia tria super ens addant aliquid quod ens non contrahat; si enim contraherent ens, iam non essent prima. Hoc autem esse non potest nisi addant aliquid secundum rationem tantum: hoc autem est vel negatio, quam addit unum (ut dictum est), vel relatio ad aliquid quod natum sit referri universaliter ad ens; et hoc est vel intellectus, ad quem importat relationem verum, aut appetitus, ad quem importat relationem bonum".

53. *Gloss on ¶ 297.* The fundamental awareness or apprehension is neither of existence as such nor of intelligibility—"essence" or "possibility"—as separate from existence, but simply of a prospective intelligibility given in and through experience: "Dices: Potest attingi ab intellectu quidditas singularitatis quoad an est, et non quoad quid est, et sic facilius cognoscetur ipsum an est singularitatis quam naturae. Sed esto ita sit, quod intellectus incipiat cognoscere quidditatem sui obiecti non quidditative, sed quoad an est, ita quod neque de ipsa natura neque de ipsa singularitate attingat aliud praedicatum quam ipsum an est, tamen hoc ipso non cognoscitur singulare ut singulare est, sed sub confusione et ratione quadam communissima ipsius esse, ita quod de ipsa singularitate non cognoscit nisi quod sit ens. Hoc autem est cognoscere aliquid commune ipsi singulari et ipsi naturae; de utroque enim datur cognitio quoad an est, et sic ipsum esse seu an est ut concretum seu applicatum alicui singulari sensibili erit primum cognitum intellectus. Quare (quod valde advertendum est) quando intellectus cognoscit aliquid quoad an est, non praescindit a quod quid seu a quidditate, hoc enim est impossibile, cum sit formale eius obiectum et primo et per se intelligibile, sed solum non cognoscit quidditative, id est penetrando constitutionem propriam quidditatis et causas essendi, sed in ipsa quidditate solum attingit praedicatum quoddam valde commune et confusum, quod est ipsum ess; et hoc est, quod tunc cognoscit ut quod quid.

"Et licet sensus immediate moveat intellectum, tamen quia non movet ad cognoscendum singulare eo modo, quo sensus, nec sub eadem ratione formali obiecti, sed per modum intelligibilem, id est per modum quidditatis, ideo intellectus non respicit ut primo cognitum ipsum singulare sub modo et exercitio singularitatis, cum tamen in sensu singularitatis sit conditio obiecti sensibiliter moventis, ita quod obiectum non per quidditatem nec per abstractionem, sed ut hic et nunc movet ad sui cognitionem" (Poinsot 1633: 23b34-24a41).

54. First Gloss on ¶ 298. Poinsot 1633: 32b37-33a13: "formalis ratio cognoscendi intellectus, in quo a sensu distinguitur, non est ipsa singularitas, sed ipsa quidditas, cuius singularitas est modus. Sed tamen quia intellectus non attingit ipsam quidditatem nisi dependenter a phantasmatibus, convertendo et coordinando se illis, ut dicitur 3. de Anima textu 32. [c. 7, 431b2], ideo attingit singularia, ut sunt quaedam connotationes quidditatis abstractae a phantasmatibus, ad quae dicit ordinem. Et ita sensus et intellectus contrario modo procedunt, quia sensus primo et per se respicit accidentia, a quibus pendet individuatio quidditatis, intellectus autem primo et per se respiciat quidditatem, quae talibus accidentibus et individuatione connotatur et designatur, et ideo potest proprie distincte attingere illa, non tamen immediate et directe".

55. Second Gloss on ¶ 298. Aquinas, c.1265: de pot. q. 9. art. 7. ad 15: "secundum philosophum, 'multitudo est prior uno secundum sensum, sicut totum partibus et compositum simplici': sed unum est prius multitudine naturaliter et secundum rationem. Hoc autem non videtur sufficere ad hoc quod unum opponatur multitudini privative, nam privatio est posterior secundum rationem cum in intellectu privationis sit eius oppositum per quod definitur: nisi forte hoc referatur solum ad nominis rationem, prout hoc nomen unum significat privative, nomen vero multitudinis positive; nomina enim imponuntur a nobis secundum quod congnoscimus res. Unde ad hoc quod aliquid significetur per nomen ut privatio, sufficit qualitercumque sit posterius in nostra cognitione; quamvis hoc non sufficiat ad hoc quod res ipsa sit privativa, nisi sit posterius secundum rationem. Et ideo potest melius dici, quod divisio est causa multitudinis, et est prior secundum intellectum quam multitudo; unum autem dicitur privative respectu divisionis, cum sit ens indivisum, non autem respectu multitudinis. Unde divisio est prior, secundum rationem, quam unum; sed multitudo posterius. Quod sic patet: primum enim quod in intellectum cadit, est ens; secundum vero est negatio entis; ex his autem duobus sequitur tertio intellectus divisionis (ex hoc enim quod aliquid intelligitur ens, et intelligitur non esse hoc ens, sequitur in intellectu quod sit divisum ab eo); quarto autem sequitur in intellectu ratio unius, prout scilicet intelligitur hoc ens non esse in se divisum; quinto autem sequitur intellectus multitudinis, prout scilicet hoc ens intelligitur divisum ab alio, et utrumque ipsorum esse in se unum. Quantumcumque enim aliqua intelligantur divisa, non intelligetur multitudo, nisi quodlibet divisorum intelligatur esse unum, et sic etiam patet quod non erit circulus in definitione unius et multitudinis" (Cf. Deely 1982: 153-155 n. 1).

56. Gloss on ¶ 300. Poinsot 1632a: First Preamble, Art. 2, 60/7-25, and Book 1, Quest. 2, 141/12-14: "not every mind-dependent objective relation is a second intention, because even though every mind-dependent relation results from cognition, yet not every such relation denominates a thing only in the state of a cognized being, which is a second state, but some also do so in the state of an existence independent of cognition, as, for example, the relations of being a doctor, being a judge. For the existing man, not the man as cognized, is a doctor or a judge, and so those mind-dependent relations [being a doctor, judge, teacher, etc.] denominate a state of existence.

"You may gather from what has been said that even in the case of stipulated signs the rationale of sign must be explained by a relation to a signified."

57. Gloss on ¶ 306. The Latins called these elements of physical being as internally codetermined "transcendental relatives", a difficult term discussed in detail in Poinsot 1632a: esp. Second Preamble, Arts. 1 and 2, and in Deely 1990: esp. 35-46, but best summarized by Baer as an aid to understanding "how objects become signs in experience" (Baer 1992: 353): "Transcendental relations constitute a given thing, say, a rock, and provide thus the possibility of understanding it, once it becomes an object in experience. Ontological relations characterize the interactions a thing may assume in addition to being a thing. Here thing becomes a little tricky", Baer notes, "because it is often difficult to say what exactly a thing is, since", as we saw in ¶s 38-60 particularly, "things are accessible only by becoming objects in our experience, and the 'thingness' in objects might precisely be the element which resists our understanding. It is perhaps best to say that transcendental relations", as I would put it, in the sense relevant to semiosis, "constitute things in the first place which then may or may not engage in additional relations with other things already established in their own right. These additional relations would then be ontological relations. They exist not as things but 'between things'". Baer concludes (ibid.):

> While transcendental relations provide the possibility for our understanding a thing as thing (say, a rock as a rock), ontological relations provide the possibility of experiencing that thing as an object in various contexts, not all of which need be physically real. A rock can become a weapon; I would say, it then assumes for the time being an ontological relation with perhaps tangible physical results. But what happens if it becomes a tombstone, one of the oldest signs of humankind, distinguishing the human species clearly from all others? Here the ontological relation reveals its true essence as an imperceptible relation which nevertheless makes a huge difference in relating a rock to the memory of the dead. A rock can be weapon, tombstone, furniture or, as in the case of our paleontology student, a piece of scientific information. Semiosic relations are ontological relations which provide the possibility for experiencing objects as bringing other objects into view. A rock recognized by the appropriate interpretant as a fossil bone begins to tell a story. (See further Baer 1977.)

58. First Gloss on ¶ 308. Thomas Aquinas, c.1266: I. q. 84. art. 7c: "impossibile est intellectum nostrum . . . aliquid intelligere in actu, nisi convertendo se ad phantasmata. Et hoc duobus indiciis apparet. Primo quidem quia . . . ad hoc quod intellectus actu intelligat, non solum accipiendo scientiam de novo, sed etiam utendo scientia iam acquisita, requiritur actus imaginationis et ceterarum virtutum. . . . Secundo, quia hoc quilibet in seipso experiri potest, quod quando aliquis conatur aliquid intelligere, format aliqua phantasmata sibi per modum exemplorumm, in quibus quasi inspiciat quod intelligere studet. Et inde est etiam quod quando alium volumus facere aliquid intelligere, proponimus ei exempla, ex quibus sibi phantasmata formare possit ad intelligendum. . . . Et ideo necesse est ad hoc quod intellectus actu intelligat suum objectum proprium, quod convertat se ad phantasmata, ut speculetur naturam universalem in particulari existentem".

59. Second Gloss on ¶ 308. Aquinas, c.1254-1256: 1 Sent. dist. 19. q. 5. art. 1. ad 7, p. 55: "cum sit duplex operatio intellectus: una quarum dicitur a quibusdam 'imaginatio intellectus', quam philosophus nominat 'intelligentiam indivisibilium', quae consistit in apprehensione quidditatis simplicis, quae alio etiam nomine formatio dicitur; alia 'est quam dicunt fidem', quae consistit in compositione vel divisione propositionis: prima operatio respicit quidditatem rei; secunda respicit esse ipsius. Et quia ratio veritatis fundatur in esse, et non in quidditate, . . . ideo veritas et falsitas proprie invenitur . . . non in prima, vel signo ejus quod est definitio, nisi secundum quid; sicut etiam quidditatis esse est quoddam esse rationis, et secundum istud esse dicitur veritas in prima operatione intellectus: per quem etiam modum dicitur definitio vera. Sed huic veritati non adjungitur falsitas per se, quia intellectus habet verum judicium de proprio objecto, in quod naturaliter tendit, quod est quidditas rei, sicut et visus de colore; sed per accidens admiscetur falsitas, scilicet ratione affirmationis vel negationis annexae, quod contingit dupliciter: vel ex comparatione definitionis ad definitum, et tunc dicitur definitio falsa respectu alicujus et non simpliciter, sicut definitio circuli est falsa de triangulo; vel in respectu partium definitionis ad invicem, in quibus implicatur impossibilis affirmatio; sicut definitio vacui, quod est locus in quo nullum corpus est; et haec definitio dicitur falsa simpliciter, ut in 9 metaph. dicitur. Secundae autem operationi admiscetur falsitas etiam per se: non quidem quantum ad primas affirmationes quas naturaliter intellectus cognoscit, ut sunt dignitates, sed quantum ad consequentes: quia rationem inducendo contingit errare per applicationem unius ad aliud".

60. *Gloss on* ¶ *309.* Peirce 1908a: 6.476: "Animals of all races rise far above the general level of their intelligence in those performances that are their proper function, such as flying and nest-building for ordinary birds; and what is man's proper function if it be not to embody general ideas in art-creations, in utilities, and above all in theoretical cognition? To give the lie to his own consciousness of divining the reasons of phenomena would be as silly in a man as it would be in a fledgling bird to refuse to trust its wings and leave the nest, because the poor little thing had read Babinet, and judged aerostation to be impossible on hydrodynamical grounds. Yes; it must be confessed that if we knew that the impulse to prefer one hypothesis to another really were analogous to the instincts of birds and wasps, it would be foolish not to give it play, within the bounds of reason". (And we do know.)

61. *Gloss on* ¶ *310.* Poinsot 1632a: Book 1, Quest. 1, 117/28-118/18: "And we speak here of ontological relation—of relation according to the way it has being—not of categorial relation, because we are discussing the sign in general, as it includes equally the natural and the social sign, in which general discussion even the signs which are mental artifacts—namely, stipulated signs as such—are involved. And for this reason, the rationale common to signs cannot be that of a categorial being, nor a categorial relation, although it could be an ontological relation, according to the point made by St. Thomas in the Summa theologica, I, q. 28, art. 1, and explained in our Preamble on Relation—to wit, that only in the case of these things which exist toward another is found some mind-independent relation and some mind-dependent relation, which latter relation plainly is not categorial, but is called a relation according to the way relation has being (an ontological relation), because it is purely a relation and does not import anything absolute".

Appendix: The Ethics of Terminology

Here follows the complete list of rules which C. S. Peirce was led to formulate (1903) on the basis of his knowledge of and reflections upon the *history of ideas* (italics added; for general discussion of the rules, see Gloss 14 above):

"*First*. To take pains to avoid following any recommendation of an arbitrary nature as to the use of philosophical terminology.

"*Second*. To avoid using words and phrases of vernacular origin as technical terms of philosophy.

"*Third*. To use the scholastic terms in their anglicised forms for philosophical conceptions, so far as these are strictly applicable; and never to use them in other than their proper senses.

"*Fourth*. For ancient philosophical conceptions overlooked by the scholastics, to imitate, as well as I can, the ancient expression.

"*Fifth*. For precise philosophical conceptions introduced into philosophy since the middle ages, to use the anglicised form of the original expression, if not positively unsuitable, but only in its precise original sense.

"*Sixth*. For philosophical conceptions which vary by a hair's breadth from those for which suitable terms exist, to invent terms with a due regard for the usages of philosophical terminology and those of the English language but yet with a distinctly technical appearance. Before proposing a term, notion, or other symbol, to consider maturely whether it perfectly suits the conception and will lend itself to every occasion, whether it interferes with any existing term, and whether it may not create an inconvenience by interfering with the expression of some conception that may hereafter be introduced into philosophy. Having once introduced a symbol, to consider myself almost as much bound by it as if it had been introduced by somebody else; and after others have accepted it, to consider myself more bound to it than anybody else.

"*Seventh*. To regard it as needful to introduce new systems of expression when new connections of importance between conceptions come to be made out, or when such systems can, in any way, positively subserve the purposes of philosophical study."

To which I would add, for the speculative and historical reasons spelled out in *New Beginnings* (Deely 1994), an

Eighth. To scrutinize contemporary epistemological problems in the light of late Latin developments which the moderns neglected, as an aid in determining the choices of terminology most suitable for postmodern considerations.

Since, as has now been discovered, the major developments in semiotic and epistemological theory during the Latin epoch occurred not in central Europe during the middle ages, but in Iberia during the sixteenth and seventeenth centuries, we are able to see concretely, by comparing the early modern development with the late Latin development in these very areas, how true it is that (Ketner 1981: 336) "to reject a fairly well developed terminology, created by a working body of scientific intelligences" as the Iberian scholastics were, "would involve a later generation of scholars in arbitrarily throwing away the results of earlier scientific study, and hence would be a major moral sin against the development of a science", in this case, the doctrine of signs.

I would also comment, regarding Peirce's stricture in Rule 6 against employing terms that may "create an inconvenience by interfering with the expression of some conception that may hereafter be introduced into philosophy", that I take this to be a *monitum* against proposing terminology designed and intended to block further inquiry, such as the analytic attempt to rule discussion of mind out of philosophy, the behaviorist attempt to rule discussion of consciousness out of psychology, or the attempt of the officers of the Linguistic Society of Paris to rule discussion of the origin of species-specifically human language out of linguistics, rather than a requirement, obviously preposterous, to divine the particulars of future developments of human understanding.

References

ALMEDER, Robert
   1979. "Peirce on Meaning", *Synthese* 41.1, 1-24, as reprinted in *The Relevance of Charles Peirce*, ed. Eugene Freeman (La Salle, Il: Monist Library of Philosophy, 1983), 328-347, to which reprint reference is made.

ANDERSON, Myrdene, John DEELY, Martin KRAMPEN, Joseph RANSDELL, Thomas A. SEBEOK, and Thure von UEXKÜLL.
   1984. "A Semiotic Perspective on the Sciences: Steps toward a New Paradigm", in *Semiotica* 52.1/2, 7-47.

AQUINAS, Thomas.
   i. 1252-1273. *S. Thomae Aquinatis Opera Omnia ut sunt in indice thomistico*, ed. Roberto Busa (Stuttgart-Bad Cannstatt: Frommann-Holzboog, 1980), in septem volumina:
     1. In quattuor libros Sententiarum;
     2. Summa contra Gentiles, Autographi Deleta, Summa Theologiae;
     3. Quaestiones Disputatae, Quaestiones Quodlibetales, Opuscula;
     4. Commentaria in Aristotelem et alios;
     5. Commentaria in Scripturas;
     6. Reportationes, Opuscula dubiae authenticitatis;
     7. Aliorum Medii Aevi Auctorum Scripta 61.
   c. 1254-1256. *In quattuor libros sententiarum Petri Lombardi]*, in Busa ed. vol. 1.
   c. 1256-1259. *Quaestiones Disputatae de Veritate*, in Busa ed. vol. 3, 1-186.
   c. 1265-1267. *Quaestiones Disputatae de Potentia*, in Busa ed. vol. 3, 186-269.

c. 1266-1273. *Summa theologiae,* in Busa ed. vol. 2, 184-926.
c. 1268-1272. *In duodecim libros metaphysicorum Aristotelis expositio,* in Busa ed. vol. 4, 390-507.

ARAÚJO, Francisco de.
1617. *Commentariorum in universam Aristotelis Metaphysicam tomus primus* (Burgos and Salamanca: J. B. Varesius).

ARDENER, Edwin.
1977. "Comprehending Others", originally presented at a Wenner-Gren Symposium and reprinted in the collection of Ardener's essays, *The Voice of Prophecy,* which appeared two years after Ardener's death under the editorship of Malcolm Chapman (Oxford, England: Basil Blackwell, 1989), 159-185.

ARISTOTLE.
c. 348-347BC. *Posterior Analytics,* trans. G. R. C. Mure in Oxford Vol. I, Ross Ed. 1928: 71a1-100b17.
c. 330BC. *On the Soul,* trans. J. A. Smith in Oxford Vol. III, Ross Ed. 1931, 402a1-435b26.

ASHLEY, Benedict M.
1952. "Research into the Intrinsic Final Causes of Physical Things", in *ACPA Proceedings* XXVI, 185-194.

BACON, F.
1620. *Novum Organum,* ed. Thomas Fowler (Oxford, 1889); English trans. ed. Fulton H. Anderson, *The New Organon* (Indianapolis, IN: Bobbs-Merrill, 1960).

BAER, Eugen.
1977. "Things Are Stories: A Manifesto for a Reflexive Semiotics", *Semiotica* 25.3/4, 293-205.
1981. "Thomas A. Sebeok's Doctrine of Signs", in *Classics of Semiotics* (English edition of *Die Welt als Zeichen: Klassiker der modernen Semiotik,* Berlin: Wolf Jobst Siedler Verlag), ed. Martin Krampen, Klaus Oehler, Roland Posner, Thomas A. Sebeok, and Thure von Uexküll (New York: Plenum Press, 1987), 181-210.
1988. *Medical Semiotics* (= Sources in Semiotics VII; Lanham, MD: University Press of America).
1992. "Via Semiotica", review of Deely 1990, *Semiotica* 92—3/4, 351-357.

BAKHTIN, Mikhail.
1963. *Problemy poetiki Dostoevskogo* (Moscow), revised and expanded version of *Problemy tvorchestva Dostoevskogo*

(Leningrad 1929), trans. as *Problems of Dostoevsky's Poetics* by R. W. Rotsel (Ann Arbor, MI: Ardis, 1973), and retranslated under the same title by Caryl Emerson (Minneapolis: University of Minnesota Press, 1984; Theory and History of Literature Series, Vol. 8), to which 1984 retranslation page references are keyed in this essay.
- 1970-1971. "From Notes Made in 1970-1971", a section within the posthumous collection *Estetika slovesnogo tvorchestva* (Moscow, 1979), trans. by Vern W. McGee as *Speech Genres and Other Late Essays*, ed. Caryl Emerson and Michael Holquist (Austin: University of Texas Press, 1986), 132-158.
- 1975. *Voprosy literatury i estetiki* (Moscow), trans. by Caryl Emerson and Michael Holquist as *The Dialogic Imagination; Four Essays by M. M. Bakhtin*, ed. Michael Holquist (Austin: University of Texas Press, 1981), to which translation page reference is made.

BALDWIN, James M., Editor.
- 1901-1902. *Dictionary of Psychology and Philosophy*, "giving a terminology in English, French, German, and Italian. Written by many hands and edited by J. M. Baldwin", in 3 Volumes, the 3rd being a Bibliography of Philosophy, Psychology, and cognate subjects compiled by Benjamin Rand (original ed. New York: Macmillan; vols. 1 and 2 reissued by Peter Smith, New York, 1940, vol. 3, 1949).

BALLY, C.
- 1965. *Le langage et la vie* (Geneva: Droz).

BARTHES, Roland.
- 1964. *Elements de Sémiologie* (Paris: Seuil), trans. by Annette Lavers and Colin Smith as *Elements of Semiology* (New York: Hill and Wang, 1967), to which translation page reference is made in this essay.
- 1970. *S/Z* (Paris: Seuil), trans. with title unchanged by Richard Miller (New York: Farrar, Straus and Giroux, 1974), to which translation page reference is made in this essay.

BASSO, Keith H.
- 1976. "'Wise Words' of the Western Apache: Metaphor and Semantic Theory", in Basso and Selby 1976: 93-121.

BASSO, Keith H., and Henry A. SELBY.
1976. *Meaning in Anthropology* (Albuquerque: University of New Mexico Press).

BERKELEY, Bishop George.
1710. *The Principles of Human Knowledge*, in *The Works of George Berkeley, Bishop of Cloyne*, ed. A. A. Luce and T. E. Jessop (London: Nelson, 1948ff.).

BEUCHOT, Mauricio.
1980. "La doctrina tomista clásica sobre el signo: Domingo de Soto, Francisco de Araújo y Juan de Santo Tomás", *Critica* XII.36 (México, diciembre), 39-60.
1983. "Lógica y lenguaje en Juan de Sto. Tomás", *Diánoia* 17.
1987. *Metafísica: La Ontología Aristotelico-Tomista de Francesco de Araújo* (Mexico City: Universidad Nacional Autónoma de México).

BOURDIEU, Pierre.
1977. *Outline of a Theory of Practice*, (Cambridge, England: Cambridge University Press), trans. by Richard Nice from *Esquisse d'une théorie de la pratique, précédé de trois études d'ethnologie kabyle* (Switzerland: Librairie Droz, 1972), with refinements, omissions, and recastings.

BRENT, Joseph.
1993. *Charles Sanders Peirce. A Life* (Bloomington: Indiana University Press).

BRIGGS, Charles L.
1986. *Learning How To Ask. A sociolinguistic appraisal of the role of the interview in social science research* (Cambridge, England: Cambridge University Press).

BÜHLER, Karl.
1934. *Sprachtheorie: Die Darstellungsfunktion der Sprache* (reprint ed.; Stuttgart: Gustav Fischer, 1965).

BURKS, Arthur W.
1958. "Bibliography of the Works of Charles Sanders Peirce", in *The Collected Papers of Charles Sanders Peirce*, Volume VIII ed. Arthur W. Burks (Cambridge, MA: Harvard University Press, 1958), 249-330.

CAJETAN, Thomas de Vio.
c. 1493. *Commentaria in De Ente et Essentia*, ed. M. H. Laurent (Turin, Italy: Marietti, 1934).
1507. *Commentaria in summam theologicam. Prima pars* (Rome),

reprinted in *Sancti Thomae Aquinatis Doctoris Angelici Opera Omnia*, vols. 4 and 5 (Rome: Leonine, 1888-1889).

CAPUTO, John.
1987. *Radical Hermeneutics. Repetition, Deconstruction, and the Hermeneutic Project* (Bloomington: Indiana University Press).

CERTEAU, Michel de
1984. *The Practice of Everyday Life*, (Berkeley, CA: University of California Press), trans. by Steven F. Rendall of *Arts de faire*, Part I of *L'Invention du quotidien* (Part II, *Habiter, Cuisiner*, having been written by Luce Giard and Pierre Mayol; Paris: Union Général d'Editions, 1980).

COLAPIETRO, Vincent, and Thomas OLSHEWSKY.
1994. *The Doctrine of Signs* (Berlin: Mouton de Gruyter).

COLLINI, Stefan, Editor.
1992. *Interpretation and Overinterpretation* (Cambridge, England: Cambridge University Press).

COMPTON-CARLTON, Thomas.
1649. "De Signo", *Logica*, Disp. 42, in *Philosophia Universa* (Antwerp).

CON DAVIS, Robert.
1985. "The Case for a Post-Structuralist Mimesis: John Barth and Imitation", in *The American Journal of Semiotics* 3.3, 49-72.

CORRINGTON, Robert S.
1987. *The Community of Interpreters. On the Hermeneutics of Nature and the Bible in the American Philosophical Tradition* (Macon, GA: Mercer University Press).
1992. *Nature and Spirit. An Essay in Ecstatic Naturalism* (New York: Fordham University Press).
1992a. "Peirce's Abjected Unconscious: A Psychoanalytic Profile", in *Semiotics 1992*, ed. John Deely (Lanham, MD: University Press of America, 1993).
1993. *An Introduction to C. S. Peirce: Philosopher, Semiotician, and Ecstatic Naturalist* (Lanham, MD: Rowman & Littlefield).

CRICK, Malcolm.
1976. *Explorations in Language and Meaning. Towards a Semantic Anthropology* (New York: John Wiley & Sons).

CULLER, Jonathan.
   1981. *The Pursuit of Signs. Semiotics, Literature, Deconstruction* (Ithaca, NY: Cornell University Press).
   1982. *On Deconstruction. Theory and Criticism after Structuralism* (Ithaca, NY: Cornell University Press).
   1992. "In Defence of Overinterpretation", in Collini Ed. 1992: 109-123.

DANOW, David.
   1984. "Dialogic Perspectives: Bakhtin and Mukarovsky", in *Semiotics 1984*, ed. John Deely (Bloomington IN; Lanham, MD: University Press of America, 1985), 3-11.
   1984a. "M. M. Bakhtin's Concept of the Word", in *The American Journal of Semiotics* 3.1, 79-97.
   1985. "M. M. Bakhtin in Life and Art", in *The American Journal of Semiotics* 3.3, 131-141.
   1987. "Text and Subtext", in *Semiotics 1987*, ed. John Deely (Lanham, MD: University Press of America, 1988).
   1991. *The Thought of Mikhail Bakhtin: From Word to Culture* (New York: St. Martin's Press).

DEELY, John N.
   1966. "The Emergence of Man: an inquiry into the role of natural selection in the making of man," *The New Scholasticism* XL (April), 141-176; reprinted in *The Problem of Evolution. A Study of the Philosophical Repercussions of Evolutionary Science*, ed. John N. Deely and Raymond J. Nogar (New York: Appleton-Century-Crofts, 1973), 119-145.
   1971. "Animal Intelligence and Concept Formation", *The Thomist* XXXV.1 (January), 43-93.
   1971a. "The Myth as Integral Objectivity", *ACPA Proceedings* XLV, 61-76.
   1978. "Semiotic and the Controversy over Mental Events", *ACPA Proceedings* LII, 16-27.
   1981. "Cognition from a Semiotic Point of View", in *Semiotics 1981*, ed. John N. Deely and Margot D. Lenhart (New York: Plenum), 21-28.
   1982. *Introducing Semiotic, Its History and Doctrine* (Bloomington: Indiana University Press).
   1985. *Logic as a Liberal Art* (Victoria University of the University of Toronto: Toronto Semiotic Circle Monograph, Summer).
   1986. "A Context for Narrative Universals, or: Semiology as a Pars Semeiotica", *The American Journal of Semeiotics* 4.3-4, 53-68.

1986a. "Semiotic as Framework and Direction", in Deely, Williams and Kruse 1986, 264-271, notes 287-288.
1986b. "John Locke's Place in the History of Semiotic Inquiry", in *Semiotics 1986*, ed. Jonathan Evans and John Deely (Lanham, MD: University Press of America, 1987), 406-418.
1986c. "Doctrine", terminological entry for the *Encyclopedic Dictionary of Semiotics*, ed. Thomas A. Sebeok et al. (Berlin: Mouton de Gruyter), 214.
1986d. "The Coalescence of Semiotic Consciousness", in Deely, Williams, and Kruse 1986: 5-34.
1986e. "Idolum. Archeology and Ontology of the Iconic Sign", in *Iconicity: Essays on the Nature of Culture*, Festschrift volume in honor of Thomas A. Sebeok, edited by Paul Bouissac, Michael Herzfeld, and Roland Posner (Tubingen: Stauffenburg Verlag), 29-49.
1987. "On the Problem of Interpreting the Term 'First' in the Expression 'First Philosophy'", in *Semiotics 1987*, ed. J. Deely (Lanham, MD: University Press of America), 3-14.
1989. "The Grand Vision", presented on September 8 at the September 5-10 Charles Sanders Peirce Sesquicentennial International Congress at Harvard University, forthcoming in Colapietro and Olshewsky 1994.
1989a. "A Global Enterprise", Preface to Sebeok 1989, q.v.: vii-xiv.
1988. "The Semiotic of John Poinsot: Yesterday and Tomorrow", *Semiotica* 69.1/2 (April), 31-127.
1990. *Basics of Semiotics* (Bloomington: Indiana University Press).
1990a. *Semiótica Básica* (Ática Éditora: São Paulo, Brazil).
1990b. "Sign, Text, and Criticism", *The American Journal of Semiotics* 7.4, 41-81.
1991. "Semiotics and Biosemiotics: Are Sign-Science and Life-Science Coextensive?", in *Biosemiotics. The Semiotic Web 1991*, ed. Thomas A. Sebeok and Jean Umiker-Sebeok (Berlin: Mouton de Gruyter, 1992), 45-75.
1991a. "Modeling Anthroposemiosis", in *On Semiotic Modeling*, ed. Myrdene Anderson and Floyd Merrell (Berlin: Mouton de Gruyter, 1991), 525-593. This is the text of an early draft for the present book, which was further expanded and used in manuscript form under the title "Elements of Anthroposemiosis" as the basis for a graduate course taught by the author as Visiting Fulbright Professor at the Brazilian Federal University of Minas Gerais in Belo Horizonte in the winter 1989.

1992. "The Supplement of the Copula", in *The Review of Metaphysics* 46.2 (December), 251-277.
1992a. "Philosophy and Experience", in *ACPQ* LXVI.3 (Summer), 299-319.
1992b. "From Glassy Essence to Bottomless Lake: Reflections on the Problem of Saying 'What Consciousness Is'", in *Semiotics 1992*, ed. John Deely (Lanham, MD: University Press of America, 1993), 150-158.
1994. *New Beginnings. Early Modern Philosophy and Postmodern Thought* (Toronto, Canada: University of Toronto Press).

DEELY, John N., Brooke WILLIAMS, and Felicia E. KRUSE, Editors.
1986. *Frontiers in Semiotics* (Bloomington: Indiana University Press).

DOUGHERTY, Janet W. D., and James W. FERNANDEZ.
1981. "Introduction to Symbolism and Cognition", in a Special Issue of *American Ethnologist* 8.3, 413-421.

ECO, Umberto.
1962. *Opera aperta* (Milan: Bompiani), partially presented in English along with additional material as *The Open Work*, trans. Anna Cancogni (Cambridge, MA: Harvard University Press, 1989).
1977. "The Code: Metaphor or Interdisciplinary Category?", *Yale Italian Studies* 1.1 (Winter), 24-52.
1979. "Proposals for a History of Semiotics", in *Semiotics Unfolding*, ed. Tasso Borbé (Berlin: Mouton de Gruyter), 75-89.
1990. *The Limits of Interpretation* (Bloomington: Indiana University Press).
1992. "Interpretation and History", in Collini ed. 1992: 23-43.
1992a. "Overinterpreting Texts", in Collini ed. 1992: 45-66.
1992b. "Between Author and Text", in Collini ed. 1992: 67-88.
1992c. "Reply", in Collini ed. 1992: 139-151.

ECO, Umberto, and Manfred BIERWISCH.
1986. "Interpretant", entry in *The Encyclopedic Dictionary of Semiotics*, ed. Thomas A. Sebeok et al. (Berlin: Mouton de Gruyter), Vol. 1, 385-387.

FABIAN, J.
1983. *Time and the Other: How Anthropology Makes Its Objects* (New York: Columbia University Press).

FISCH, Max H., Kenneth Laine KETNER, and Christian J. W. KLOESEL.
1979. "The New Tools of Peirce Scholarship, with Particular Reference to Semiotic", in *Peirce Studies* 1 (Lubbock, TX: Institute for Studies in Pragmaticism), 1-17.

FRENCH, A. P., and P. J. KENNEDY, Editors.
1985. *Niels Bohr: A Centenary Volume* (Cambridge, MA: Harvard University Press).

GANNON, Timothy J.
1991. *Shaping Psychology: How We Got Where We're Going* (Lanham, MD: University Press of America).

GEERTZ, Clifford.
1988. *Works and Lives: The Anthropologist as Author* (Stanford, CA: Stanford University Press).

GLEICK, James.
1987. *Chaos: Making A New Science* (New York: Viking).

GOULD, Stephen J., and Elisabeth S. VRBA.
1982. "Exaptation—A Missing Term in the Science of Form", *Paleobiology* 8.1 (Winter), 4-15.

HARDWICK, Charles, Editor.
1977. *Semiotics and Significs. The Correspondence between Charles S. Peirce and Victoria Lady Welby* (Bloomington: Indiana University Press, 1977).

HAWKES, Terrence.
1977. *Structuralism and Semiotics* (Berkeley: University of California Press).

HEIDEGGER, Martin.
1927. *Sein und Zeit* (10th ed.; Tübingen: Niemeyer, 1963), originally published in the *Jahrbuch fur Phanomenologie und phänomenologische Forschung*, ed. Edmund Husserl; trans. John MacQuarrie and Edward Robinson as *Being and Time* (New York: Harper & Row, 1962), to which page reference is made in the present work.

HERZFELD, Michael.
1985. *The Poetics of Manhood. Contest and Identity in a Cretan Mountain Village* (Princeton, NJ: Princeton University Press).

1987. *Anthropology through the Looking-Glass. Critical Ethnography in the Margins of Europe* (Cambridge, England: Cambridge University Press).

HJELSMSLEV, Louis.
1961. *Prolegomena to a Theory of Language*, being the second, revised translation by Francis J. Whitfield of *Omkring sprogteoriens grundlaeggelse* (Copenhagen: Ejnar Munksgaard, 1943), incorporating "several minor corrections and changes that have suggested themselves in the course of discussions between the author and the translator" (Hjelmslev and Whitfield 1961: v).

HJELMSLEV, Louis, and Francis J. WHITFIELD.
1961. "Preface" to Hjelmslev 1961: v.

HOBBES, Thomas.
1651. *Leviathan*, ed. Michael Oakeshott, reprinted with an Introduction by Richard S. Peters (New York: Macmillan, 1962).

HOUSER, Nathan.
1989. "La Structure Formelle de l'Experience selon Peirce", *Études Phénoménologiques* 9-10, 77-111.

JACOB, François.
1982. *The Possible and the Actual* (Seattle: University of Washington Press).

JAKOBSON, Roman.
1960. "Closing Statement: Linguistics and Poetics", in *Style in Language*, ed. Thomas A. Sebeok (Cambridge, MA: M.I.T. Press), 350-377.
1974. "Coup d'oeil sur le devéloppement de la sémiotique", in *Panorama sémiotique/A Semiotic Landscape*, Proceedings of the First Congress of the International Association for Semiotic Studies, Milan, June 1974, ed. Seymour Chatman, Umberto Eco, and Jean-Marie Klinkenberg (The Hague: Mouton, 1979), 3-18. Also published separately under the same title by the Research Center for Language and Semiotic Studies as a small monograph (= Studies in Semiotics 3; Bloomington: Indiana University Publications, 1975).
1980. *The Framework of Language* (Ann Arbor: Michigan Studies in the Humanities).

JAMESON, Frederic.
    1972. *The Prisonhouse of Language: A Critical Account of Structuralism and Russian Formalism* (Princeton, NJ: Princeton University Press).

JOHANSEN, Jorgen Dines.
    1982. "Sign Concept, Meaning, and the Study of Literature", in *Semiotics 1982*, ed. John Deely and Jonathan Evans (Lanham, MD: University Press of America, 1987), 473-482.
    1985. "Prolegomena to a Semiotic Theory of Text Interpretation", *Semiotica* 57.3/4, 225-288.
    1993. *Dialogic Semiosis* (Bloomington: Indiana University Press).
    1993a. "Let Sleeping Signs Lie. On signs, objects, and communication", *Semiotica*, forthcoming.

JOSEPH, Roger and Terri.
    1987. *The Rose and the Thorn* (Tucson: University of Arizona Press).

JOYCE, James.
    1939. *Finnegans Wake* (London: Faber & Faber).

KANT, Immanuel.
    1781, 1787. *Kritik der reinen Vernunft* (1st and 2nd ed.; Riga), correlated and trans. by Norman Kemp Smith as *Kant's Critique of Pure Reason* (New York: St. Martin's Press, 1963).

KARP, Ivan.
    1986. "Agency and Social Theory: A Review of Anthony Giddens", in *Amerincan Ethnologist* 13.1 (February), 131-137.

KARP, Ivan, and Martha KENDALL.
    1982. "Reflexivity in Fieldwork", in Secord, Ed. 1982: 249-273.

KETNER, Kenneth Laine.
    1981. "Peirce's Ethics of Terminology", *Transactions of the Charles S. Peirce Society* (Fall), XVII.4, 327-347.

KETNER, Kenneth Laine, Editor.
    1992. *Reasoning and the Nature of Things: The 1898 Cambridge Conference Lectures by C. S. Peirce* (Cambridge, MA: Harvard University Press). *See* Peirce 1898.

KETNER, Kenneth Laine, and Hilary PUTNAM.
 1992. "The Consequences of Mathematics", *Introduction to Peirce* 1898, q.v.: 1-19.

KING, Terrance.
 1987. "Text and Object: Distinguishing Them as Interpretations", in *Semiotics 1987* (Lanham, MD: University Press of America, 1988), 99-106.

KINTZ, Linda.
 1987. "On Learning Deconstruction: Postmodernist Pedagogy", in *Semiotics 1987*, ed. John Deely (Lanham, MD: University Press of America, 1988), 157-164.

KLOESEL, Christian J. W.
 1983. "Peirce's Early Theory of Signs (1863-1885): The First Barrier", *The American Journal of Semiotics* 2.1-2, 109-119.

KOELB, Clayton, and Virgil LOKKE, Editors.
 1988. *The Current in Criticism. Essays on the Present and Future of Literary Theory* (West Lafayette, IN: Purdue University Press).

KONKLE, John.
 1992. *Aristotle and John Philoponus on Beginningless Change* (unpublished doctoral dissertation from the Princeton University Department of Philosophy, available from University Microfilms, 300 North Zoeb Road, Ann Arbor, MI 48106).

KRISTEVA, Julia.
 1967. "Bakhtine, le mot, le dialogue et le roman", *Critique* 239, 438-385, trans. by Thomas Gora, Alice Jardine, and Leon S. Roudiez as "Word, Dialogue, and Novel" in *Desire in Language; A Semiotic Approach to Literature and Art*, ed. Leon S. Roudiez (New York: Columbia University Press, 1980), 64-91, to which translation page reference is keyed.

LEACH, Edmund R.
 1954. *Political Systems of Highland Burma* (Cambridge, England: Cambridge University Press).
 1964. "Introductory Note to the 1964 Reprint" of Leach 1954 (Boston: Beacon Press), ix-xv.

LISZKA, James Jakób.
 1990. "Peirce's Interpretant", *Transactions of the Charles S. Peirce Society* (Winter), XXXVI.1, 17-62.

LOCKE, John.
    1690. *An Essay Concerning Humane Understanding* (London: Thomas Bassett). The original text of the concluding chapter introducing the term "semiotic" is reproduced in full from this original edition in Deely, Williams, and Kruse 1986: 2-4.

LOKKE, Virgil.
    1988. "Contextualizing the Either/Or: Invariance/Variation and Dialogue in Jakobson/Bakhtin", in Koelb and Lokke, eds., 1988: 243-264.

MACKINNON, D. L.
    1926. *Theoretical Biology*, being an attempted translation of von Uexküll 1920 (New York: Harcourt Brace). Hopefully, another attempt will be made, this time within the perspective of semiotic.

MARITAIN, Jacques.
    1957. "Language and the Theory of Sign", originally published as Chapter V of the anthology *Language: An Enquiry into Its Meaning and Function*, ed. Ruth Nanda Anshen (New York: Harper), 86-101, is reprinted with the addition of a full technical apparatus explicitly connecting the essay to Maritain's work on semiotic begun in 1937 and to the text of Poinsot 1632 on which Maritain centrally drew, in Deely, Williams, and Kruse 1986: 51-62, to which reprint page references are keyed.
    1964. *Notebooks*, Chapter 3 (translated by Joseph W. Evans; New York: Albany, 1984), 81-99.

MAYR, Ernst.
    1974. "Teleological and Teleonomic: A New Analysis" in *Methodological and Historical Essays in the Natural and Social Sciences*, 4, ed. Robert Cohen and Marx W. Wartofsky (Dordrecht, Holland: D. Reidel Publishing Co.), 91-117.
    1983. Adaptation of 1974 entry with unchanged title as Chapter 25 of *Evolution and the Diversity of Life. Selected Essays* (Cambridge, MA: The Belknap Press of Harvard University Press), 383-404.

MERRELL, Floyd.
    1988. "An Uncertain Semiotic", in *The Current in Criticism. Essays on the Present and Future of Literary Theory*, ed. Clayton Koelb and Virgil Lokke (West Lafayette, IN: Purdue University Press), 243-264.

MORGAN, Thais.
1985. "Is There an Intertext in This Text: Literary and Interdisciplinary Approaches to Intertextuality", *The American Journal of Semiotics* 3.4, 1-40.

MORRIS, Charles.
1946. *Signs, Language and Behavior* (Englewood Cliffs, NJ: Prentice-Hall), reprinted in *Writings on the General Theory of Signs*, ed. Thomas A. Sebeok (=Approaches to Semiotics 16; The Hague: Mouton, 1971), 73-397.

PARMENTIER, Richard J.
1986. Review of Deely, Williams and Kruse 1986, in *Poetics Today* 7.4, 771-772.
1987. *The Sacred Remains: Myth, History, and Polity in Belau* (Chicago: University of Chicago Press).
1991. Review of Deely 1990 in *American Anthropologist* 93.4 (December), 965-966.

PEIRCE, Charles Sanders.
Note: The designation CP abbreviates *The Collected Papers of Charles Sanders Peirce*, Vols. I-VI ed. Charles Hartshorne and Paul Weiss (Cambridge, MA: Harvard University Press, 1931-1935), Vols. VII-VIII ed. Arthur W. Burks (same publisher, 1958). The abbreviation followed by volume and paragraph numbers with a period between follows the standard CP reference form. Unpublished mss. are cited by number, using the pagination made by the Institute for Studies in Pragmaticism at Texas Tech in Lubbock. Chronology and identification of the Peirce materials is based on Burks 1958, Fisch et al. 1979, Hardwick 1977, and Robin 1967, 1971, as indicated at specific points.

The designation W followed by a volume, period, and page number refers to the *Writings of Charles Sanders Peirce: A Chronological Edition*, published in 5 volumes so far (Bloomington: Indiana University Press, 1982, 1984, 1986 bis, 1993).
1867. "On a New List of Categories", CP 1.545-559 (Burks p. 261).
1868. "Questions Concerning Certain Faculties Claimed for Man", *The Journal of Speculative Philosophy* 2, 103-114; reprinted in CP 5.264-317 (Burks p. 261).
1868a. "Some Consequences of Four Incapacities", *The Journal of Speculative Philosophy* 2, 140-157; reprinted in CP 5.264-317 (Burks p. 261).

c. 1890. "A Guess at the Riddle", CP 1.354-368, 1.373-375, 1.379-416 (Burks p. 276).

1891. "The Architecture of Theories", *The Monist* 1 (January), 161-176; reprinted in CP 6.7-34 (Burks p. 276).

1892. "Man's Glassy Essence", *The Monist* 3 (October), 1-22; reprinted in CP 6.238-271.

1897. "The Logic of Relatives", *The Monist* 7 (January), 161-217; reprinted in CP 3.456-552 (Burks p. 287).

c. 1897. An unidentified fragment printed in CP 2.227-229 with the editors' title of "Ground, Object, and Interpretant" (Burks p. 287).

1898. *Reasoning and the Logic of Things*, lectures delivered in the series of Cambridge *Conferences*, February 10-March 7; ed. Kenneth Laine Ketner (Cambridge, MA: Harvard University Press).

1901. A passage editorially deleted from the "Sign" entry for Baldwin 1901-1902 (q.v.), Vol. 2, pp. 527-528, printed in CP 2.303-304 (Burks p. 292).

1901-1902. Multiple entries for Baldwin, Ed. 1901-1902, q.v.

c. 1902. Ms. 599, "Reason's Rules" (Robin p. 74).

c. 1902a. "Syllabus" (never published), CP 2.274-277, 2.283-284, 2.292-294, 2.309-331 with 2.309 continuing 2.294 are from it (Burks p. 296).

c. 1902b. "Minute Logic", cited passages are in CP 1.204-276, 2.92, 5.538 (Burks pp. 293-294).

1903. "The Ethics of Terminology", from *A Syllabus of Certain Topics of Logic* (Boston: Alfred Mudge & Son), pp. 10-14; reprinted in CP 2.219-2.226 continuing 1.202 (Burks p. 295).

1903a. Lowell Lectures (at Harvard) given under the general title "Some Topics of Logic Bearing on Questions Now Vexed". Citations are from Lecture IIIa entitled "Lessons from the History of Philosophy" in CP 1.15-26, from draft 3 of Lecture III entitled "Degenerate Cases" in 1.521-544, and from Lecture VIII, "How to Theorize", in CP 5.590-604 (Burks p. 295).

1903b. "Lectures on Pragmatism", citation is from Lecture V, "The Three Kinds of Goodness", in CP 5.120-150 (Burks pp. 204-205).

1903c. "What Makes a Reasoning Sound?", the first of the Lowell lectures of this year, in CP 1.591-610, 1.611-615, and 8.176 except n3 (Burks p. 295).

1903d. "On Phenomenology, or The Categories", Draft 3 of Lecture 2 for the March-May Harvard lecture series on Pragmatism, in CP 5.59-65 (Burks p. 294).

c. 1903. "Nomenclature and Divisions of Triadic Relations, as far as they are determined", CP 2.233-272 continuing

CP 3.608 (the second part of a two-part work, the first part being "Nomenclature and Divisions of Dyadic Relations", CP 3.588-608: see Burks p. 295-296).
c. 1904. From a draft of a book review printed in CP 8.191-193 under the editors' title "On Pragmatism, from a review of a book on cosmology" (Burks n.1 on p. 148 of CP 8).
1904. Letter to Charles Augustus Strong, numbered 427 in the Robin catalogue (p. 199), cited according to the pagination of the Institute for Studies in Pragmaticism.
1904a. Manuscript materials for *The Monist* 1905-1906 series on pragmaticism (Robin p. 29).
1905. "Issues of Pragmaticism", *The Monist* 15, 481-489, in CP 5.438-463, except 448n1, which is part of 1905-1906 below (Burks p. 296).
1905a. "Prolegomena to an Apology for Pragmaticism", *The Monist* 16 (October), 492-546, with an errata in vol. 17 (January, 1907, p. 160), published in CP 4.530-572 with additional material in notes.
1905b. Letter of 3 July from Peirce to Francis C. Russell; L387, pp. 00274-00280 (cited in Brent 1993: 300n.84).
c. 1905. "Pragmaticism, Prag. [4]", in CP 5.502-537 (with a deletion) under the title "Consequences of Critical Common-Sensism" (Burks p. 298).
1905-1906. Ms. 283, partially published under the title "The Basis of Pragmaticism" in CP 1.573-574 (=ms. pp. 37-45), 5.549-554 (=ms. pp. 45-59), and 5.448n.1 (=ms. pp. 135-148) (Burks p. 328 and 298).
1906. March 9. 52-page draft letter to Lady Welby (under Robin L463, p. 200), ms. pp. 24-30 excerpted in Hardwick 1977: 195-201, to which published excerpt page reference is made in this essay.
c. 1906. Excerpt from "Pragmatism (Editor [3])", published under the title "A Survey of Pragmaticism" in CP 5.464-496. (Burks p. 299).
1907. Ms. 320, incomplete draft on Pragmatism (Robin p. 37).
1908. Letter to Lady Welby begun December 14 (in Hardwick 1977: 66-73) and continued December 23 (ibid. 73-86); the "sop to Cerberus" passage occurs in the latter part.
1908a. "A Neglected Argument for the Reality of God", *The Hibbert Journal* 7 (October), 90-112; reprinted in CP 6.452-485 (Burks p. 300).
c. 1909. "Some Amazing Mazes, Fourth Curiosity", CP 6.318-348.
1913. Ms. 681, "A Study of How to Reason Safely and Efficiently" (Robin p. 86).

PETRILLI, Susan.
1990. "On the Materiality of Signs", Appendix II to Ponzio 1990: 365-392, q.v.

PHILODEMUS.
 c. 54BC. *Peri Semeioseon*, trans. Phillip Howard De Lacy and Estelle Allen De Lacy with Greek text facing as *Philodemus: On Methods of Inference*, ed. rev. with the collaboration of Marcello Gigante, Francesco Longo Aurricchio, and Adele Tepedino Buerra (Naples: Bibliopolis, 1978), 27-131.

PITTENDRIGH, Colin S.
 1958. "Adaptation, Natural Selection, and Evolution", Chapter 18 of *Behavior and Evolution*, ed. Anne Roe and George Gaylord Simpson (New Haven: Yale University Press), 390-416.

PLANT, James Stuart.
 1950. *The Envelope. A Study of the Impact of the World Upon the Child* (New York: Commonwealth Fund).

POINSOT, John.
 Note: A complete table of all the editions, complete and partial, and in whatever language, of Poinsot's systematic works in philosophy and theology is provided in Deely 1985: 396-397. The principal modern editions referred to in this work are abbreviated as follows:

 R followed by a volume number (I, II, or III) and pages, with column (a or b) and line indications as needed = the *Cursus Philosophicus Thomisticus*, ed. by B. Reiser in 3 volumes (Turin: Marietti, 1930, 1933, 1937).

 S followed by a volume number (I-IV) and page numbers = the five volumes of the incomplete critical edition of the *Cursus Theologicus* ed. at Solesmes (Paris: Desclée, 1931, 1934, 1937, 1946; Matiscone: Protat Frères, 1953).

 V followed by a volume number (I-IX) = the complete edition ed. by Ludovicus Vivès published in Paris between 1883 and 1886.

 1631. *Artis Logicae Prima Pars* (Alcalá, Spain). The opening pages 1-11a14 of this work and the "Quaestio Disputanda I. De Termino. Art. 6. Utrum Voces Significant per prius Conceptus an Res" pages 104b31-108a33, relevant to the discussion of signs in the *Secunda Pars* of 1632 (entry following), have been incorporated in the 1632a entry (second entry following, q.v., pp. 4-30 and 342-351 "Appendix A. On the Signification of Language", respectively), for the independent edition of that discussion published by the University of California Press. From R I: 1-247.

1632. *Artis Logicae Secunda Pars* (Alcalá, Spain). From R I: 249-839.

1632a. *Tractatus de Signis*, subtitled *The Semiotic of John Poinsot*, extracted from the *Artis Logicae Prima et Secunda Pars* of 1631-1632 (above two entries), using the text of the emended second impression (1932) of the 1930 Reiser edition (Turin: Marietti), and arranged in bilingual format by John Deely in consultation with Ralph A. Powell (First Edition; Berkeley: University of California Press, 1985), as explained in Deely 1985, q.v. Pages in this volume are set up in matching columns of English and Latin, with intercolumnar numbers every fifth line. (Thus, references to the volume are by page number, followed by a slash and the appropriate line number of the specific section of text referred to—e.g., 287/3-26.)

1633. *Naturalis Philosophiae Prima Pars* (Madrid, Spain). In R II: 1-529.

1634. *Naturalis Philosophiae Tertia Pars* (Alcalá, Spain); in R II: 533-888.

1635. *Naturalis Philosophiae Quarta Pars* (Alcalá, Spain); in R III: 1-425.

1637. *Tomus Primus Cursus Theologici* (Alcalá, Spain). V I & II; S I complete & II through p. 529.

PONZIO, Augusto.
1990. *Man as a Sign. Essays on the Philosophy of Language*, trans. from the Italian and ed. by Susan Petrilli (Berlin: Mouton de Gruyter).

POPPER, Karl R.
1972. *Objective Knowledge. An Evolutionary Approach* (Oxford: Clarendon Press).

POPPER, Karl R., and John ECCLES.
1977. *The Self and Its Brain* (Berlin: Springer Verlag).

POWELL, Ralph Austin.
1983. *Freely Chosen Reality* (Lanham, MD: University Press of America).

PREWITT, Terry J.
1991. "Geometry and the Hidden Algorithm of Discourse", in *Semiotics 1991*, ed. John Deely and Terry Prewitt (Lanham, MD: University Press of America, 1992), 27-33.

QUINE, Willard Van Orman.
　1965. *Elementary Logic* (rev. ed. of 1941 text; Cambridge, MA: Harvard University Press).
　1987. "Mathematosis," in Quiddities (Cambridge, MA: Harvard University Press), 127-129.

RANSDELL, Joseph.
　1977. "Some Leading Ideas of Peirce's Semiotic", *Semiotica* 19:3/4, 157-178.
　1986. Entry for "Peirce, Charles Sanders" in *The Encyclopedic Dictionary of Semiotics*, ed. Thomas A. Sebeok et al. (Berlin: Mouton de Gruyter), Vol. 2, 673-695.

REY, Alain.
　1984. "What Does Semiotics Come From?", *Semiotica* 52, 79-93.

RICOEUR, Paul.
　1981. *Hermeneutics & the Human Sciences*, ed. and trans. John B. Thompson (Cambridge: Cambridge University Press).

RIFFATERRE, Michael.
　1985. "The Interpretant in Literary Semiotics", *The American Journal of Semiotics* 3.4, 41-55.

RIORDAN, Michael.
　1987. *The Hunting of the Quark* (New York: Simon & Schuster).

ROBIN, Richard S.
　1967. *Annotated Catalogue of the Papers of Charles S. Peirce* (Worcester, MA: University of Massachusetts Press).
　1971. "The Peirce Papers: A Supplementary Catalogue", *Transactions of the Charles S. Peirce Society* VII.1 (Winter), 37-57.

ROE, Anne, and George Gaylord SIMPSON, Editors.
　1958. *Behavior and Evolution* (New Haven, CT: Yale University Press).

ROSS, W. D., Editor.
　1928-1952. *The Works of Aristotle Translated into English*, in XII vols. (Oxford: Clarendon Press).

RUSSELL, Anthony F.
　1982. "The Semiosis Linking Human World and Physical Reality", in *Semiotics 1982*, ed. John Deely and Jonathan

Evans (Lanham, MD: University Press of America, 1987), 591-600.

RUSSO, Adelaide M.
1982. "The Rhetoric of the Interpretant: Eco, Riffaterre, and the Triangle", in *Semiotics 1982*, ed. John Deely and Jonathan Evans (Lanham, MD: University Press of America, 1987), 175-190.

SAHLINS, Marshall.
1976. *Culture and Practical Reason* (Chicago: University of Chicago Press).

SANTAELLA BRAGA, Lúcia.
1992. "Time as the Logical Process of the Sign", *Semiotica* 88—3/4, 309-326.
1993. *Percepcão. Teoria Semiótica* (São Paulo, Brasil).

SAUSSURE, Ferdinand de.
i. 1906-1911. Lectures delivered at the University of Geneva and published from auditors' notes by Charles Bally and Albert Sechehaye under the title *Cours de linguistique générale* (Paris: Payot, 1915), trans. by Wade Baskin as *Course in General Linguistics* (New York: McGraw-Hill, 1966).

SCHILLER, Claire H.
1957. "Note by the Translator" to *Instinctive Behavior. The Development of a Modern Concept* (New York: International Universities Press, 1957), with particular reference to von Uexküll 1934, q.v.

SCHOLES, Robert.
1982. *Semiotics and Interpretation* (New Haven, CT: Yale University Press).

SEBEOK, Thomas A.
1972. *Perspectives in Zoosemiotics* (The Hague: Mouton).
1974. "Semiotics: A Survey of the State of the Art", in *Linguistics and Adjacent Arts and Sciences*, Vol. 12 of the Current Trends in Linguistics series, ed. T. A. Sebeok (The Hague: Mouton), 211-264; reprinted in Sebeok 1985: 1-45, to which page reference is made.
1976. "Foreword" (pp. ix-xiii) to original publication of Sebeok 1985 following.
1977. "Ecumenicalism in Semiotics", in *A Perfusion of Signs*,

ed. Thomas A. Sebeok (Bloomington: Indiana University Press), 180-206.
1979. "Looking in the Destination for What Should Have Been Sought in the Source", Chapter 5 of *The Sign & Its Masters* (=Sources in Semiotics VIII; Lanham, MD: University Press of America, 1989), 84-106. Corrected reprint, with a new Author's Preface and an added Editor's Preface [Deely 1989], of the University of Texas Press, 1979, original imprint), 272-279.
1982. "Foreword" to *Introducing Semiotic* (Deely 1982), ix-xi.
1984. "Signs of Life", *International Semiotic Spectrum* 2 (June), 1-2.
1984a. "Vital Signs", *The American Journal of Semiotics* 3.3, 1-27.
1985. *Contributions to the Doctrine of Signs* (=Sources in Semiotics IV; reprint of 1976 original with an extended Preface evaluating the book in light of major reviews; Lanham, MD: University Press of America).
1987. "Language: How Primary a Modeling System?", in *Semiotics 1987*, ed. John Deely (Lanham, MD: University Press of America, 1988), 15-27.
1991. *American Signatures. Semiotic Inquiry and Method*, edited by Iris Smith (Norman: University of Oklahoma Press).

SEBEOK, Thomas A., General Editor; Paul Bouissac, Umberto Eco, Jersy Pelc, Roland Posner, Alain Rey, Ann Schukman, Editorial Board.
1986. *Encyclopedic Dictionary of Semiotics* (Berlin: Mouton de Gruyter), in 3 volumes.

SEBEOK, Thomas A., and Robert ROSENTHAL, Editors.
1981. *The Clever Hans Phenomenon: Communication with Horses, Whales, Apes, and People* (New York: New York Academy of Sciences).

SEBEOK, Thomas A., and Jean UMIKER-SEBEOK, Editors.
1980. *Speaking of Apes. A Critical Anthology of Two-Way Communication with Man* (New York: Plenum).

SECORD, Paul F., Editor.
1982. *Explaining Human Behavior: Consciousness, Human Action, and Social Structure* (Beverly Hills, CA: Sage Publications).

SIMPSON, George Gaylord, Colin S. PITTENDRIGH, and Lewis H. TIFFANY.
1957. *Life. An Introduction to Biology* (New York: Harcourt, Brace and Co.).

SINGER, Milton.
   1978. "For a Semiotic Anthropology", in *Sight, Sound, and Sense*, ed. Thomas A. Sebeok (Bloomington: Indiana University Press), 202-231.
   1984. *Man's Glassy Essence: Explorations in Semiotic Anthropology* (Bloomington: Indiana University Press, 1984).

SOTO, Dominic.
   1529, 1554. *Summulae* (1st ed., Burgos; 3rd rev. ed., Salamanca; Facsimile of 3rd ed., Hildesheim, NY: Georg Olms Verlag).

TODOROV, Tzvetan.
   1981. *Mikhail Bakhtine: Le Principe Dialogique Suivi de Écrits da Cercle de Bakhtine*, trans. from the French by Wlad Godzich as *Mikhail Bakhtin: The Dialogical Principle* (Minneapolis: University of Minnesota Press, 1984).

TOEWS, John E.
   1987. "Intellectual History after the Linguistic Turn: The Autonomy of Meaning and the Irreducibility of Experience", *American Historical Review* 82.4, 879-907.

TOULMIN, Stephen.
   1982. "The Construal of Reality: Criticism in Modern and Postmodern Science", in *The Politics of Interpretation*, ed. W. J. T. Mitchell (Chicago: University of Chicago Press).

von UEXKÜLL, Jakob.
   1920. *Theoretische Biologie* (Berlin; 2nd ed. 1928, reprinted Frankfurt a. M.: Suhrkamp 1970).
   1934. *Streifzüge durch die Umwelten von Tieren und Menschen* (Berlin), trans. by Claire H. Schiller as "A Stroll through the Worlds of Animals and Men" in *Instinctive Behavior: The Development of a Modern Concept*, ed. by Claire H. Schiller (New York: International Universities Press, Inc., 1957), 5-80. The Schiller translation has recently been reprinted in a Jakob von Uexküll Special Issue of *Semiotica* 89.4 (1992), 319-391, with T. von Uexküll 1981 (below) reprinted as "Introduction", 279-315.
   1940. "Bedeutungslehre", *Bios* 10 (Leipzig), trans. by Barry Stone and Herbert Weiner as "The Theory of Meaning" in *Semiotica* 42.1 (1982), 25-82.

von UEXKÜLL, Thure.
   1981. "The Sign Theory of Jakob von Uexküll", in *Classics of Semiotics* (English edition of *Die Welt als Zeichen: Klassiker der modernen Semiotik*, Berlin: Wolf Jobst Siedler

Verlag), ed. Martin Krampen, Klaus Oehler, Roland Posner, Thomas A. Sebeok, and Thure von Uexküll (New York: Plenum Press, 1987), 147-179.

VOLOSINOV, V. N.
1926. "Slovo v zhini i slovo v poezii", *Zvezda* 6, 244-267, rendered "Discourse in Life and Discourse in Art (Concerning Sociological Poetics)" in *Freudianism: A Marxist Critique*, trans. and ed. by I. R. Titunik in collaboration with Neal H. Bruss (New York: Academic Press, 1976), 93-116, to which translation page references are keyed.
1929. *Marksism i filosofiia iazyka. Osnovnye problemy sotsiologicheskogo metoda v nauke o iazyke*, translated by Ladislav Matejka and I. R. Titunik as *Marxism and the Philosophy of Language* (New York: Seminar Press, 1973), to which translation page references are keyed.

WALDROP, M. Mitchell.
1992. *Complexity: The Emerging Science at the Edge of Order and Chaos* (New York: Simon & Schuster).

WILLIAMS, Brooke.
1985. "What Has History To Do with Semiotic?", *Semiotica* 54.3/4, 267-333.
1985a. "Challenging Signs at the Crossroads", prefatory essay to Sebeok 1985: xv-xlii.
1990. "Uma década de debates: História e Semiótica nos anos 80", *Face* 3.1 (janeiro/junho), 11-28; translation by Júlio Jeha (UFMG).
1991. "History and Semiotics in the 1990s", *Semiotica* 83.—3/4, 385-417.

WILLIAMS, Brooke, and William PENCAK, Guest Editors.
1991. *Special Issue: History and Semiotics, Semiotica* 83.—3/4.

Index of Persons Mentioned

Key to Index: *Arabic numbers* in this index preceded by a G refer to the *Paragraphal Glosses*; all other arabic numbers refer to *Paragraph Numbers*, not pages. Key expressions that are set off in bold typeface are usually followed by a further breakdown into specific propositions. The occasional abbreviation "q.v." is the standard "quod vide", or "have a look at".

Adam (mythical first human male): 296
Almeder, R.: 223
Anderson, M.: xii, 254
Aquinas, T.: 42, 290, 293, 299, 302, 308, G34, G36, G46, G47, G52, G55, G58, G59, G61
Araujo, F.: 68
Ardener, E.: 287
Aristotle: 41, 205, 213
Ashley, B.: 95
Augustine of Hippo: v
Avicenna: G47

Babinet: G60
Bacon, F.: G14
Baer, E.: xii, 25, 51, 52, 57, 58, 113, epigraph before 134, 150, 151, 169, 195, 283, G21, G38, G57
Bakhtin, M.: 246, 256, 270, 279, G27, G39
Bally, C.: 147
Barthes, R.: 165, 171, 172, 179, 232, 256, 258, G27
Basso, K. H.: 10

Berkeley, G.: 35
Beuchot, M.: 68
Bohr, N.: G23
Bourdieu, P.: 19, 139, 147-150, 263, 279
Bühler, K.: 176

Caesar, J.: 246
Cajetan, T.: G46
Caputo, J.: 254
Caruso, P.: G1
Certeau, M. de: 6
Cinderella: 53, 76
Cleopatra: 301
Compton-Carlton, T.: 200
Con Davis, R.: 265
Corrington, R.: xii, 146, 224, 284, G14, G24, G46
Crick, M.: G27
Culler, J.: 165, 218, 221, 250, 265

Danow, D.: 142, 246, 263
Darwin, C.: G45
Deely, Williams, and Kruse: 122
Derrida, J.: 85, 179, 232

199

Dougherty and Fernandez: G43

Eco, U.: 84-86, 88, 131, 161, 168, 181, 200, 228, 232, 244, 251, 278, G5, G6, G7, G26
Eco and Bierwisch: 72

Fabian, J.: 10
Firth, R.: 202
Fisch, M.: xii
French and Kennedy: G23

Galilei, G.: 36
Gannon, T.: 83
Geertz, C.: 9
Giddens, A.: 4, 9
Gleick, J.: G33
Guha, S.: xii

Hawkes, T.: 259
Hamlet: 301
Heidegger, M.: 263, 276, G17, G25, G38
Heraclitus: G36
Herzfeld, M.: xii, 200, 285
Hjelmslev, L.: 162, 165
Hobbes, T.: G45
Holems, S.: 301
Houser, N.: xii, 78
Hume, D.: 82

Jacob, F.: 127
Jakobson, R.: 66, 173, 176, 178, 251
Jeha, J., xii
Johansen, D.: 132, 145, 172, 178-190, 261, 267-272, 282, G7, G22, G25, G27, G28
Johnson, M.: xii
Joseph and Joseph: 92
Joyce, J.: 142

Kant, I.: 117, G17, G42
Karp, I.: 9
Karp and Kendall: 4
Ketner, K.: 201, G14, Appendix
Ketner and Putnam: 201
King, T.: 267
Kintz, L.: 85
Kloesel, C.: 67
Konkle, J.: G33
Kristeva, J.: 240

Leach, E.: 198, 202
Liszka, J.: 72
Locke, J.: 17, 26, 79, 235, 262, G14, G42

MacKinnon, D. L.: G17
Maritain, J.: 133, 137, 238, 246, 279
Mayr, E.: 95
Merrell, F.: 238, 253
More, T.: 126
Morgan, T.: 258
Morris, C.: 122, 132, 231

Occam, W.: 42

Parmentier, Richard: xii, 151, G2, G28, G31
Paul, St.: 123
Peirce, C. S.: xii, 26, 58, 67, 68, 70, 71, 72, 77, 78, 79, 80, 88, 89, 97, 98, 99, 105, 107, 111, 112, 114, 116, 117, 146, 155, 158, 162, 169, 171, 172, 179, 180, 181, 190, 201, 223, 224, 239, 257, 258, 261, 272, 284, 293, 294, 296, 310, G4, G5, G7, G14, G15, G19, G22, G24, G25, G27, G28, G30, G32, G35, G37, G40, G42, G51, G60
Percy, W.: 181
Petrilli, S.: G27
Pittendrigh, C. S.: 95
Plant, J.: 195
Plato: 126
Poinsot, J.: 26, 38, 68-70, 79, 80, 88, 107, 112, 129, 131, 138, 166, 190, 226, G48-51, 254, 277, 302, 310, G1, G4, G9, G11, G13, G15, G18, G22, G33, G46, G53, G54, G56, G57, G61
Ponzio, A.: G16
Popper, K. R.: G1
Popper and Eccles: G1
Powell, R. A.: 144, 156
Prewitt, T.: 183-188
Putnam, H.: G14

Quine, W. V. O.: 271, G14

Radcliffe-Brown, A. R.: xi
Ransdell, J.: 87, 97, 98, 114
Ricoeur, P.: 256

Riffaterre, M.: 181
Riordan, M.: 125
Roe and Simpson: 209
Royce, J.: G24
Russell, A.: G30, 272
Russell, B.: G14
Russell, F. C.: 180
Russo, A. M.: 181

Santaella-Braga, L.: 110, G19, G43
Saussure, F. de: 149, 179
Schaefer, T.: 301
Schiller, C. H.: G17
Scholes, R.: 258
Sebeok, T. A.: xi, 21, 22, 24, 25, 138, 169, 176, 177, 181, 186, 187, 232, 254, 259, 268, G12, G33
Sebeok and Rosenthal: 187
Sebeok and Umiker-Sebeok: 187
Simpson, Pittendrigh, and Tiffany: 95

Singer, M.: 284, G2
Soto, D.: 26
Suárez, F.: 42

Thom, R.: 195
Todorov, T.: 279
Toews, J. E.: 200
Touissant: G35
Toulmin, S.: 253

Uexküll, J. von: 21, 117, 121, 181, 190
Uexküll, T. von: 121

Volosinov, V. N.: G29

Waldrop, M. M.: G33
Williams, B.: xii, 122, 253, 254
Williams and Pencak: 253
Wilson, R.: 271
Wittgenstein, L.: G14

Index of Conceptions

Key to Index: *Arabic numbers* in this index preceded by a G refer to the *Paragraphal Glosses*; all other arabic numbers refer to *Paragraph Numbers*, not pages. Key expressions that are set off in bold typeface are usually followed by a further breakdown into specific propositions. The occasional abbreviation "q.v." is the standard "quod vide", or "have a look at".

Abduction, abductive hypothesis, abductive inference: 130, 222, 224, 243, 269
Abductive inference to the formal sign: 130
Abductive spiral: 224, 243
Abstract: 39, 87, 109, 139, 177, 189, 227, 237, 282, G15, G51
Abstraction: 111, 133, 272, 293, G51, G53, G54
Abstraction, negative process of: G51
Abstraction, scientific: G51
Acid test: 285
Acoustical phenomena: 74
Action and being as coextensive: 3
Action and structure: 3, 4
Action follows on being: 3
Action is coextensive with being: 3
Action of signs (*see also* Semiosis; Virtual semiosis): 13, 20, 24, 57, 75, 77-79, 91, 92, 96, 98, 100, 112, 163, 234, 252, 253, 310, G2, G4, G22, G25, G40

Action of signs, criterion for explaining: 93, 99, 110
Action of signs, difference of within anthroposemiosis and zoösemiosis: 150, 241, G25
Action of signs contrasted with physical interaction: 75-115, 130, G22
Action of signs vs. action of bodies: 77; principles underlying difference 79, 80
Action specifically proper to signs: 110
Actions, antecedent and sustenative: 4 (*see also* Causes)
Actual world: 123, 222, 229, 230
Actual world as precipitate of semiosis: 229
Actual world of experience: 123
Actual world of physical environment: 222
Acupuncture: 277
Ad infinitum: 202, 238 (*see also* Infinite process; Unlimited semiosis)

202

Ad placitum: 25, 240, 245, 250 (*see also* Stipulated)
Adam (mythical first human male): 228
Admixture: *see* linguistic admixture
Agent: 9, 77, 79, 81, 96, G1, G22 (*see also* Efficient Causality; Productive causality)
Aliquid stans pro aliquo, classic formula for sign: 65, 130
Alterity: 263, G16 (synonym for "Otherness", *q.v.*)
Alternative embodiments: 237 (*see also* Embodiment)
Ambiguity of sign-vehicles: 201
America: 199
Amplification: 170
Analogy and sympathy as principles of drift: 84
Analytic philosophy: G14, Appendix
Anesthesia: 277
Angels: 62 (*see also* Imperceptible; Spirit)
Animalia sine sermone ("animals lacking discourse"): 185
Anthropic behavior: 11
Anthropic content: 17
Anthropologist: 143
Anthropology: 1, 2, 6, 8-10, 15, 20-22, 27, 28, 186, 188, 216, 221, 224, 247, 257, 285-287, 309-311, G2, G24
Anthropology, adequate object of: 287
Anthropology, assimilation of other to self and self to other in: 287
Anthropology, focus of: 15, 20, 22
Anthropology, new keys for: 309
Anthropology, object of: 20, 311
Anthropology, object of compared with literature: 311
Anthropology, scientific object richest in: 311
Anthropology, shared ground with history, sociology, and psychology: 309
Anthropology, unique task of: 285, 309-310
Anthropos: 2, 8, 9, 11-14, 24, 25, 56, 147, 168, 229, 233, 244, 309-311

Anthropos, assigning reasons for being distinctive of: G60
Anthropos, proper function of: G60
Anthropos as codifying animal: G3
Anthroposemiosis: 10, 14, 17, 18, 19, 22, 24, 26, 28, 48, 110, 138, 150, 178, 181
Anthroposemiosis, processes differentiative of: 189
Anthroposemiosis, what is definitive for: 158
Anthroposemiosis as exception to J. von Uexküll's functional cycle (*q.v.*): 190
Anthroposemiosis as fulfillment of human nature: 281
Anthroposemiosis as local field of natural semiosis: 266
Anthroposemiosis in its integrity ("adequately considered"): 178, 185
Anthroposemiosis not autonomous: 232
Anthroposemiotic objectivity: 179
Ape language: 233, G45
Apes: 187, 188, 233
Appearance for nonhuman animals: 296
Application of consistent thought: 230
Apprehensive action can dimanate cognition-independent relations: 166
Aquinas on essences as models: 308
Arbitrary: 135, 156, 160, 193, 194, 196, 197, 202, 203, 213, 232, 245 (*see also* Conventional)
Arbitrary, meaning of: 203
Arbitrary as prospectively natural: 193
Arbitrary elements and language: 196
Arbitrary signifiers: 156, 245 (*see further* Relationship of signification; Sign vehicle; Stipulated)
Arbitrary signs, ground of: 134-135
Arbitrary signs, how experienced as natural: 135
Arc de Triomphe: 47, 48
Architect: 105
Architecture: 92, 101, 105, 123 (*see also* Structure)

Art as nonrepresentative: 105
Artifacts, artifactual transformation: 11, 17, 74, 92, 96, 103, 105, 108, 110, 143, 166, 189, 216, 218, 261, 287, G10, G61
Artist: 105
As signified: see *Ut significata*
Aspect, aspectual: 7, 26, 36, 41, 43, 52-54, 56, 58-60, 68, 74, 90, 92, 121, 122, 125, 127, 130, 133, 164, 171, 182, 186, 189, 194, 196, 198, 199, 201, 211, 216, 218, 229, 243, 251, 263, 268, 271, 277, 286, 292, 293, 298, 300, 302, 310, G2, G17, G18, G19, G27, G40
Aspectual identity: 52, 53
Aspectual inconsistency of individuals: 6
Aspectual vs. total distinction: 52
Assigning reasons for being as distinctive of anthropos: G60
Assimilation, assimilative: 87, 98, 166, 167, 196, 229, 248, 287, G47
Assimilative, semiosis as: 87
Association: 82, 88, 89, 141, 156, 161, G5, G17, G35
Association and semiosis: 88 (*see also* Drift)
Association of ideas: 82, 89
Association vs. stipulation: 141, 156, 161
Associationism: 82, 83, 88
Associationism, doctrine of: 82-86
Asymptotic: 72, 223, 233, 235, 262, 287 (*see also* Syncategorematic)
Asymptotic circumscription of significates: 72
Atomism: 189
Attention: 106, 109, 253, 268, 293, G3, G35
Autism, autistic: 85, 260
Autonomous, autonomy: 14, 26, 165, 195, 199, 232, 236, 269, 311
Awareness: 19, 75, 76, 130, 132-134, 159, 190, 197, 241, 242, 288, 290, 292, 297, G53
Awareness, difference of human: 290
Awareness, fundamental ground of as human: G53 (*see also* Primum cognitum)
Awareness, intelligence as mode of within perception: 288 (*see also* Perception; Understanding)
Awareness, line separating what is and is not independent of: 19
Awareness, permeation of as intellectual: 292
Awareness as ground of encoding: 242
Awareness behind differentiation of Umwelt as human (*see* Anthroposemiosis; Lebenswelt)
Awareness enabling stipulation of sign-vehicle: 135
Awareness motivating the question "What": 297
Awareness nascent of idea of reality: 190
Awareness of environmental aspects as objects and as signs: 76, 132
Awareness of relation of signification: 133 (*see also* Anthroposemiosis; Relationship of signification)
Awareness of signs: 75
Awareness productive of stipulable signs: 134 (*see also* Stipulable; Stipulated)
Awareness resulting in critically controlled intersubjectivity: 159

Background: 109
Balinese: 28
Barbarism: 285-286
Barbarism, first: 286
Barbarism, risk of: 285
Barbarism, second: 285-286
Bare suspicion differentiating intellect from sense: 128
Barthes' fallacy: 171
Basics of Semiotics (=Deely 1990): xi, 67, 70, 112, 113, 272, G2, G4, G17, G18, G57
Basis of semiosic relation: 130
Behaviorist: 218
Being: 3-8, 12-18, 20, 21, 29, 31-37, 39, 41, 48, 53, 54, 59-63, 65-67, 74, 76, 77, 80, 81, 88-93, 96, 98-103, 107, 109-112, 115-123, 125, 127, 128-133, epigraph before 134, 136, 138, 139, 144, 145, 147, 151, 155-158, 161-164, 167, 169,

172, 187, 191, 194, 197, 198, 203-206, 208-213, 215-217, 222-224, 232, 239-241, 252, 262, 263, 265, 278, 283, 293, 294, 296, 297, 299, 300-304, 308, 310, G1, G2, G4, G7, G11, G15, G18, G19, G25, G33, G34, G35, G47, G51, G56, G57, G61 (*see also* Action; Ens, Human being; Mind-dependent; Mind-independent; Primum cognitum, Reality; Relation)

Being, understanding of term: 293-294, G47

Being and action are existentially simultaneous: 3-4

Being as divided into natural and mind-dependent: 302

Being as first known (*ens ut primum cognitum*): 293, 296, 308, 310

Being as first known, notions derivative from: 293, G47

Being-in-the-World as Umwelt codified linguistically: G25

Being objectively taken: 8

Being proper to experience: 15-16, 33

Being proper to signs: 116, 144, 310, G15

Being proper to signs equivalent of real and unreal relations: 144

Belief: 18, 60, 62, 95, 146, 156, 157, 251, 277, 309

Belief, point of view of: 146

Belief in spiritual beings: 60

Big Bang theory: 209

Billboards: 132

Binary opposition: 261

Biological heritage: 25, 122, 136, 156, 157, 160, 163, 165, 177, 186, 193, 198, 199, 220, 233, 240, 244, 296

Biological heritage underdetermines linguistic interaction: 122 (*see also* Anthroposemiosis)

Biology: 98, 107

Biosphere: 19, 115, 167, 171, 209, 283, G33

Blind force of nature: 108 (*see also* Secondness)

Bone: 108, 113, 262, 306, 307, G57

Boundary: 35, 53, 85, 112, 126, 163, 223, 230, 233, 259, 261

Boundary line between physical and objective: 230

Bourdieu's aim: 148-149

Bourdieu's complaints: 149

Bourdieu's critique of Saussure: 149

Bourdieu's fact (or counterfactual): 263, 279

Brontosaurus: 108, 306

Brute fact: 89, 130 (*see also* Secondness)

Brute force: 118, 216, 297 (*see further* Secondness)

Brute secondness: 81 (*see also* Interaction; Physical interaction; Secondness)

Bugs: 59

Bühler's model of speech: 176

Burma: 199

Cambridge Conferences: 201

Camel: G22

Cancer: 87

Capacity: 28, 65, 67, 138, G21, G22, G27, G46

Capacity for language: 28, 165, G21

Capacity of the understanding ("capacitas intellectus"): G46

Carthage: 123

Cascade of signs: 129

Categorial relation: G61 (*see also* Physical relation)

Category as objective modality: 287

Cathexis: 118, 131

Causality: 79-112, 115, 159, 211, 218, 228, G1, G8, G13, G22, G33, G34 (*see further* Cause; Causes)

Causality, objective: 79, 80, 106, 108, 109, 112, 228, G13

Causality, prime requirement of semiosic: 93, 99

Causality, role of in order of subjective being: 102, G9

Causality as intrinsic and extrinsic, first aspect: 92

Causality as intrinsic and extrinsic, second aspect: 94-98

Causality as intrinsic and extrinsic, third aspect: 99

Causality in Aristotle: 90

Cause: 69, 79, 80, 82, 91-94, 97, 99, 101-109, 162, 206, 208, 211, 215, 296, G10, G33, G34, G35, G37 (*see further* Agent; Causality; Causes; Efficient causality; Exemplary causality; Extrinsic formal causality; Final cause; Formal causality; Ideal causality; Material causality; Objective causality; Productive causality; Specifying causality)
Cause, early and later modern notions of: 81-82
Cause, efficient and final, how extrinsic: 102
Cause, equivocal: G34
Cause, *loci* for research into classical discussions of among Latins: G13
Cause as constant conjunction: 82
Cause of sign distinguished from effect of sign: 162
Cause-effect relation differentiated from sign-relation: 69, 129
Causes: 15, 93, 102, 206, 208, 211, 215, 218, 219, 223, G4, G34
Causes, classical four: 90
Causes, sustaining and initiating distinguished: 211
Causes distinguished from principles: 102, G11
Causes essentially subordinated: 206, 208, 211
Causes productive but not preservative: 211
Causes which are and causes which are not also principles of being: 102
Causes which are preservative: 211
Celestial spheres: 36, 53, G33
Cerberus, sop to: 261, 272
Chain: 114, G6, G33
Chain of signs: G6
Chance: 164, 209, 307
Channels of causality structure interaction: 111
Chaos: G33
Characters, real and invented: 301
Check on interpretation: 86
Chemistry: 76, 77, 107, 130, 163, G14

Chemistry, physical: 76
Chemistry, semiosic: 76-77
Chew toy: 307
Child consciousness: 137
China: 229
Choices, role of in trajectory of linguistic signs: 142
Circumcision: 277
Civilization defined by artifacts and customs: 166
Classic formula for sign: 65
Classical modern philosophy: 190
Clever Hans fallacy (or effect): 187
Cleverness, excess: 236
Code: 13, 17, 25, 26, 126, epigraph before 134, 140, 141, 145, 153, 158-162, 164-169, 172, 173, 177, 179, 186, 194, 195, 197, 198, 200, 221, 232, 239, 240, 244, 245, 250, 258, 263, 265, 279, 283, G2, G20, G27, G39, G57
Code, consequence of: 159
Code, how different from idea: 158
Code, how established: 158
Code, how it functions: 159, 164
Code, material effects distinguished from formal constitutive: 164
Code, more than wake of the past: G27
Code, problematic of: 153
Code, role of in the signification of imperceptible objects: 140
Code, what it does: 240
Code, what it is anthroposemiotically: 158, 169, 177
Code, zoösemiotic notions of: 161
Code and environment: 169
Code and familiar path: 169
Code and idea: 145-146, 153, 159, 162
Code and idea, sameness and difference: 159, 162
Code and scarring of environment: 169
Code anthroposemiotically vs. zoösemiotically: 177
Code as accumulation of past conceptions in public experience: 196
Code as correlation: 158, 161, 165

Code as differentiative of objective order: G2
Code as system of contrastive relations: 263
Code broader than linguistic code: 166
Code in broadest sense anthroposemiotically taken: 166
Code is an interpretant: 169, 172
Code Napoléon: 126
Code transforms Umwelt to Lebenswelt: 166, 199
Codes, basis for development of: 239
Codes, cumulative residuality of: 200
Codes, invasion of: G26
Codes and alien Umwelts: 167
Codes and nature of the human animal (anthropos): 168
Codes as conventional involve more than convention: 232
Codes demarcating culture: 196
Codes virtually operative: 200, 280 (*see also* Virtual semiosis)
Codifiable is function of stipulable: G3
Codification, codify: 13, 14, 21, 182, 198, G3, G14
Codifying animal: 13, G3, 14
Codifying behavior: 13
Coextensive: 3, 16, 61, 98, 115, 128, 195, 247
Coextensiveness of textuality with objective world of human experience: 247
Cognitional structure of experiencing: G19
Cognitive map (*see also* Innenwelt): 117
Coliseum: 47, 48
Combustion, history of: 215
Cominterpretant: 171
Commens: 171, 174 (*see also* Intersubjective moment)
Common feature of mind-dependent and mind-independent relations: 300
Common feature of perception and understanding: 45
Common measure for perceptual disagreements: G7

Communicational interpretant: 171, 172
Communicative intent or purpose: 164-166, 191, 193, 196, 203, 220
Communicative intention and biological heritage: 165
Communicative intention and the arbitrary: 194
Communist Party: 246
Community of inquirers: 86
Comparative nonexistence: G22
Comparison of signs to onions: 58
Competence: 26, 136, 228
Competence, biblical: 228
Competence, biological: 136
Competence, linguistic: 136
Competence, semiotic: 26
Comprehension-extension distinction: G38
Concept, conception: 32, 34, 38, 39, 60, 69, 82, 87, 97, 117, 120, epigraph before 134, 134, 137, 157-159, 162, 173, 179, 188, 193, 196, 198, 205, 208, 224, 233, 237, 272, 292-294, 295, 297, G1, G2, G14, G15, G28, G32, G37, G38, G41, G47, G50 (*see also* Idea; Intraorganismic factor)
Conception, first species-specifically human one: 292-293
Conceptions within perceptions are species-specifically human: 158
Concepts, how understood as signs: 134
Conduct as interpretant of thought: 158, G37
Conjecture: 166, 205
Connotative neoplasm: 85
Consciousness: 126, 145, 148, 158, 190, 200, 214, 221, 223, 239, 248, 257, 309
Consciousness, heart of the constructivity of: 190
Consistency: 230
Conspecific: 27, 28, 118, 125, 145, 152, 185, 193, 237, 279, 283, 287, 288, 309
Conspecific anthroposemiotically defined: 145, 193
Constitution, biological: 121
Contemplation (*see also* Functional cycle; Musement): 154

Content of knowledge: 107
Context: 13, 32, 34, 50, 53, 60, 65, 66, 67, 85, 95, 106, 107, 110, 114, 150, 151, 165, 166, 168, 169, 173, 186, 211, 261, 265, 266, 277, G4, G12, G13, G17, G24, G27, G29, G33, G57
Context as regards signification: 67
Context of appearance: 50
Context specified: 65
Contingent exaptation, zone of: 231
Continuum: 201, G32
Contrast: 2, 5, 7, 9, 14, 15, 32, 34, 35, 45, 59, 61, 75-79, 143, 147, 154, 156, 163, 173, 197, 198, 202, 204, 205, 211, 234, 239, 240, 241, 245, 251, 254, 262, 263, 280, 288, 289, 298, 300-301, G2, G4, G19
Contrast of actual and virtual semiosis: 113
Contrast of ancient with modern cosmology: G33
Contrast of anthropos: 2, 14
Contrast of causes as excluding and not excluding infinite process: 211
Contrast of code with idea: 239
Contrast of criticism to empirical research: 202
Contrast of *doctrina* and *scientia*: 254
Contrast of essentially and accidentally embodied objects: 59
Contrast of free play of thought to requirements of communication: 203
Contrast of images to ideas: 137, 164 (*but see also broadest sense of idea*: 134)
Contrast of immediate and dynamic object: G19
Contrast of Lebenswelt with Umwelt: 154, 163, 173, 241, 262
Contrast of logos and mythos: 204
Contrast of material existence to physical existence: 60
Contrast of objective as such to objective as textual: 240, 280
Contrast of objective constructs based on relations to those based on individuals: 300-301
Contrast of objective to biological and physical: 145, 197, 241, 280
Contrast of objective to physical existence: 59, 280
Contrast of objective to psychological and physical subjectivity: G2, 198
Contrast of perception to sensation: 45, 289
Contrast of perception to understanding: 288, 298
Contrast of real and unreal: 145
Contrast of science focused on physical with science extended to objective in its proper being: 204-205
Contrast of sign action to action of bodies and efficient causality: 75, 77-79, G4
Contrast of sign with other objective structures: 32
Contrast of sign-vehicle with physical object as such: 76
Contrast of signs which reduce to stipulations and signs which reduce to perceptual associations: 156
Contrast of sustaining to initiating causes: 211
Contrast of things to objects and signs: 35, 147
Contrast of Umwelt to environment: 234
Contrast of what does and what does not reduce to my experience of it: 147
Contrast of what is first and what is derivative in understanding: 254
Contrast of written and spoken word: 143
Convention: 140, 142, 156, 164, 165, 198, 232, 233, 245
Conventional: 133, epigraph before 134, 164, 166, 213, 232, 233, G37
Conventional, bare sense of: 232
Conventions as communitized individual choices: 197
Copernican system: 125
Correlating, Correlation, Correlative: 7, 101, 135, 136, 157, 158,

161, 165, 195, 240, 241, G19, G51 (*see also* Code)
Correlation with a biological heritage: 240 (*see further* Biological heritage)
Correlativity of sign, semiosis, and object: 131-132
Correspondence: 179, 203-205, G4
Correspondence with the physical: 205
Cosmology, ancient: G33
Cosmology, modern: G33
Counterfactual supposition: 47-48, 263
Creation, difference of technological from artistic: 143
Creation, literary, artistic, or technological: 143
Critical: 9, 10, 18, 26, 72, 120, 142, 143, 163, 193, 203, 221, 234, 240, 244, 252, 285, 286, 296
Critical activity a subspecies of semiotic competence: 26
Critical activity presupposes anthroposemiotic codes: 193
Critical control: 9, 10, 72, 120, 143, 163, 203, 221, 240, 244, 285, 286
Critical control, discursive: 244
Critical control, form of objectification most subject to: 143
Critical control, reflexive element of: 9, G50
Critical control of objectification: 9, 10, 72, 121, 221, 244
Critical control of objectification as expanding coincidence of objective with physical: 120 (*see also* Science)
Critical control of relation of signification: 141, 143
Critical inquiry: 10
Critical perspective: 18
Critical understanding, ground of: 296
Critically controlled relativities artifactually embodied: 143
Criticism: 17, 18, 26, 30, 97, 129, 157, 178, 191-196, 202, 213, 226, 227, 231, 236, 264, 279, 280
Criticism, intelligibility of: 264, 267
Criticism, Kantian: *see* Kantian criticism
Criticism, place within anthroposemiosis: 192
Criticism, prospective contribution of: 280
Criticism, roles for: 231
Criticism, sense in which least independent of intelligent activities: 196
Criticism, starting point of: 193
Criticism as response to dilemma of culture's openness to infinite process: 221
Criticism distinctive of anthroposemiosis: 196, 221
Criticism in most general sense: 195-196, 221
Criticism within anthroposemiosis: 236
Critick (general term for analysis and evaluation of codes): 17, 26, 191, 194, 221, 231, 236, 264, 280
Critick, domain of: 231
Critick, subject matter of: 196
Critique: 17, 22, 149, 266
Critique of Prewitt's models: 184-189
Critique of Saussure by Bourdieu: 149
Critique of Sebeok's model: 177
Cross-purposes: 200
Cul de sac: 260
Cultural and scientific creation as proper function of anthropos: G60
Cultural coding, superstructurally unique aspects of: 189
Cultural life as web of codes: 168
Cultural semiosis: *see* Semiosis, cultural
Cultural semiotics, naive assumption equating semiotics with: 258
Cultural units: 72
Cultural world: 151
Culture: 17, 28, 47, 73, 87, 103, 108-110, 122, epigraph before 134, 142, 156, 163, 167, 169, 193, 197, 216-219, 221, 228-234, 246, 257, 260, 271, 273, 279, 281, 287, 293, 300, 310, G2, G3, G26, G28
Culture, collisions of: 229

Culture, firstness of: 217
Culture, foundations of: 219
Culture, how in its totality a text: 142, 151
Culture, internal being of: 217
Culture, nature's human part: 169, 257
Culture, scientific: 281
Culture, semiotic equivalent of: 122
Culture, umbrella term for texts: epigraph before 134
Culture as minuscule segment of nature: 169, 273
Culture distinct from social world: 193
Culture involves a pure thirdness: 217
Culture superstructural to zoösemiotic socialization processes: 189

Dark underlying something: G15 (*see also* Essences of material things)
Darwinian: 156, 174, 242
Dasein: G25
De anima (Aristotle): 41
Death: 224, G35
Deception, ontological ground of: 308
Deconstruction: 9, 83, 96, 108, G8
Deconstruction as dyadic: 89
Deconstruction as method is semiotically neutral: G8
Deconstruction as tracing of extrinsic formal causality: 108
Deconstruction presupposes semiosis: G8
Deconstructionist: 85, 213, 227
Deduction: 224, 236
Definition: 13
Demonstration: 227
Dependence on action of being and being-known: 12
Dependency in being illustrated through semiosis: 88-90 (*see also* Causality, Cause)
Derridean drift: 84
Determinate causes: 211
Diachronic: 230, G33
Dialectic, dialectical: 19, 148, 195
Diaphanous medium: 165

Dicisign: 271-272
Dicisignificative utterance: 271
Difference between objects and things: 39-40 (*see also* Objective)
Difference between objects of experience which are only objects and which are also things: 115
Difference between possession vs. exercise of knowledge: 41
Dimanation, dimanate: 4, 112, 164, 173, G1, G19
Dimanation, what it is: G1
Dimanation as triadic dimension epiphenomenal to dyadic interaction: G1
Dinosaur bone perceived: 307
Dinosaurs: 108, 306, 307
Dipyramid: 183
Diremption: 120
Discontinuity of paths anthroposemiotically and zoösemiotically familiar: 169, 177
Discriminations experientially imposed within the objective world: 115
Discursive: 59, 183, 197, 201, 205, 240, 244, 287, 309
Discursive conspecificity: 287, 309
Discursive conspecifics, what they are: 309
Discursive critical control: 244 (*see also* Critical control)
Distinction of literary and nonliterary discourse questioned: 265
Division of objects: 162
Division of reality: 19
Divisions of objectivity vary with relative independence of the differences among objects in the dimension of physical being: 201
Doctrine: 17, 26, 79, 82, 83, 107, 117, 129, 131, 155, 234, 235, 299, G17, G37, G42
Doctrine of associationism: 82-83
Doctrine of signs: 17, 26, 79, 107, 117, 129, 131, 155, 234, 235, G17
Doctrine of signs, experimental point of departure for: 155
Dog: 138, 140, 170, 238
Dog, idea of: 238
Double break: 19

Double hermeneutic: 9
Doubly related distinguished from two relations: 66
Dragonflies: 127, 128
Drift: 84-86, 88, 89, 201, 229, G8
Drift, associative: 83
Drift, deconstructive: 85
Drift, mechanisms of: 84
Drift, not necessarily triadic: 89
Drift, process of: 84
Drift and extrinsic formal causality: G8
Drift contrasted with semiosis: 86
Dyadic interactions: 81 (*see also* Efficient causality; Secondness)
Dynamic object: 52, 54, G7, G19, G37
Dynamical action: 77, 78, 80, 91, 112, 114, 130, 147, 163, 303 (*see also* Interaction)
Dynamical interpretant: G37

Effect, how constituted as an entity in its own right: 102
Effectual interpretant: 171
Efficient causality: 81, 91, 92 (*see also* Productive causality)
Embodiment: 36, 47, 59, 62, 115, 132, G37, G46
Embodiment, material requirements of: 164
Embodiment as sensorially accessible base for a given object: 143, G46
Embodiment as sensorially accessible base for sharing of ideas: 155
Emergent levels: 283
Emotion: 173
Encoding through anthroposemiosis: 242
Ens commune: G51
Ens praedicamentale: 310
Ens primum cognitum distinguished from *ens reale, ens quantitativum, ens commune, ens ut sic, ens transcendentale*: G51
Ens primum cognitum is sui generis notion: G51
Ens quantitativum: G51
Ens reale: 191, 235, G51
Ens transcendentale: G51

Ens ut primum cognitum as Firstness: 296 (*see also* Primum cognitum)
Ens ut sic: G51
Entitative, entity: G1, 53, 59, 62, 74, 76, 92, 101-103, 110, 132, 197, 234, 304, G7, G9, G12, G22, G25, G47
Envelope of language: 195
Environment: 5-8, 11, 15, 19, 24, 33, 35, 38, 63, 65, 76, 77, 91, 115, 117, 118, 121, 123-126, 130, 144, 147 154, 163, 166, 169, 177, 198, 203, 213, 215, 216, 230, 234, 239, 263, 271, 274, 288, 289, 293, 296, 300, 302, 306, G7, G17, G18, G25, G34 (*see also* Physical world; Subjective being)
Environment, notion of as prejacent physical: G25
Environment (physical surroundings as such): 54
Environment as common physical surroundings: 300
Environment reconstituted structurally in experience: 115
Environmental factors objectified: 130, 147
Environmental structure experienced: G19 (*see also* Structure)
Environmentality: 263
Epicycles: 236
Epistemology and semiotics: 106, G12, G37
Equilibrium: 198
Equivocal model: 186
Errors in science: 215
Essence: 38, 59, 77, 229, 237, 262, 265, 284, 298-299, 305, 308, G57, G14, G39, G53
Essence as a construct of relations (Aquinas): 299, 304-308, G51
Essence as model (Aquinas): 308
Essence as prospectively definable structure: 294
Essence of material things, in what it consists: 298-299, 308, G49-51
Essence of perceptible objects: 294 (*see also* Essence of material things)
Essences as known: 304-308
Essences as models: 308

Essential distinction between thing and object: 39, 51
Essentially subordinate: 206, 208, 218, 223, G33, G34 (*see further* Infinite process)
Essentially subordinate series as regional only: G33 (*see also* Cause; Infinite series)
Essentially subordinated sustenative causes: 223 (*see also* Cause)
Ethics: 17
Ethics of terminology: 107, 294, G1, G14, Appendix
Ethnic: 200, G24
Ethnic groupings: G24
Ethno-, ethnographic, ethnography, ethnology: 10, 247, 285, 287, 311, G24
Ethnocentrism: 286
Eurocentrism: 285-287
Evolution: 202, 209, 272, G33
Evolutionary causal chain: G33
Exaptation: 134, 139, 149, 164, 166, 186, 203, 220, 230, 231, 274, 290
Exaptation of language, how accomplished: 230
Exaptation of language to communicate: 134, 139, 177, 149, 164-166, 185, 203, 220, 230, 231, 262, 274, 290
Exaptibility of species-specifically human language: 139
Exemplary causality: 105, 107, 109, 303, G11, G13 (*see also* Extrinsic formal causality, first type)
Existential facts and thought: 89
Existential simultaneity of relations and being: 4
Experience: 11, 15, 16, 19, 20-22, 24, 25, 32-39, 41-45, 47, 50, 52-55, 57-65, 71, 75-78, 80, 82, 87, 110, 112, 115, 117, 119, 120, 123, 125, 126, 128, 129, 131, 132, 135, 136, 137, 140-142, 144, 145, 147, 151, 152, 154-158, 160, 162-164, 166, 172, 177, 179, 181, 182, 185, 191, 193-197, 199-203, 205, 212-214, 223, 224, 228, 230, 231, 234, 237, 239-241, 243-247, 249, 251-254, 257, 263, 265, 267-269, 275-277, 279, 284, 286, 289, 297, 299, 300, 301, 308, G2, G3, G15, G19, G27, G35, G38, G42, G43, G51, G53, G57
Experience, abductive spiral of: 224
Experience, cognitional structure of: G19
Experience, content of: 32
Experience, corrective of: 38
Experience, difference on which depends: 57
Experience, diversity of: 129
Experience, element of: 44
Experience, formal constituent of: 63
Experience, invariant at base of: 34
Experience, paradigm case of: 38
Experience, primacy of Umwelt for: 151
Experience, role of as ground of understanding: 253
Experience, semiosic structuring of: 71
Experience, semiotic notion of: 22
Experience, structure of: 197
Experience, viewpoint of: 128, 212
Experience as distinctive to the human Umwelt: 128
Experience necessary to any universe of discourse: 268
Experiences, possible: 123
Experiential point of view: 155
Experiment, experimental: 76, 120, 155, 215, G45
Experiments, critically controlled: *see* Critical control
External reality: 19, 41, 86, 96, 105, 128, 162, 201, 216, 218, 227, G3, G7, G44
Extinction of physical stimulus: 121 (*see also* Functional cycle)
Extra-: 28, 86, 143, G14, G33, G47
Extralinguistic items: 86
Extrasemiotic: 86
Extraterrestrial life: 28, 119, 143, 154, 167, 309 (*see also* Intelligent life)
Extrinsic formal causality: 79, 105, 106, 108, 109, 159, G5 (*see also* Causality; Cause; Formal causality)

Extrinsic formal causality, first type (exemplary causality): 105, 109
Extrinsic formal causality, second type (objective causality): 106-109
Extrinsic formal causality and authorial control of text: G8
Extrinsic formal causality as exercised by an objective cause (second mode): 108
Extrinsic formal causality concretely illustrated in discourse: 109
Extrinsic specificative, object as: G22

Fact: 34, 52, 55, 60, 72, 89, 93, 97, 100, 103, 106, 114, 116, 119, 120, 132, 141, 149, 150, 168, 171, 173, 183, 195, 198, 199, 201, 202, 206, 226, 232, 243, 251, 257, 259, 263, 265, 269, 277, 279, 291, 308, G4, G11, G15, G34, G37, G40
Fact as perceptually accessible: 199, 203
Facts, empirical: 199
Facts as belonging to relational systems: 198, 251
Fakery: 138
Fallacy, *pars pro toto*: see Pars pro toto fallacy
Familiar path: 169
Fancies: 155, 157, 275 (*see also* Fantasy; Fiction)
Fancies divided into images and ideas: 157
Fantasy, fantasies: 283 (*see also* Fiction)
Fashion: 124
Feminism: 126
Fiction: 53, 199, 252, 264, 269, 283, 284
Field of infinite possibilities: 238 (*see also* Infinite process; Unlimited semiosis)
Field research: 202
Final cause: 90, 93, 94, 96-105, G10; as twofold: 94 (*see also* Causality; Cause)
Final cause, apologetic uses of: 95
Final cause, extrinsic dependency of: 96
Final cause, intrinsic dependency of: 95

Final cause as intrinsic to an effect: G10
Final causality, extrinsic: 96
Final causality, intrinsic: 95, 97
Finnegans Wake: 142
First human animals: 146
First intention: 300, G56
First intentions are sometimes mind-dependent relations, sometimes mind-independent ones: G56
First intentions characterize objects as directly experienced, not objects as reducible to things: 300, G56
First intentions include mind-dependent relations: 300
First of all species-specifically human conceptions not a temporal first: 292
Firstness: 78, 217, 293, 294, 296, 297, 310
Firstness defined: 293, 296
Focus of attention: 291
Foreground: 173, 176
Formal causality: 100-106, 108-110, 159, G8, G13 (*see also* Causality; Cause)
Formal causality, first mode of externality: 105
Formal causality, how exercisable according to a nonexistent source: 104, 112
Formal causality, intrinsic: 101
Formal causality, objective exercise of in semiosis: 110
Formal causality, second mode of externality: 106, 108
Formal causality and intrinsic constitution of entity: 102-104, 110
Formal rationale distinguishing understanding within sense perception: 298, G54
Formal sign: *see* Idea; Intraorganismic factor; Image
Fossil bone: 108, 113, G57
Fossil bone as extrinsic specifier (objective cause): 108
Foundation: 7, 26, 28, 112, 130, 138, 140, 165, 245, 296, G1 (*see also* Fundament; Ground; Interpretant)

Foundation of semiosic relation: 130
Foundational: 1, 8, 10, 113, 186, 255, 257, 272
Foundational anthropology: 1, 10, 186
Frame of reference, historical: G25
Frame of reference, mechanistic: G25
Framing, linguistic: 120
Free: 84, 89, 122, 123, 141, 143, 144, 145, 156, 165, 169, 203, 205, 220, 265, 280, 296, G27, G35
Freedom: epigraph before 134, 165, 283
Freedom of the intellect: 165, 280, 283
Freely chosen reality: 142, 144, 145, 156
French Empire: 126
French Revolution: 122
Functional cycle, anthropic transcendence of: 121, 128, 154, 181, 190, 263
Fundament: 7, G19 (*see also* Foundation; Fundament; Ground; Interpretant)
Fundamental intellectual awareness is neither of essence nor existence: G53 (*see also entries under* Primum cognitum)
Future: 45, 111, 125, 126, 143, 155, 163, 211, 222, 224, 235, 280, G27, G33
Future, orientation toward: G27
Future outcomes: 163

Geisteswissenschaften: 18
General rule regarding need for physical lining of objectivity: 63
Generation, generating: 110, 231, 269, G27, G33
Generating cause: G1 (*see also* Efficient causality; Productive causality)
Genus and difference as defining human Umwelt: 163
German: 120
Given: 7, 20, 32, 33, 44, 60, 73, 86, 93, 99, 112, 114, 126, 128, 129, 132, epigraph before 134, 139- 141, 147, 156-159, 162, 164, 182, 184, 197, 200, 206, 211, 218, 223, 224, 226-230, 232, 247, 251, 262, 267, 272, 273, 275, 276, 285, 286, 293, 299-301, 303, G5, G8, G27, G33, G34, G42, G44, G53, G57
Glass slipper: 53
Glassy essence: 284
Glottocentric: 259
God, existence of: G33
Government: 31, 122
Government, constitutional forms of: 122
Grand view of semiosic progression in nature vs. culture: 110
Grand Vision: G41
Graven images: 62
Ground: 17, 19, 28, 41, 66, 69, 112, 120, 130, 133, 134-137, 141, 147, 149, 151, 157, 158, 159, 162-164, 169, 170, 193, 232, 234, 253, 298, 310, G1, G2, G4, G19, G25, G26, G60 (*see also* Foundation; Fundament; Ground; Interpretant)
Ground and terminus of relation distinguished: 133
Ground arms!: G4
Ground distinguished from relation: 133
Ground for sign relations, how interchangeable within human semiosis: 134
Ground of semiosic relation: 130
"A Guess at the Riddle": G42

Habit, difference from disposition: 155
Habit-patterns naturalize linguistic signs: 142
Habits grounded in imperceptible stipulation vs. perceptible association: 156 (*see also* Association)
Heart of anthroposemiotic coding: 161
Heidegger's question concerning present-at-hand vs. ready-to-hand answered: 263, 296
Here and now (*hic et nunc*): 19, 37, 39, 43, 45, 46, 60, 121, 130, 166, 197, 203, 206, 208, 210, 211, 212, 220, 250, 293, G15, G33, G53

Heritage: *see* Biological heritage
Hermeneutics: 9, 253-254
Hermetic drift: 84, 85, G8 (*see also* Drift)
Heterogeneity of existential relations: 6
Heuristic: 184, 185, 268
Hic et nunc: *see* Here and now
Hierarchy: 142
Highland Burma: 199
Historical: 17, 106, 122, 136, 151, 191, G26
Historical causation: 209
Historical context: 251, 277
Historical deformations: 259
Historical environment: 271
Historicity: 271
Historicizing sign: 151
History, centrality of: 253, 279
Hoover Dam: 48
Horizon: 149
Human act: 246
Human ancestors: 146
Human awareness as species-specifically differentiated: 290
Human being: 11, 12, 48, 126, 232, 245, G34 (*see also* Anthropos)
Human communication as species-specifically differentiated: 290
Human communication species-specifically differentiated: 290
Human practice as anthropic: 150
Human sciences: 18, 126, 191, 202, 216, 248, 249, 250, 251, 252, 277, 278, 279
Human Umwelt: 120, 123, 125, 128, 139, 144, 154, 171, 173, 174, 240, 241, 243, 263, G2 (*see also* Lebenswelt; Objective world; Umwelt)
Human Umwelt, gradual differentiation of within biosphere: 171, 243
Human Umwelt, how different: 241
Human use of signs, what distinguishes: 144 (*see also* Contrast; Human Umwelt; Lebenswelt)
Humanities: 154, 247-250, 253, 279
Hunches and guesses: 222
Hydrodynamical grounds: G60
Hypothesis: 49, 62, 98, 130, 147, 149, 222, 243, 289, 309, G32, G60

Iberian semiotics: 26, 68, Appendix
Iceberg, tip of: G15
Icon, iconic: 114, 157, 173, 232, 233
Icon of semiosis: 114
Iconicity, problematic character of: 233
Idea: 21, 35, 42, 43, 47, 62, 82, 89, 98, 134, 137, G2
Idea, how shared: 153, 193
Idea, how understood as sign: 134
Idea, psychological sense of: G2 (*see also* Intraorganismic factor; Subjectivity)
Idea and code contrasted: 153, 239
Idea as determining outward sign: 158
Idea as intraorganismic factor: 137
Idea as private: 152
Idea as sharable: 158-160
Idea conceived fundamentally: 239 (*see also* Sign fundamentally; Intraorganismic factor)
Idea in the anthroposemiotic sense: 138, 153, 164
Idea in the most general sense not restricted to anthroposemiosis: 134
Idea is an interpretant: 170
Idea is to Innenwelt as code to Umwelt: 153
Ideal and final causality distinguished: 98 (*see also* Extrinsic formal causality, second sense)
Ideal being at work in all of nature: 169
Ideal causality: 98, 105, 107, 109, 169 (*see also* Extrinsic formal causality; *and esp.* Specifying causality)
Ideal causality, Latin sense of: 98, 105, 107 (*see also* Extrinsic formal causality, first sense)
Ideal causality as specifying distinguished from ideal causality as exemplary: 107, 109
Ideal final interpretant: 114
Idealism, idealistic philosophy: 120, 199, 260, 261, G17
Idealism, German: G17
Idealism, Kantian: 117, 120, G17

Idealism and perspective proper to semiotics: 261
Idealisms, classical modern: G17
Ideas, origin of: 137-139
Ideas, primitive order of: G55
Ideas, species-specific human sense of: 158, 164
Ideas codified: 193
ideatum: 238 (*see also* Object)
Identification without identity: 194
Ideology, ideological: 60, 188, 231-233, 280
Ideological phenomenon par excellence: 231
Ignorance: 113, 260, 293, 307, G35, G48
Ignorance, effect of on perception: 307
Ignorance, negative sense of: 260
Ignorance, positive sense of (Aristotle): 260
Ignorance and error prove individual existence: G35
Illusion, illusory: 26, 115, 120, 199, 202, 236
Illusion of critical autonomy, basis for: 202
Image: 62, 69, 134, 137, 157, 164, 246, G35
Image as intraorganismic factor: 134, 137
Images, how understood as signs: 134
Images as distinguished from conceptions or ideas: 137, 157, 164
Images essential to functioning of ideas in specifically anthroposemiotic sense: 246
Immediate experience: 275
Immediate interpretant: G37
Immediate needs: 121
Immediate object: 52, 54, 131, G4, G7, G15, G19, G35, G37
Immediate proportion of knowing and known: 294
Imperceptible in principle: 138, 161, 198, 243, 295, G21, G51, G57
Imperceptible objectivities are rendered public through deliberate coding: 245 (*see also* Anthroposemiosis; Critical control)
Imperialism of natural science: 253
Impossible: 40, 142, 308, G36, G53, G58, G59, G60 (*see also* Possible)
Improbable language: 144
Inconsistency: 7, G17
Inconsistent: 7, 209, G17
Incorporeal being: 136
Indeterminacy: 223, 265, G33
Indeterminacy among causes: G33 (*see also* Infinite process; Infinite regress)
Indeterminacy among signs: 223
Indeterminacy of meaning: 265 (*see also* Vagueness)
Index: 232, 233, G4, G22, G28, G46
Indexical: 232
Indian tribes: 229
Indifference, indifferent: 43, 139, 144, 157, 170, 186, 187, 234, 310, G33
Indifference distinguishing perception and understanding from sensation: 43
Indifference enabling semiosis: 234
Indifference of relation: 234
Indifference of relation to subjective ground: 144, 304-308, 310
Indifference of signs derivative from formally relative rationale: 144
Indifference of signs to what is and is not: 144
Indifference proper to signs: 144, 304-308, 310
Indifference to physical presence: 43
Indifference to subjective ground: 134-135, 157, 164
Indifferent sender and receiver: 139
Individual: 4-7, 15, 20, 31, 35, 41, 56, 81, 86, 95, 96, 101, 114, 115, 117, 126, 128, 142, 146-148, 152, 153, 158, 171, 181, 183, 190, 197, 200, 202, 212, 218, 224, 227, 279, 287, 294, 300, 302, 307, G22, G27, G33, G43
Individual consciousness: 148, 158, 190
Individual creativity and language: 171
Individual mind as source of subsequently common notions: 152

Individual subsistent in contrast to substance: 5
Individual-universal distinction: 41
Infallible sign: 214 (*see also* Infinite process)
Inference as producing error: 260
Infinite: 86, 87, 123, 133, 138, 202, 206, 208-211, 214, 218, 219, 222-224, 226, 227, 229, 230, 238, 239, 263, G14, G32, G33, G34, G40, G46, G47 (*see also* Infinite process; Infinite series; Progress toward the infinite)
Infinite, physical and mathematical arguments concerning: G33
Infinite, progress toward the: 86, 138
Infinite divisibility: 201
Infinite process: 206, 208, 209-211, 214, 218, 222, 230, G32, G40 (*see also* Unlimited semiosis)
Infinite process, Corrington on: 224
Infinite process, no intrinsic repugnancy to in culture: 219
Infinite process, Poinsot on: G33
Infinite process, Ransdell on: 227
Infinite process, sense of as incompatible with intelligible causality: 210, G34
Infinite process, senses of compatible with causality: 211
Infinite process, form of unique to the objective order: 214
Infinite process, where required: 223
Infinite process among cultural relations: 218
Infinite process and Big Bang theory: 209
Infinite process and counterfactuals: 230
Infinite process and intelligibility: 211
Infinite process and semiotic consciousness: 214
Infinite process argument: G33
Infinite process in objective world: 222-223
Infinite process in physical environment: 222-223

Infinite process in physical world vs. objective world: 222
Infinite process unavoidable in semiosis: 214-227
Infinite regress: 219, 222, 223 (*see also* entries under Infinite)
Infinite regress, point of the exclusion of: 207-227
Infinite regress and scientific understanding: 206
Infinite regress not denied in every form: 208
Infinite series: 208, G33 (*see also* Infinite process; Progress toward the infinite; Series; Unlimited semiosis)
Infinite series, Poinsot on: G33
Infinite series in modern cosmology: G33
Infinities involved in semiosis: 87
Infinity: 133, 138, 211, 224, 226, 239, G34 (*see also* Infinite)
Infinity of semiosis virtual and syncategorematic: 226, G33 (*see also* Unlimited semiosis)
Informational semiosis: 271
Initial anthropological moment: 147, 149
Initiative, radically new: G17
Innenwelt: 116, 117, 147, 149, 153, 156, 159, 163, 164, 172, 237, 241, 242, 263, 264, G2, G19 (*correlate* of Umwelt; Lebenswelt, *q.v.*)
Inner speech: G39
Inner vs. outer: 155
Innovation: 170
Insight-without-parts: 273, G42
Instability in the sign: 33, 34, 58
Instability of objects as signs and signs as objects: 33, 58
Instinct, instinctive: G37, G60
Instinct for preferring better hypotheses: G60
Instrument: 79, 115, 120, 121, 143, 154
Instrument for discriminating true from false: 115
Integrity as a virtue: 228
Integrity of individual: 227
Integrity of object as semiosic: 228
Intellect, intellectual: 26, 87, 97,

111, 114, 165, 227, 228, 280, 283, 289-295, 298, 299, G14, G44, G46-G55, G58, G59 (*see also* Understanding)
Intellect, capacity contrasted to situation of vital response: G46
Intellectual apprehension differentiated from perceptual: 295, 298
Intellectual justice in use of terms: G14
Intelligence: 27, 136, 166, 196, 231, 288, 308, G3, G4, G44, G60
Intelligence, what it is as linguistic competence: 136
Intelligent life: 154, 167 (*see also* Extraterrestrial)
Intelligibility: 7, 103, 104, 110, 201, 261, 264, 287, 292, 295, 298, 309, G53 (*see also* Intelligible; Primum cognitum; Unintelligible prospect)
Intelligibility, how constituted: 296
Intelligibility, what it primordially consists in: 292, 296
Intelligibility, where it begins: 296, G53
Intelligibility as distinct and irreducible aspect of cognition: 292, 298
Intelligibility determined through relations: 6-7
Intelligible: 142, 196, 290, 291, 293, 296, 298, G29, G32, G51 (*see also* Intelligibility; Primum cognitum; Unintelligible prospect)
Intelligible, outer limit of: 142
Intelligible contrasted to sensible: 296
Intelligible world a mixture of mind-independent and mind-dependent relations: 296 (*see also* Objective world; Umwelt)
Intension: G38
Intent, problem of: 85
Intention: 50, 164, 165, 193, 194, 300, G56
Intention, first: *see* First intention
Intention, second: *see* Second intention
Intentional interpretant: 171
Intentionality: 9

Interaction: 9, 24, 31, 38, 43, 51, 55, 60, 75-78, 80, 81, 111, 112, 115, 118, 119, 121, 122, 126, 130, 147, 149, 163, 181, 193, 194, 197, 200, 201, 220, 221, 242, 244, 271, 310, G1, G3, G12, G27, G29, G33, G57
Interaction, biological: 197
Interaction, causal: G33
Interaction, communicative: 242
Interaction, dialogic: G27
Interaction, law-governed: 163
Interaction, objective: 118, 197
Interaction, physical: 51, 55, 60, 75, 76, 77, 118, 121, 130 (*see also* Secondness; Dynamical action)
Interaction, semiotic: 271
Interaction, social: 31, 115, 122, 149, 151, 193, 194, 200, 220, 244, 287, G3, G29
Interaction linguistically mediated is disproportionate to biological heritage: 122
Interactions, spiral of: 310
Internal correlation of formal and material cause: 101
Interplay between objective and physical being: 80
Interpretant: 67-72, 77, 87, 89, 113, 114, 158, 159, 169-172, 181, 224, 227, 261, 270, G4, G8, G37, G57
Interpretant, cases where mental: 69
Interpretant, cases where not mental: 70
Interpretant, demonstration of role of mental: 69
Interpretant, dynamical: G37
Interpretant, effectual: 171
Interpretant, final: 114
Interpretant, ideal final: 114
Interpretant, immediate: G37
Interpretant, indifferently physical or mental: 170
Interpretant, intentional: 171
Interpretant, Johansen's model as: 270
Interpretant, logical: 159, 169-171
Interpretant, role of, holds equally for natural signs and cultural symbols: 69
Interpretant, role of in structuring experience: 71

Interpretant, species of: 171
Interpretant, theoretical need for: 68
Interpretant as "an equivalent or more developed sign": 67
Interpretant as species of thirdness: 71, 78
Interpretant as the effect proper to the sign as such: 261
Interpretant idea: 158
Interpretant in general: 170
Interpretant need not be mental: 67
Interpretant-object distinction, importance of: G37
Interpretants, function of: 170
Interpretants, subsequent: G37
Interpretants, where given: 170
Interpretants of percepts: G37
Interpretation, interpreting: 84-86, 89, 145, 147, 170, 172, 181, 189, 190, 223-226, 228, 229, 239, 244, 250, 251, 253, 250, 251, 253, 254, 261, 265, 268-275, 272-274, 277, 279, 285, G7, G8, G17, G24, G27, G33, G37, G39, G40
Interpretation, intellectual as differentiating zoösemiosis from within: 285
Interpreter: 84, 85, 89, 171, 181, 189, 190, 228, 239, 269, 271, G8, G24, G40 (*see also* Interpretant)
Interpretive structures: 273
Intersemioticity: 269
Interspecific: 273
Intersubjective, intersubjectivity: 159, 166, 167, 193, G17
Intersubjective moment: 159, 171-172
Intertext, intertextuality: 194, 251, 258, 260, 269
Intraorganismic: 130, 137, 239
Intraorganismic factor distinct from object as such: 130
Intraorganismic factor grounding semiosic relations: 137
Intraorganismic factor required for objectification: 130
Introducing Semiotic: xi, 254
Intuition determined by previous cognition: G35
Investigator, investigation: 22, 195, 251, 253, 276, 277, 285, 291, 294, 311, G38, G50
Irreducibility: 38, 181, 182, 199 (*see further* Irreducible)
Irreducibility of experience to existence of things: 44, 47, 55, 63
Irreducibility of individuals to relational webs: 4, 7
Irreducibility of other to object pole of individual experience: 181
Irreducible: 205, 16, 38, 44, 63, 115, 119, 125, 141, 145, 150, 156, 157, 172, 185, 197, 199, 205, 232, 262, 274, 275, 286, 292, G2, G19, G51
Irreducible channels of cognition: 292
It: 293-294

Jakobson's factorial model: 173
Jakobson's functional model: 173
Johansen model, peculiar interest of: 178-179
Johansen/Deely model: 180, 183
Judgment, conjectural nature of: 223
Judgment of existence: G59
Jurisdictional boundaries: 126

Kantian: 117, 120, 129, G17, G42
Kantian context: G17
Kantian criticism as it departs from semiotic critick: 129
Kantian idealism: 120
Kline bottle: 183
Klüger, Hans: 187
Knowledge, object of, distinguished from interpretant of knowledge: G37
Knowledge, scientific: 307
Kritik der Reinen Vernunft: 117

Laboratory technique: 202
Lamarckian: 156, 165, 174
Language: 9, 14, 17, 28, 36, 59, 75, 86, 120-122, 133, 139, 144, 146, 147, 151, 164, 166, 171-173, 185, 187, 195, 197, 198, 201, 203, 213, 220, 221, 228, 230, 233, 237, 245, 246, 249, 251, 262, 265, 270, 271, 273, 274, 279, 287, 290, 293, 300, G1, G2, G6, G8, G14, G17, G21, G27, G45

Language, birth of as species-specifically human: 133
Language, capacity for: 28
Language, essence of (prior to exaptation): 237
Language, existential definition of: 133
Language, ground sense of: 164
Language, larger and more fundamental notion required for: 244-245
Language, origin of exaptibility for communication: 139
Language, privileged place of: G31
Language, propositional aspect of: 271
Language, structural peculiarity of: 165
Language, what the term covers: 246
Language and the individual: 171
Language as a form of life: 195
Language as aspect of modeling species-specifically human: 121
Language as exapted, material requirements of: 164, 203
Language as exapted, unique function of: 164
Language as publicly available coding of Umwelt: 165
Language as reflective of intellect: 165
Language as species-specific: 151
Language in root sense: 195
Language not an autonomous system: 165
Language-dependent activities (see also Postlinguistic): 17
langue: 149, 263, G14
langue as communicative exaptation of anthropic Innenwelt: 149
Latin tradition, contribution to problem of primum cognitum: 293
Law: 130, 163, 244, 282, 297, G14, G35
Laws of physics and chemistry: 130
Lebensform: 195
Lebenswelt (general term for Umwelt as species-specific to anthropos): 125, 154, 165, 166, 167, 171, 173, 174, 177, 187, 194, 198, 240, 252, 262, 263, 274, 278, 286, 295, 296, 309 G2, G27
Lebenswelt as different from Umwelt: 194; root cause of: 295
Legal systems: 126
Legendary heroes: 62
Leprechauns: 54
Levels, semiosic interdependence of: 283
Life, dependence on co-operating causes: G34
Life, highest expression of: 274
Life and semiosis: 111
Lifeworld (*see also* Lebenswelt): 129, 129, 153, 154
Line between mind-independent and mind-dependent being: 265
Line between what is and what is not: 283
Line between what is dependent upon and independent of interpretive activity: 265, 275
Linguistic: 13, 17, 21, 22, 24, 25, 27, 28, 59, 62, 109, 120, 122, 135, 146, 143, 144, 151, 156, 165, 172, 173, 181, 185, 186, 195, 199, 213, 221, 227, 230-232, 237, 245, 247, 258, 260, 261, 263, 269, 287, 290, 310, G3, G17, G26
Linguistic admixture: 165, 172, 181, 246, 247, 269
Linguistic animal: 13, 24, 25
Linguistic code is subspecies of anthroposemiotic coding: 172
Linguistic codes: *see* Code
Linguistic forms, extraterrestrial: 28
Linguistic mediation, thesis of: 195
Linguistic sign: 109, 134, 144, 227, 230, 231, 245
Linguistic signs, role of choices in trajectory of: 142
Linguistic signs naturalized through habit-patterns: 142
Linguistic Society of Paris: Appendix
Linguistic texture: 260
Linguistic understanding of signs, what it is: 136
Linguisticization of experience: 25
Lining of objective world: 54, 63,

119, 123, 129, 191, 276 (see also Environment; Physical; Physical being)
Linkage: 68, 71, 110, 133, 237
Literal meaning: 228
Literary, literature: 17, 18, 26, 36, 132, epigraph before 134, 141, 143, 178, 181, 247, 248, 251, 257, 258, 260-262, 265, 266-269, 271, 273, 275, 279-281, 287, 311
Literary, requirements for intelligibility of: 261
Literary criticism: 18
Literary genre: 247
Literary semiotics: 181
Literary text: 267
Literature: 18, 178, 247, 258, 265-267, 271, 280, 311, G40
Literature, case of: 265
Literature, creation of extends semiosis of nature: 266
Literature as presuppositioned phase of anthroposemiosis: 267
Living speech: 250, 279
Logic, logical: 3, 4, 7, 60, 98, 114, 159, 170, 171, 182, 184, 185, 205, 227, 271, G19, G38, G51
Logical atom: 114
Logical incoherence vs. existential conflict and sustenance: 7
Logical interpretant: 159, 169-171
Logical relations, impersonal aspect of: 182
Logical symbolizations: 271
Logos and mythos: 204
Loose ends: 197, 200-201
Loose-endedness: 200-201
Loras College: 271

Major tradition of semiotic development: 132, 178, 232, 235, 234, 268, G38
Mark linguistically: 181 (see also Functional cycle)
Markers, verbal: 121
Mars: 49
Material causality: 91, 92
Material change and objective change contrasted: 77
Materialists: 60
Matrix: 252, 271, 278, 279

Maximum contingency embodied in linguistic signs: 230
Meaning, literal: 228
Meaning, zero degree: 228
Meaning-plan: 25
Mediating role of signs beyond physical dynamics: 80
Medieval doctrine concerning essences: 299
Mental: 67, 69, 71, 87, 89, 170, 173, 279, G4, G35, G37, G42, G61
Mental operations, logic of: G37
Mental processes, can be cancerous: 87
Mental representations, how understood as signs: 134
Mental synthesis and analysis: G34
Mere noises: 109
Message: 149, 173, 221, 250, 279
Metalinguistic: G27 (see also Postlinguistic)
Metaphysical, metaphysics: 138, 162, 254, 293, G51, G32, G47, G51
Microcosm: 311
Mind-dependent: 15, 201, 293, 296, 300-304, 308, G32, G47
Mind-dependent being consists only of relations: 302
Mind-dependent relations constitutive of language: 201
Mind-independent: 15, 41, 191, 203, 217, 293, 296, 300, 303, 304, 308, G47 (see also Environment; Physical)
Mind-independent and mind-dependent relations are univocal as objective: 308 (see also First intentions)
Mind-independent being consists both of relations and of related individuals: 300-302
Minor tradition in semiotics: 178, 179, 235, G38
Minotaur: 36, 53
Mistakes in science swept under rug: 215
Misunderstanding: 286, G17, G19, G39 (see also Ignorance)
Model: 4, 9, 14, 21, 24-26, 29, 92, 105, 109, 121-129, 139, 147, 156, 164, 168, 173, 175-190, 195, 198,

237, 260, 262, 265, 268, 269, 274, 283, 284, 308, G3
Model, biological and linguistic notions of: 2
Model, connotations of not appropriate to Umwelt: 127
Model, in what sense true or false: 308, G59
Model of poetic language: 173
Model of textuality, derivation of: 173
Model of textuality, shortcomings: 175
Model world: 123, 127, 128, 156, 198
Models, role of in understanding: 308
Models, two-dimensional vs. three-dimensional: 187
Models as example: G58
Modeling: 21, 24-26, 121, 122, 125-129, 164, 184, 265, 283, G3
Modeling anthroposemiosis, crucial point for: 182
Modeling procedure exhibited in hard and soft sciences: 125-126
Modeling system: 21-22, 24, 25, 121, 127, 128, 164, 283
Modeling system, primary: 121
Modeling system, secondary: 121
Modeling system, tertiary: 121
Modern, early notion of cause: 81
Modern, later notion of cause: 82
Monarchy, hereditary aspect of primarily cultural: 122
Monarchy derived from primate social interaction: 122
Morality, origin of: 128
Morley triangle model of discourse (Sebeok): 176
Mores as distinct from morality: 128
Mountain stream: 53, 54, 163
Movement from signification to textuality: 191
Multifaceted individuals and relations: 7
Multivoicedness: G27
Muscular effort: 155 (see also Secondness)
Musement: 145 (see also Contemplation)

Mutually invisible objective worlds: 118
Myth: 62, 151, 204, 265, 269

Naive ethnocentrism: 286
Native speaker: 228
National language: G1, G14
Natural language: 9, 167, 271
Natural sign: 63, 249, 251, 277 (see also Relationship of signification)
Natural sign-relation different from causal relation: 69, 129
Natural sign-relation different from similarity: 69
Nature: see Environment; Physical being
Necessary partial coincidence of objects with things: 41
Necessity, in experience of nature: 117
Negation distinguished from relation only as a special case of relation: 302
Neoscholastic opinion that *ens ut primum cognitum* is simply *ens reale ut obiectum*: G51
Neoscholastics, shabby practice of: G44
Network of signs: 142
New Beginnings: Appendix
New List of Categories: G51
New Yorkers: 28
Newtonian system: 125
Node: 117, 142, 193, 202, 251, 273, G33
Nominalists: 42
Nonexistent objects, what able to specify: G22
Nonliterary discourse: 265
Nonrepresentative art: 105
Nontransitivity of Prewitt model vis-à-vis Johansen model: 187
Nonverbal: 195, 269,
Notions derivative from primum cognitum: G47
Novel, novelty: 131, 270, 283, G17
Novel, language of: 270
Nucleus in theory of linguistic interpretation: 172 (see also Intersubjective moment)

Object: 25, 30, 32-34, 36, 40, 41, 47, 52-54, 58, 59, 66, 69, 73, 76, 80, 82, 86, 87, 105, 107, 111, 114, 129, 130-133, epigraph before 134, 135, 137-139, 144, 157, 161, 162, 170, 181, 182, 223, 224, 227, 237, 239, 251, 252, 262, 267, 274, 276-278, 285, 287, 289, 292-294, 296, 300, 311, G4, G7, G15, G17, G19, G22, G42, G57
Object, presence and absence of: G7
Object, rationale of distinguished from rationale of sign: 131
Object, role of in semiosis: 145
Object as dissolving into cascades of signs: 129, G15
Object as presupposed to sign: 131, G15, 132
Object of a sign: G15
Object of perception as act of interpretation: G7
Object sometimes in principle imperceptible: 161
Object specifies: 107
Object/sign distinction: G15
Object/thing distinction: 52
Objectification: 9, 10, 72, 109, 121, 125, 147, 152, 244, 293, 309, G32
Objective: 2, 3, 5, 7-11, 15, 16, 19, 20, 22, 32, 34, 53, 54, 58, 59, 61-64, 66, 77, 79, 80, 92, 106-110, 112, 115, 118, 120, 121, 123, 125-129, epigraph before 134-136, 139-141, 143-145, 147, 148, 154-160, 162, 163, 165-167, 169, 172, 173, 177, 181, 182, 186, 189, 191, 193, 196, 197-202, 204, 214-219, 222, 223, 228, 230, 231, 234, 237, 239-244, 247, 252, 264, 265, 274, 280, 282, 284, 286-288, 292, 293, 295-300, 302-305, 307-310, G2, G13, G14, G15, G17, G19, G27, G51, G56 (*see also* Purely objective beings)
Objective, concept of as inclusive of but irreducible to subjective being: G2
Objective, partial coincidence of with physical: 120
Objective as applied to anthropology: 310

Objective as essential category for the experienced as such: 115
Objective as prospectively intersubjective: G17
Objective aspects experienced as not reducible to experience: 125
Objective being opposed to psychic depths of individual existence: 115
Objective causality: 79-80, 106-109, 112, 228, G13
Objective causality, how virtually operative within secondness: 112
Objective causality in culture: 108 (*see also* Causality, objective)
Objective causality in nature: 108, 112 (*see also* Causality, objective)
Objective cause: 79, 108, 219
Objective constructs as such are relational: 300-301
Objective content: 11
Objective creations mistaken for proper causes: 215
Objective elements: 20
Objective embodiment vs. essence of object embodied: 59, 62, 76
Objective entities as physical: 59
Objective equals whatever exists as known: 115
Objective exhibition, permanence of: 143
Objective possibilities not prefigured as such in biological heritage: 165
Objective protrusions of physical: 154, 181, 214
Objective relations: 8, 22, 139, 143, 148, 158-160, 166, 288, 302, 303, 308, 309, G56 (*see also* Relationship of signification)
Objective relations, conventionalizing of: 166
Objective relations are both physical and psychical: 303
Objective relations in their detachability: 158
Objective structure: 10, 11, 32, 34, 63, 120, 126, 140, 141, 148, 156, 158, 240-242, 282 (*see also* Structure)
Objective structure and physical relations: 63

Objective structure and zoösemiosis: 282
Objective structure as text: 141
Objective structures understandable but not perceptible as such: 140
Objective vagueness: 223-224, G37 (*see also* Indeterminacy)
Objective world: 54, 63, 115, 118, 128, epigraph before 134, 136, 143, 144, 145, 147, 162, 163, 165-167, 172, 177, 186, 189, 193, 200, 201, 222, 230, 234, 241-244, 247, 252, 264, 265, 274, 286, 292, 294-299, 309, G17
Objective world, subject as center of web comprising: 115
Objective world, why different for each species: 144
Objective world and physical world: 54, 91, 130
Objective world as subsumptive of the physical: 144, 154, 161, 234, 293
Objectivism, problematic of: 148, 151
Objectivist mode of knowledge: 148, 151
Objectivity: 34, 45, 53, 56, 60, 61, 129-131, 140, 145, 146, 149-151, 156-159, 163, 177, 179, 182, 185, 186, 197, 201, 203, 204, 216, 217, 221, 240, 245, 250, 253, 280, 292, G2, G3, G27
Objectivity and code as related notions: G2
Objectivity as central category for anthropology: 310-311, G2
Objectivity as stipulatable: 203
Objectivity, emergence of as different from the physical: 130
Objectivity, fabric of: 45
Objectivity, importance of revised notion for anthropology: G2
Objectivity in its proper being: 151
Objectivity key to argument of book: G2
Objectivity, need and importance of reorienting notion: G2
Objectivity proper to culture: 217
Objects: 10, 32-35, 37, 41, 43, 45, 48, 50-53, 55-59, 62, 75, 76, 110, 111, 113, 115, 121, 125, 127, 131, 133, epigraph before 134, 135, 140-144, 147, 152, 156, 157, 159, 161, 162, 164, 170, 201, 223, 225, 237, 241-245, 265, 267, 275, 289, 294, 296-298, 300, 301, 311, G14, G21, G37, G38, G48, G49, G53, G57
Objects, dependence of on semiosis: 131
Objects, neutral: 121, 127
Objects, origin of distinction between things which are objects and objects which are not things: 36-37, 39, 40, 52
Objects, understanding of which excludes a proper sensory instantiation: 289
Objects and representations: 55
Objects and signs: 34, 57, G15
Objects and things: 33, 57, G15
Objects as essentially vs. accidentally embodied: 115
Objects as self-representations vs. signs as other-representations: 57
Objects by definition independent of body: 59
Objects of human experience both textual and natural: 144
Objects signified though not present in the perceptible sign-vehicle: 140
Observation: 11, 198
Observer: 9, 73, 115, 125, 191, 211, 275, 307
Observer, standpoint of: 211Onion: 58, G15
Ontological relation: G21, G57, G61
Opacity of individuals: 7
Opera aperta (Eco): 232
Opinion: 35, 120
Opinion strangely prevailing amongst men: 35
Opposition of present-at-hand to ready-to-hand: 263, 296
Order of primitive intellectual concepts: G55
Original anthroposemiosic moment: 149
Ostension: 73, 86

Other: 2, 3, 12, 15, 22, 30-34, 36, 43, 48, 55, 56, 59, 64, 66, 69, 73, 75-77, 79, 84, 88, 92, 101, 111, 113, 115, 117-121, 130, 132, 133, 134, 138, 139, 143, 144, 150, 152, 154, 158, 159, 162, 164, 165, 170, 172, 181, 182, 186, 187, 189, 190, 195, 196, 200, 211, 215, 218, 221, 223, 226, 229, 246, 252, 254, 265, 271, 284, 285, 287, 288, 290, 292, 297, 301, 303, 306, 307, 309, G7, G17, G27, G31, G33, G34, G35, G37, G45, G47, G51, G57
Other as unique to anthroposemiosis: 182, 297 (*see also* Alterity; Otherness)
Otherness: 27, 44, 182, 285, 287, 288, 297, 309-310, G27
Otherness, arisal of notion: 297
Otherness as alternate subjectivity: 44
Otherness created within conspecificity: 288
Outlandish terms: G14, G17
Overlaps: 114, 118, 159, 226, 230
Over-modeling: 184
Oxford Dictionary: G1

Paleontologist: 108, 113, 307
Panpsychism: 98-99
Paradigm: 38, 245, 260, 261, G25
Paradox in notion of thing: 40, 50
Parliament: 247
Parmentier's objection: G28
Pars pro toto fallacy discussed: G38
Pars pro toto fallacy illustrated: 235, 256, 261
Parsimony semiotically considered: 188-189
Past: 45, 110, 125, 195, 196, 200, 211, 222, 224, 231, 267, 306, 307, G27, G33
Pelikan 120 pen: xiii
Peirce, contribution of to overall task of anthropology: 310
Peirce and Poinsot compared on problem of nonexistent signifieds: G1, G22
Percept: 130, 134, 155, 161, G15, G19, G37
Percept, function of: 130

Percept, use of term in Peirce analyzed (Santaella-Braga): G19
Percept distinguished from object: 130, G19
Percept functioning in manner of semiosis: 130
Perceptible: 25, 64, 74, 75, 112, 140, 141, 145, 163, 164, 194, 198, 201, 241, 295, 298, G51 (*see also* Imperceptible)
Perceptible dimension of sign-structure contrasted to text dimension: 145
Perceptibly objectifiable: 112
Perception: 20, 42, 43, 45, 69, 120, 121, 140, 157, 158, 201, 243, 285-288, 292-296, 298, 300, G7, G27, G37, G44
Perception and understanding, respective tasks of: 298
Perception in contrast to sensation: 45
Perceptive acquaintance: G7
Perceptual: 133, 138, 156, 159-161, 173, 193, 199, 233, 243, G15
Perceptual activity, sensory core of: G15
Perceptual apprehension: 146
Perceptual facts: G15
Perceptual field: 199
Perceptual items: 243
Perceptual judgment: G37
Perceptual link: 161
Perceptual mechanisms perceiving resemblance: 233
Perceptual universe: 138, G37 (*see also* Umwelt; Zoösemiosis)
Perceptually shared objectivity: 159, 173, 193
Perihermenias: 254
Perspective: 17, 18, 96, 186, 189, 200, 235, 252, 254, 256, 257, 259-262, 276, 277, 280, G17
Perspective opened by sign: 260
Perspective opened by sign developed from within: 261
Perspective proper to sign: 262
Perspectivization: 286
Phantasm: G58 (*see also* Fancy; Fantasy; Percept; Perception)
Pheme: G37

Phenomenal being: 133, G17, G35
Phenomenal being, in what it principally consists: 133, G35
Philosophy, classical modern: 117 (*see also* Cause, early and later modern notions of)
Philosophy, German: 117
Phlogiston: 215
Phoenix: G22
Physical: 2, 3, 6-9, 11, 14-16, 19, 20, 33, 35, 36, 38, 41, 43, 44, 50, 51, 53-55, 58-63, 65, 66, 73, 74, 76, 77, 79-81, 91, 93, 99, 101, 109, 110, 112, 115, 118-121, 122, 125, 127-130, 131-133, 135, 136, 140-145, 147, 154, 158, 162-167, 169, 170, 172, 181, 191, 194, 197-199, 201-206, 212, 214, 216-218, 223, 230, 234, 239-243, 252, 262, 263, 265, 272-274, 276, 278, 280, 282, 283, 288, 289, 293, 296, 299-304, 306-308, 310, G1, G2, G7, G15, G17-G19, G22, G25, G27, G30, G32, G33, G51, G57
Physical, medieval application of term to objects: 59
Physical as environmental: 115
Physical aspects of being external to culture in its proper being: 216
Physical being: 36, 53, 54, 61, 63, 65, 76, 80, 118-120, 123, 128, 145, 147, 172, 191, 194, 205, 206, 223, 240, 252, 278, 303, G1, G19, G57
Physical being as internally determined: 306, G9, G57
Physical being as modelable within the Umwelt: 128
Physical being as residue of an objectivity not only itself: 150
Physical being as transcendentally relative: G57
Physical being proper to objectivity vs. not: 53
Physical chemistry: 76
Physical constitution relative to technological vs. artistic creations: 143
Physical elements of phenomenal being: 133
Physical entities ex hypothesi bodiless: 62

Physical environment: 6, 8, 11, 19, 63, 76, 115, 118, 121, 130, 144, 163, 216, 230, 234, 274, 288, 289, 293, 296, 300, G7, G19, G25 (*see also* Thing; *contrast with* Object; Objective world; Umwelt; World of experience)
Physical environment as incorporated within Umwelt: 144, 154, 234, 293
Physical lining: 119
Physical relation: 63, 118, 125, 132, 166, 300, 302, 303, 308
Physical relation, how different from sign relation: 132
Physical structures, how made to be texts: 141
Physical vs. objective: 2, 7-9, 15, 19, 20, 26, 59, 61
Physical vs. objective structure: 52
Physical world: 54, 91, 115, 121, 133, 199, 306 (*see also* Environment; *contrast with* Objective world; Umwelt)
Physical world, how properly called physical: 115
Physical world as experienced is properly called objective: 115
Physical world exists within world of experience: 115
Physics: 74, 107, 125, 130, 163, 215, 253, 279, G51
Physics (Aristotle): G34
Physics of light waves: 74
Physiological, physiology: 74, G12
Physiology of optic nerves: 74
Physiosemiosis: 14, 19, 110, 169, 178, 181, 188, 229, 232, 282, G1 (*see further* Semiosis; Virtual semiosis)
Plane of dicisigns: 272
Planes of anthroposemiosis: 269
Planetarium: 125
Play as human: 145
Pleistocene: 113
Plethora: 234, 284
Pluto: 50
Poetic language: 172
Political: 9, 107, 199
Political science: 107

Political systems of Highland Burma: 199
Polyvalency: 199
Popular consciousness: 248, 257
Positivism: 188, 253
Positivism, heritage of: 253
Positivism, ideology: 188
Possibilities, possible: 10, 18, 22, 26, 27, 3059, 78, 79, 84, 112, 114, 116, 119, 120-123, 131, 133, 134, 139, 147-149, 151, 161-163, 165, 167, 169, 172, 190, 191, 194, 195, 197, 201, 202, 204, 210, 211, 214, 223, 228, 229, 238, 250, 263, 268, 269, 272, 274, 283, 310, G6, G8, G17, G27, G29, G38, G46, G51, G53, G57 (*see also* Impossible)
Possibilities, infinite: 238 (*see also* Infinite process)
Possibility of meaning: 269
Possible experiences: 123, 223
Possible illusion: 202
Possible world: 191, 197, 201, 300, G32
Postlinguistic: 13, 28, 122, 144, 151, 156, 164, 231, 287, 293, G3
Postlinguistic as tertiary modeling system: 122
Postlinguistic behaviors: 287
Postlinguistic codes of culture: 13, 28
Postlinguistic signs: 144
Postlinguistic structures: 122, 163
Postmodern: 191, Appendix
Potential inferences: 113
Potential infinity: 133
Practical, practice: 6, 56, 86, 134, 150, 151, 155, 220, 221, 227, 229, 251, 273, 275, 277, 287, G6, G44
Practical consequence of difference between sign-vehicle and sign-relation: 134
Practical effect distinguished from semiosic effect: 86, G1
Practical effects need not be semiosic: 86
Practical functions, functions of communication or knowledge not identical with: 150
Practical limits, theoretical importance of: 229

Praesidium: 247
Praeter: 25, 165, 191
Praeter-biological: 25
Praeter-objective character of experienced aspects of environment: 191
Praeterphysical means of correlating costs: 165
Pragmatic maxim: 86
Pragmaticism: G37, G40
Predication, prior conditions for: 293-294, G51
Predication, what makes possible: G51
Prejacent: 52, 115, 123, 126, 154, 172, 203, 205, 262, 275, 279, 283, G17, G20, G25, G39 (*see also* Reality)
Prejacent codes: G20
Prejacent context of German philosophy: G17
Prejacent given: 275 (*see also* Given)
Prejacent physical being as derivative from Umwelt: 123
Prejacent physical dimensions or elements: 52, 115, 123, 126, 154, 172, 203, 205, 262, 275, 279, 283, G17, G25, G39
Prescission, prescision: 42, 43, 177, 190, G51
Prescission compared with Latin idea of *abstractio negativa*: G51
Prescission of code anthroposemiotically taken: 177
Prescission of sensation from perception: 42-43
Prescission of the role of ideas as signs: 190
Present: *see* Here and now
Present-at-hand: 263
Present-at-hand vs. ready-to-hand, answer to Heidegger's question concerning: 263, 296
Present being virtually signifies past and future: 110
Present in general: 293
Presto chango: 55
Prewitt's attempted reduction of Johansen's pyramid: 183
Prewitt's critique of Johansen/Deely model: 183

Primary modeling system: 120
Primate social interaction: 122
Primum cognitum: 293, 296, 308, G47, G48, G51, G53 (*see also* Fundamental intellectual awareness)
Primum cognitum, difficulty of question concerning: 291
Primum cognitum, Latin expression for ground of species-specifically human apprehension: 293
Primum cognitum, why not a predicate: 294, G48-50
Primum cognitum includes mind-dependent relations: G52 (*see also* First intention)
Primum cognitum intellectus is neither essence nor existence: G53
Primum intelligible, visibile, audibile: 290 (*see also Primum cognitum*)
Primum mobile: G33
Principle: 79, 80, 84, 88, 102, 103, 112, 114, epigraph before 134, 155, 161, 162, 167, 194, 198, 229, 287, 294, G1, G11, G14, G21, G35, G47
Principle as different from cause: 102, G11
Principles of dimanation: G1
Principles underlying difference between action of signs and action of bodies: 79-80
Private: 115, 152, 164, 166, G17
Private as illusory: 115
Private ideas: 152, 166 (*see also* Idea, psychological sense of; Intraorganismic factor)
Private/public as matter of degree: 115
Processus ad infinitum absolute repugnat, primary import of maxim: 211-212; secondary meaning: 214
Processus ad infinitum absolute repugnat, scholastic maxim or adage: 206 (*see also* Infinite process)
Productive causality: 79, 81, 91, 92
Progress toward the infinite: 86, 138
Proper being of Umwelt as enculturated: 198
Proper function of anthropos: G60
Proper functions of a species: G60

Proper object defined: G51
Proportion of object with power: 294, G48-50
Proposition, propositional: 10, 113, 182, 223, 271, G15, G32, G37, G59
Proposition of existence: G37
Propositions and verification: 10
Propositions express belief: G59
Propositions ordinarily a generalization from perceptual facts: G15
Propositional plane, uniqueness of: 271
Prospective: 19, 135, 174, 193, 205, 226, 229, 239, 240, 250, 252, 257, 294, G17, G33, G53 (*see also* Virtual semiosis)
Prospective intelligibility: G53
Prototypical causality: 107
Protrusions: 122, 154, 214, G15
Provenance: 156, 166, 199, 242
Psychic, psychological: 9, 77, 80, 83, 98, 107, 108, 115, 116, 129, 166, 194, 198, 201, 202, 234, 303, 309, G2, G12, G15, G27, G37 (*see further* Subjective; Subjectivity)
Psychic depths of individual existence as one form of the two forms of subjective being: 115
Psychology: 98, 107, Appendix
Pterodactyl: 108, 306
Ptolemaic system: 125
Public, publicly: 158, 159, 165, 166, 193, 196, 201, 245
Public as real: 115
Pumpkins: 53, 76
Pure possibilities: 78 (*see also* Firstness)
Purely objective beings: 53, 62, 110, 126, 136, 147, 307, G4, G17 (*see also* Objective being, Objectivity; *contrast with* Environment, Physical being, Thing)
Purely objective phenomena: 126 (*see cross-references under* Purely objective beings)
Puzzle of culture: 216
Pyramid: 179-181, 183, 184, 185, 187, 189, 268, 270
Pyramid of anthroposemiosis (after Johansen): 180, 182, 268

Quantum level: 163
Quarks: 125
Question-begging: G44
Quiddity: 299, 305, 308, G9, G47, G49, G50, G51, G53, G54, G59 (*see also* Essence)

Rationale unifying all signs: 135
Reading: 74
Ready-to-hand: 263
Real: 35, 46, 58, 97, 117, 115, 127, 137-138, 144, 145, 172, 190, 198, 235, 300, 301, 308, G4, G9, G15, G17, G20, G22, G25, G35, G42, G51, G57
Real, accessible as entities: G25
Real, idea of: 190-191
Real and unreal as physical objectified and purely objective: 145
Real universe: 146
Realism: 162, 261, 265, G17
Realism, naive: 162
Realism-idealism debate: 261
Reality: 16, 19, 59, 66, 102, 123, 128, 144, 146, 147, 152, 156, 160, 185, 191, 212, 235, 263-265, 275, 286, 288, 297, 302, 308, G15, G17, G19, G23, G24, G25, G27, G30
Reality, a paradigmatic meaning of: G25
Reality, accessibility of: G25
Reality, ancient paradigm for: G25
Reality, diverse notions of: G24
Reality, idea of is original idea of otherness: 288 (*see also* Physical World; Thing)
Reality, origin of idea of as physical being: 146, G23
Reality, postmodern idea of: 191
Reality, reductive idea of: 263
Reality, semiotic idea of: 191
Reality, various senses of: 275
Reality as a common thought: 146
Reality as a product of semiotic convergence: 146-147
Reality as anthroposemiotically unique conception: 152, 297 (*see further* Thing)
Reality as mind-independent being: 191
Reality as prejacent physical environment: G24
Reality as species-specific objective world: 264
Reality as text of species-specifically human experience: 191
Reality as transcendence of boundary of Umwelt as purely objective: 128
Reality as what does not reduce to our experience of it: 147, 297
Reality is also a word we must learn to use: G23
Reality, meaning of: G23
Reality of direct experience: 275 (*see also* Umwelt)
Reality of experience: 19, 151
Realm: 78, 81, 87, 115, 125, 197, 217, 221, 228, 234, 275, G17
Reciprocal preconditions of anthroposemiosis and zoösemiosis: 195
Reconstruction: 143, 307 (*see also* Remodeling)
Reducible: *see* Irreducible
Reducible to experience: 125, 147 (*see also* Purely objective beings)
Reductionistic: 191
Reflexive: 9, 216, 221, 253, 278, 280, 286, G50
Reflexive element of critical control: 9, G50
Reflexive methodology: 216, 221, 280
Reflexivity and ethnocentrism: 286
Reflexivity of Lebenswelt: 252, 278
Reiteration: 155
Relations, relationship: 3-8, 13, 15, 16, 22, 25, 39, 55, 63, 65-69, 73, 74, 87, 96, 107-110, 112-116, 118, 125, 130-133, epigraph before 134-141, 143, 144, 146, 148, 153, 157-166, 172, 173, 177, 182, 190, 193-195, 201, 217, 218, 224, 227, 234, 235, 237-241, 243-245, 251, 253, 262-265, 268, 277, 287, 288, 292, 293, 295, 296, 298-304, 306-310, G17, G18, G19, G21, G43, G47, G52, G56, G57, G61
Relations, abstract quality central to phenomenon of: 133, 138

Relations, being of distinguishable from sign-vehicle and signified: 139
Relations, common denominator of all: 133
Relations, consequence of abstract quality of for zoösemiosis: 133
Relations, entitative character of: 304
Relations, equivalent in the sign: 144
Relations, how different in culture: 218
Relations, how objective ones do not preclude physical ones: 129
Relations, idea of: 238
Relations, network of: 140
Relations, proper being of as imperceptible or insensible: 138
Relations, quintessential point concerning: 304
Relations, real and unreal: 144, 300
Relations, reliance of anthropology on: 287
Relations according to the way relation has being: G61
Relations and continuance in being: 4
Relations as cause of knowables: 15-16
Relations as essential to existence: 3, 5
Relations constitutive of a literary work: 143
Relations constitutive of a technological artifact: 143
Relations is sustenative of being: 3
Relations made foundation of other relations: 138, 218 (*see also* Infinite process)
Relations of an object to itself: 293
Relations of an object to itself, requirements for formation of: 293
Relations of renvoi: 73 (*see also* Renvoi)
Relations of signification: *see* Relationship of signification
Relations of "standing for": 65 (*see also* Renvoi)
Relations vs. things related: 300

Relationship of signification: 25, 69, 133, epigraph before 134, 134, 141, 143, 153, 164, 237
Relationship of signification exercised vs. known: 137
Relationship of signification in natural signs distinct from cause-effect relation: 69
Relative autonomy of meaning: 199
Religious sects: G24
Remodeling: 124, 126, 129, 173, 265, 274
Remodeling the world: 124, 126, 274
Renvoi: 66, 72, 73, 132, 251, 273-275, 277, 280
Renvoi, aspect of acquired only by relations in experience: 277
Renvoi, repetition of: 72
Repetition of renvois: 72
Replica: G22
Representation: 51, 55-58, 69-71, 114, 122, 127, 184, 186, 187, 296, G4, G15, G35
Representation, mental: 69-71
Representation relation: 114
Representations and objects: 55
Republic (Plato): 126
Resemblance, underlying mechanisms for perception of: 233
Residual oppositions: 200
Restructure: 63, 160, 234, 237, 243 (*see also* Objective world; Remodeling)
Reversibility: 161
Reversibility as unique to anthroposemiosis: 161
Reversible associations and codes: 161
Rhematic indexical sinsign: G22
Rhetoric: 234
Ritual symbolism in the contemporary politics of academe: G14
Rock: 53, 59, 65, G57
Rome: 123
Root: 25, 136, 195, 214, 233, 234, 258, G44
Rule and code: 168
Russian formalism: G39

Sacred remains: 151

Saturn: 50
Saussurean tradition: 178, 178, 310
Science: 2, 3, 7, 9, 17, 18, 74, 83, 106, 107, 120, 121, 125-127, 148, 151, 154, 191, 202, 205, 206, 215-217, 221, 234, 247-254, 258, 267, 273, 275-280, 283, 309, 311, G33, G38, G51, G57
Science, foundations for: 154, 250, G38
Science, "hard": 125, 191, 217, 247
Science, human: see Human sciences
Science, imperialism of: 253
Science, modeling aspect of: 125, 128
Science, natural 2, 18, 121, 125, 202, 205, 248, 249, 251, 252, 253, 267, 277, 280, G208
Science, origin of: 128
Science, social: 216, 250
Science, task of: 309
Science, whole of begins from idea of otherness: 309
Science, zoösemiotic basis for: 120
Science and semiotics: 250-252, 278
Science as anthroposemiotic enterprise: 121
Science as practice: 151
Science as subspecific to the human Umwelt: 128
Science as transcendence of biological functional cycle: 121, 128
Science contrasted to doctrine: 254
Science of singularity: 7
Sciences, first among: 253
Scientia: 7, 125, 254, G47, G58
Scientia as generic term for intellectual knowledge: 125
Scientia contrasted with *doctrina*: 254
Scientific: 17, 18, 111, 120, 127, 128, 162, 205, 206, 234, 244, 251, 260, 273, 275, 281, 307, 311, G14, G24, G51, G57
Scientific intellectual abstraction: 111
Scientific practice: 251
Scientific proof: 260
Scientific theories: 127
Scotists: 42
Second intentions are a subset of mind-dependent relations: G56

Secondary modeling system: 121
Secondness: 24, 38, 60, 78, 81, 112, 130, 147, 197, 215, 217, 221, 229, 233, 282, 310 (*see also* Interaction)
Secondness, dynamical processes of: 112
Secondness as ally of scientific understanding: 215
Segmented discourse model (Prewitt): 183, 187
Self: 16, 55, 57, 155, 181, 155, 224, 263. 271, 287, G15, G30 (*see also* Semiotic self)
Self, assimilation of other to and conversely: 287
Self, future, command to: 155
Self, previous, present, and future: G30
Self, reach of: G30
Self, relation of to semiosis: 224
Self as an asymmetrical sign: 224
Self as influenced by threefold structure of sign: 224
Self is an asymmetrical sign series: 224
Self-control, logic and ethics the two forms of: G30
Self-evident: G17
Self-representation: 55, 57, G15 (*see also* Object)
Self-representation and signification: G15
Seme: G37
Semeion: 70
Semeiosy: G4 (synonym for "action of signs", *q.v.*)
Semiological, semiology: 165, 232, 247, 258, 310, G30
Semiological surplus: see Semiotic surplus
Semiological system: 165, 172, 181, 247, 269
Semiosic: 20, 71, 86, 113, 149, 167, 168, 199, 233, 235, 265, G5, G7, G27, G57
Semiosic effect: 86
Semiosic nature of anthropos: 168
Semiosic networks: 20
Semiosis: 10, 13, 14, 18, 19, 20, 26, 48, 57, 77-80, 82, 84, 86-89, 91-93, 96-99, 103, 110-115, 129-133, 138, 145, 154, 165, 167, 168, 170,

172, 176, 178, 189, 214, 217, 223, 224, 226-229, 231, 232, 234, 238-240, 250-253, 256, 258, 260, 264-266, 269-274, 277, 283, 288, 303, G1, G2, G4, G5, G6, G8, G21, G29, G30, G57 (*see also* Anthroposemiosis; Biosemiosis; Physiosemiosis; Phytosemiosis; Virtual semiosis; Zoösemiosis)

Semiosis, accelerated by advent of life and of cognition: 110, 239

Semiosis, causality proper to: 115

Semiosis, character of as dynamic and (syncategorematically) infinite: 224

Semiosis, cultural: 178, 239

Semiosis, dependence on another as constitutive of: 88

Semiosis, difference between actual and virtual: 113

Semiosis, difference on which depends: 57

Semiosis, distinctive aspect of human emphasized: 138

Semiosis, extrinsic formal cause in objective sense a peripheral topic outside discussion of: 107, G13

Semiosis, first phenomenon of: 130

Semiosis, highest achievement of in physical environment: 274

Semiosis, how unlimited and how not (Eco): G5

Semiosis, in what sense unlimited: 265

Semiosis, literary: 26

Semiosis, most interesting case of: 265

Semiosis, Peirce's view on as telic: 97-99

Semiosis, processes at work in universe at large: 114

Semiosis, scope of: 163, 272

Semiosis, sense in which limited: G33

Semiosis, understanding as a form of: 89

Semiosis, understanding of: 154

Semiosis, virtual: *see* Virtual, *esp.* Virtual semiosis

Semiosis and deconstruction: 83

Semiosis and life: 111

Semiosis and limits: 226-228

Semiosis and progress toward the infinite: 86

Semiosis and the understanding of culture: 217

Semiosis as assimilative: 87, 167, 196, 229, 248, G47

Semiosis as constructive: 234

Semiosis as distinctively human: 151 (*see also* Anthroposemiosis)

Semiosis as interface between nature and culture: 103

Semiosis as outside order of productive causality: 112

Semiosis as spatio-temporal process: 110

Semiosis contrasted with dynamical interaction: G4

Semiosis in physical nature prior to life: 130

Semiosis likened to an interminable chain: 114 (*see also* Unlimited semiosis)

Semiosis of nature: 266

Semiosphere: 283

Semiotic: 9, 13, 16, 18, 19, 21, 22, 24-26, 79, 87, 97, 106, 115, 122, 136, 139, 141, 146, 147, 165, 166, 169, 179, 191, 195, 199, 200, 213, 214, 218, 224, 227, 228, 232, 234, 235, 254, 255, 258, 260, 261-263, 265, 269, 271, 274, 275, G13, G17, G24, G26, G27, G28, G31, G39, G42

Semiotic anthropology: 224

Semiotic as introduced by Locke: 235

Semiotic competence: 26

Semiotic consciousness: 214

Semiotic convergence: 146-147, G24

Semiotic net or web: 4, 15, 18-19

Semiotic notion of experience: 22

Semiotic object of investigation: 274

Semiotic objectivity: 9; anthroposemiotic: 179; zoösemiotic: 178

Semiotic point of view, what is proper to: 255

Semiotic pre-eminence of embodied linguistic elements: 165

Semiotic reality: 275

Semiotic sensitivity: 200

Semiotic subjectivity embodies as-

pects of both psychic and physical subjectivity: G27
Semiotic surplus: 165, 231, 246, 247, 269
Semiotic triangle, point of: G29
Semiotic viewpoint, first systematic expression of: 254
Semiotic web: 115
Semiotic webs, entanglement of: 115, 118
Semiótica Básica: ix
Semiotician: 1, 68, 74
Semiotics: 1, 13, 18, 26, 57, 68, 71, 74, 78, 83, 88, 103, 110, 116, 121, 132, 165, 168, 178, 179, 181, 195, 234, 237, 247-249, 252-254, 256-260, 262, 265, 269, 272, 277-280, G2, G4, G8, G12, G14, G28, G30, G38, G39
Semiotics, arc of: 257
Semiotics, doctrine or theory: 234
Semiotics, place marked out for: 272
Semiotics, scope of proper possibilities: 272
Semiotics, shift from glottocentrism: 237
Semiotics, studies sign-vehicles *as such*: 74
Semiotics, why in conflict with traditional curricular divisions: 249
Semiotics, why not confinable to cultural analyses: 103
Semiotics and deconstruction: 83
Semiotics and morality: G30
Semiotics and science: 247-254
Semiotics as a matrix: 252
Semiotics as a perspective: 252
Semiotics as field of conflicting philosophical definitions: 278
Semiotics concerned with matrix of knowledge: 279
Semiotics in relation to science and humanities: 247-254
Semiotics misunderstood from within: 256
Semiotics misunderstood from without: 256
Semiotics naively equated with study of codes: 258
Semiotics not identical with structuralism: 259

Semiotics of texts integrally pursued: 272
Sensation: 41-43, 45, 120, 296, 298, 300, G44
Sensation, channel of technically prescissed: 43
Sensation analytically prescissed from perception: 42 (*see further* Prescission)
Sensation and dynamic object: G7
Sensation and the fabric of objectivity: 45
Sense (powers of): 41, 47, 119, 128, 133, 137-138, 156, 164, 243, 289, 292, 294, 298-300, G15, G44, G45
Sense, contrast with intellect: 289, G45
Sense-intellect contrast exaggerated: G44
Sense-intellect distinction denied: 289, G45
Sensory core: G15
Series: 16, 131, 173, 206, 208, 209, 211, 223, 239, 308, G33, G35 (*see further* Infinite process)
Series, horizontal: G33
Series, infinite: G33 (*see also* Infinite series)
Series, vertical: G33
Series of essentially subordinated causes, how constituted: G33 (*see also* Causes, sustaining)
Series vertical and horizontal, metaphorical sense of: G33
Servitude: 283
Sharability of ideas: 158-160
Shift: 72, 223, 237, 265, 275, G33
Shifting boundary between objects and things: 223
Shuttlecocks: 243
Sicily: 199
Sign: 25, 30, 32, 34, 64-73, 79, 87, 88, 92, 110, 112-114, 116, 129, 131-133, 134, 137, 144, 145, 151, 153, 160, 164, 170, 171, 178, 181, 185, 186, 190, 193, 195, 223-227, 237, 249, 260, 261, 265, 273, 283, G3, G4, G7, G15, G18, G21, G22, G35, G40, G42, G56, G61
Sign, being cognized or known not essential to: G18

Sign, body vs. soul of: 111-112
Sign, dyadic notion of: 178
Sign, formal constitutive of existence as: 65
Sign, fundamental problem of: 130
Sign, how it functions: 129
Sign, indifference of as such: 144
Sign, literary: 260
Sign, proper significate outcome of: 67; always objective: 92, 93
Sign, rationale of in physical environment: G18
Sign, required broader conception of: 272, G41
Sign, role of the idea as: 190 (see also Otherness)
Sign, soul of: 111, G15
Sign, three references of: G35
Sign, what it essentially is: 111
Sign, what is required for: 129
Sign, why not itself something directly appearing: 32, 132
Sign action: 261 (see also Action of signs)
Sign as different from both objects and things: 132
Sign as doubly related: 65
Sign as having existence only in objective becoming of others: 64
Sign as role of "standing for": 73
Sign as something representative (sign-vehicle) can be productive: 112
Sign as stipulable contrasted with sign as stipulated: 160
Sign at heart of experienced objects: G42
Sign contrasted with sign-vehicle: 74
Sign experienced linguistically: 25 (see also Code; Convention; Conventional; Stipulated sign)
Sign formally considered: 112 (see also Signs, being proper to)
Sign foundationally considered: 112 (see also Sign-vehicle)
Sign fundamentally: 132, 239 (see also Sign-vehicle)
Sign presupposes correlative object: 131-132

Sign relation as three-termed: 66
Sign relation differentiated from bare physical relation: 132
Sign structure: 151
Sign use, essence of language regarding: 237
Sign-vehicle: 25, 69, 74, 92, 108, 109, 112, 121, 132, 133, 134, 136, 139, 153, 157, 158, 201, 203, 237, 243
Sign-vehicles as bodies of signs: 112
Sign-vehicles as perceptible not always correlated with perceptible significates: 138, 161, 241-243
Sign-vehicle is sign fundamentally rather than formally: 132
Signification: 24, 29
Signification, relation of: see Relationship of signification
Signification is active power to establish connection between objects: 111
Signifier: 156, 237 (see also Sign-vehicle)
Signs: 13, 17, 20, 24, 26, 29-35, 51, 55-58, 69, 71, 72, 74-82, 87, 91, 92, 96, 98, 100, 107, 109-114, 116, 117, 129, 131, 133. epigraph before 134, 134-136, 139-142, 144, 145, 150, 151, 155, 156, 161-163, 166, 170, 224, 227, 230, 232-235, 237, 241, 243-245, 251-253, 258, 272, 277, 283, 295, 310, G2, G3, G6, G7, G15, G17, G21, G22, G25, G40, G45, G56, G57, G61
Signs, being proper to: 116
Signs, communitarian purpose of: 190
Signs, conventional in fullest sense: 164
Signs, how virtual before actual: 113
Signs, indexical dimension of: 233
Signs, instability in objects as: 33, 34, 58
Signs, material representation as foundational to: 112
Signs, practical functions of: 149-150
Signs, superstructural relation as formally constitutive of: 112
Signs, threefold structure of influences contour of self: 224

Signs, uniqueness of: 32
Signs, universe perfused with: G40
Signs, virtual and actual compared: 113
Signs, what is true of in all Umwelts: 144
Signs as imperceptible: 74
Signs as indefinite series within objects: 131
Signs beneath objects: 131
Signs contrasted with perceptible entities: 74
Signs have their being in power of intermediary: 11
Signs in relation to objects and things: 32-34
Signs reducible to perceptible associations vs. to codes as imperceptible: 141
Signum ad placitum: 245 (*see further* Code; Convention; Conventional)
Silver bullet: 54
Similarity: 69, 84, 156, 190, 233, 237, 267, G1, G5, G37
Similarity as conventionalizable: G37
Similarity distinct from relationship of signification: 69, G5
Simultaneity of objects with semiosis: 131
Slavery: 123, 283
Soap bubbles: 119
Social science: 216, 250
Social interaction linguistically mediated: 122 (*see further* Interaction)
Social practice: 151
Social signs, natural, associative, and manipulative: 135
Social world: 148
Socialization: 27, 141, 189, 287
Solipsism: 85, 184, 190
Solomonic segmentation: 183, 185
Soul of a sign: 111, G15
Sounds signifying nothing: 109
Source of infinite process as objective phenomenon: 138, 218
Soviet thinkers: 121
Soviet Union: G24
Sparta: 123
Spatio-temporal entities: 92

Speaking collective, individual member of: G27
Species-specific: 9, 12, 13, 19, 25, 117, 120, 123, 129, 136, 151, 153, 156-158, 160, 163, 165, 174, 177, 189, 191, 201, 229, 232-234, 237, 241, 243, 245, 252, 262, 264, 274, 287, 290, 292, 293, G3, G21
Species-specific action: 12
Species-specific form of objectivity: 156
Species-specific objective worlds: 252 (*see also* Umwelt)
Specifying causality: 106-107
Specifying form: 79
Speculative: 273, 275
Sphere of the moon: G33
Spheres and epicycles: G33
Spiral of semiosis: 224
Spirit world: 62
Spirits: 60, 76
Square root: 136
Stars: 59
Stimulus, physical, extinction of: 121 (*see also* Functional cycle)
Stipulable, stipulability: epigraph before 134, 160, 161, 164, 166, 185, 193, 203, 230, 232, 237, 240, 242, 243, 295, G3, G20, G21
Stipulable sign as element of experience prior to conventional sign as stipulated: 160
Stipulable sign in the fullest sense realized in conventional sign: 164
Stipulability as a source of unlimited semiosis: 243
Stipulability as ground of language: G21
Stipulability becomes source in its own right of new sign-relations: 243
Stipulability of signs: 185
Stipulable sign: 164
Stipulable sign contrasted with stipulated sign: 160, 203
Stipulable signs, how they arise: 134
Stipulable signs, proper being of: 167

Stipulatable: 203, G20 (*see also* Stipulable)
Stipulated signs: 156, 160, 193, 203, G56, G61
Stipulated signs have the same rationale as any other sign, namely, relation to a signified: G56 (*see also* Relationship of signification)
Stipulated signs logically posterior to experience of signs as stipulable: 160, 164 (*see also* Anthroposemiosis; Awareness)
Stop-sign: 73, 132
Strategy: 234, 237
Strip-mining: 169
Structural peculiarity of language: 165
Structuralism: 259
Structuralist: 248, 257, G5
Structure, structures: 3, 4, 8, 10, 32, 34, 35, 50, 53, 61, 63, 71, 75, 92, 99, 101, 111, 115, 120, 122, 123, 126, 140, 141-145, 147, 148, 149, 151, 156, 158, 164, 165, 173, 174, 197, 205, 222-223, 224, 231, 234, 240, 242, 263, 273, 279, 282, 287, 294, 296, 298-300, 306-309, G19, G24
Structure, artistic: 143
Structure, cognitive: 296 (*see also* Umwelt)
Structure, Darwinian: 174, 240, 242 (*see also* Biological heritage)
Structure, environmental experienced: 147, 205, G19
Structure, hierarchical: 142
Structure, Lamarckian: 174, 242 (*see also* Lebenswelt)
Structure, objective freedom of: 145
Structure, objective superordinate to physical: 241
Structure, everyday experience and: 279 (*see also* Loose ends; Loose-endedness)
Structure, physical instantiating objectivity: 53
Structure as encoded: 242
Structure as model: 308 (*see also* Essence)
Structure as prospectively definable: 294, 298, 299 (*see also* Essence)
Structure as sensible pattern of relative intelligibility: 298
Structure embodying objectified physical relations: 63, 115, 147
Structure of experience and individual: 197
Structure of experience different zoösemiotically and anthroposemiotically: 263
Structure of experience and of nature as relatively independent variables: 61, 234
Structure of objectivity: 149
Structure of objectivity enabling exaptation of language to speech: 149
Structure of particular objects a mixture of mind-dependent and mind-independent relations: 162, 296
Structure of Umwelt and biological heritage: 296 (*see also* Biological heritage; Umwelt)
Structure publicly accessible: 158
Structures, communal: G24
Structures, formal: 92, 101
Structures, linguistic: 156
Structures, material: 75, 92, 99, 299
Structures, mobile interpretive: 273
Structures, postlinguistic: 28, 151, 156, 164, 231, 287
Structures as expressions of relationship: 4
Structures as medium of action: 4
Structures independent of experience: 205
Structures objective and physical partially coincident: 120, 144, 234
Structures of civilization as postlinguistic: 164
Structures of environment and infinite process: 222 (*see also* Infinite process)
Structures of environment internally determined in order of physical being: 306 (*see also* Physical being; Physical Environment; Thing)
Structures of experience and structures of physical nature relatively independent variables: 61, 147

Structures understandable but not perceptible: 140 (*see also* Imperceptible)
Style: 105, 108, 233, 251, G37
Style as instance of extrinsic formal causality: 108
Stylize: 233, G37
Sub-codes: 200
Subject matter: 28, 107, 228, G14
Subject matter of critick: 196
Subject-object dichotomy rendered nugatory: G17
Subjective, subjective being: 9, 91-93, 115, 152, 157, 159, 164, 166, 167, 193, 228, 239, 301, 302, 310, G14, G17, G19, G47
Subjective, sign as objectifying the: 129
Subjective (physical or psychical): 19, 26
Subjective being: 91, 92, 93
Subjective being is transcendentally relative: G57
Subjective factors assimilated to public life: 166
Subjective-objective, misleading modern opposition: G14, G17
Subjective-objective as false dichotomy: 115
Subjective-objective in Kant: G14, G17
Subjectivity: 9, 44, 53, 55, 62, 108, 129, 167, 194, 198, 201, 202, 309, G2, G27
Subjectivity, dual dimension of: 197-198, 202 (*see also* Semiotic objectivity)
Subjectivity, physical existence as basic mode of: 19, 26, 53, 54, 62
Subjectivity, psychical: 129
Subsequent interpretants: G37
Substance: 5, 92, 293, 294, 297, G47, G49, G51
Substance as the being proper to individuals: 294
Substance vs. individual subsistent: 5
Substructure: 173
Superstructure: 112, 123, 173, 174, 189, 249
Sun: 232, G34
Superordinate: 24, 109, 119, 241, 288

Suprasubjective: 234
Surplus: 165, 231, 246, 247, 269 (*see also* Semiotic surplus)
Syllogism: 227
Symbiosis: 150
Symbol, symbolic: 69, 71, 145, 220, 232, 233, 271, 287, 293, G14, G16, G33
Symbolic: 220, 232, 233, G16
Symbolic insofar as species-specifically anthroposemiotic: 233
Symbolicity: 233
Symbolization, symbolized: 271, G33
Symbolon: 71
Symbols, postlingusitic: 287, 293
Syncategorematic: 222, 226, 229, G33 (*see also* Asymptotic)
Synchronic: 230, G33
Synechistic consequence of language: 201
Synonyms for extrinsic formal causality: 107
System: 21, 24, 25, 28, 30, 121, 122, 125-127, 139, 145, 148, 161, 164, 165, 191, 195, 198, 199, 209, 214, 218, 220, 225, 225, 226, 228, 232, 247, 249, 263, 265, 270, 271, 283, 298, 308, G2, G5, G14, G31, G33
System of signs: 30
System of contrastive relations: 263
Systematic ordering in historical events involving human experiences: 199

Tartu: 21, 24
Taxonomies: 195
Teaching language to apes: 233
Technology, origin of: 128
Teleology: 94, 97, 98 (*see also* Final causality; *also* Teleonomy)
Teleonomy: 95
Telescope: 50
Terminal cleverness: 84, 89
Terminate: 114, 133, 138, 141, 262, G1, G19, G46 (*see also* Terminus)
Terminology, ethics of: 107, G14
Terminus: G19 (*see also* Terminate)
Terminus of relation distinguished from fundament or ground: 133
Text, texts: 30, 36, 53, 59, 76, 84, 85, 89, 108, 114, 113, epigraph

before 134, 139-145, 151, 153, 156, 172, 190, 191, 201, 228, 244, 246, 252, 261, 267, 269, 272, G8, G21, G42
Text, characteristic trait of: G21
Text, difference which makes possible: 139
Text, what creation of requires: 145
Text, why authorial control of is limited: G8
Text, why the written word serves as primary analogate for: 143
Text as a freely structured objectivity: 145
Text as sign-network: 76
Text not reducible to world of language: 172
Texts, actually existent only in Lebenswelt: 139
Texts, how existent: 140
Texts, not only literary: 141
Texts and physical structures: 141
Textual embodiment: 59
Textuality: 25, 30, epigraph before 134, 136, 151, 157, 161, 163, 172, 173, 179, 191, 195, 228, 231, 240, 245, 247, 258, 260, 262, 269, 289, G28
Textuality, what it means: 240
Textuality as species-specific form of objectivity: 156, 245
Textuality as specifically literary is not adequate object of semiotics: 262
Textuality defined: 163
Textuality is proximate difference in perceptual Umwelt as genus: 163
Texture: 165, 166, 252, 260
Texture of human experience: 166, 260
Thematic: 285, 286
Theoretical importance of status of formal cause as also a principle: 103
Thing, things: 31, 35-58, 60, 64-66, 73, 75, 76, 87, 88, 90, 102, 110, 113, 115, 120, 130-133, epigraph before 134, 147, 150, 197, 201, 217, 223, 291, 293, 294, 297, 298, 300, 301, 305, G4, G12, G15, G19, G21, G22, G27, G35, G47, G51, G56, G57, G61

Thing, notion of divided: 37, 50
Thing, original conception of: 35, 37, 38, 39, 42, 47, 52, 54, 60
Thing, theoretical issue for anthropos only: 56
Thing as concrete particular: 39, 46
Thing becomes object: 130
Thing experienced vs. object of experience: 52
Thing-object distinction: 130
Things accessible only through objects: G57
Things and representations: 51
Things and stories: 150
Things as self-representations: 55
Things influenced and not influenced by anthroposemiosis: 49-50
Things simply vs. objectified aspects of things: 56
Third world (Popper): G2
Thirdness: 71, 78, 110, 147, 163, 169, 215, 217, 219, 222, 223, 229, 233, 261, 282, 310
Thirdness, breakdown of: 229
Thirdness, final redoubt of: 282
Thirdness, new magnitudes of: 110
Thirdness of anthroposemiosis: 222
Thought-sign, three correlates of: G35
Token: 39, 224, 266
Tombstone: G57
Traces (indexical signs): 211, 231
Transcendence: 138, 151, 202, 234, 252, 278
Transcendence of functional cycle: 121
Transcendent, transcendental: 4, 8, 39, 60, 93, 99, 121, 130, 138, 151, 202, 234, 252, 272, 278, 283, 286, 311, G51, G57
Transcendental relatives explained (Baer): G57
Transcendentality implicit in notion of thing: 60
Trans-specific: 121
Trap of what is not: 46
Triadic: 89, 91, 176, 181, G1, G4, G29
Triadic planes: 181
Triadic relation as essential to signifying: 66, 68, 89

Triadic relations: 15, 66, 74, 112, 181, 132
Trichotomy as essential for understanding experience: 115
Trobriand islanders: 28
Truth, approach to necessarily communitarian and asymptotic: 223
Truth, the: G37, G40
Tychism: 209, 211, G34
Type: 2, 10, 15, 17, 32, 34, 39, 66, 73, 74, 75, 92, 98, 106, 108, 109, 110, 246, 275, 293, 307, G43
Type/token distinction: 39

Umwelt: 21, 25, 116-130, 139, 143, 144, 146, 147, 151, 153-156, 159, 160, 163-165, 166, 171-174, 177, 179, 181, 185, 186, 191, 193, 194, 197, 198, 199, 234, 237, 239-241, 243, 251, 252, 263, 264, 274, 277, 278, 282, 286, 293, 295, 293, G2, G17, G19, G26 (*see also* Objective, Objective world)
Umwelt, common denominator of every: 241
Umwelt, heart of difference between anthroposemiotic and zoösemiotic: 139, 154, 156
Umwelt, limits in J. von Uexküll's notion of: 129, G17
Umwelt, notion of remodeled by semiotics: 129, G17
Umwelt, problem of translating: 120
Umwelt, problem of translating the term: 120, *esp.* G17
Umwelt and Heideggerean Being-in-the-World: G25
Umwelt as actual world of everyday life: 123
Umwelt as codified linguistically: G25
Umwelt as modeling system: 283
Umwelt as objectively containing physical aspects as such of the environment: 144, 154, 161, 234, 293
Umwelt as primary modeling system: 121 (*but see* 127)
Umwelt as prospectively human: 174
Umwelt as reality of direct species-specific experience: 128
Umwelt as species-specifically determined: 121, 163
Umwelt as uniquely human: 120
Umwelt externally considered: 128
Umwelt internally considered: 128
Umwelt irreducible to physical as such: 119
Umwelt partially inclusive of physical environment: 144, 154, 234, 293, G19
Umwelts, how diverse ones interact: 118-119
Umwelts, source of: 130, 310
Umwelts compared to soap bubbles: 119
Understand, understanding: 7, 14, 19, 35, 43, 45, 53, 72, 80, 82, 84, 87, 89, 109, 120, 125, 128, 129, 134, 136, 143, 145, 153, 154, 162-165, 171, 203-205, 206, 215, 217, 219, 227, 232, 240, 245, 246, 249-251. 253, 254, 264, 265, 267, 269, 273-277, 279, 280, 282, 286, 287, 289, 290, 292, 294-296, 298-300, 308-311, G1, G2, G3, G7, G8, G17, G27, G33, G45, G46, G51, G57 (*see also* Intellect)
Understanding, centrality of history for: 279
Understanding, fundamental orientation of: 290, 296
Understanding, semiotic posing of the question of: 251
Understanding and infinite process, 206, 214, 227, G33
Understanding as different from perception: 298
Understanding of simple essences: G59
Understanding signs vs. using signs: 154
Unicorns: 36, 59
Unintelligible prospect: 211
Uniqueness of the sensible object as such: 41
Universality and linguistic code: 172
Universe, physical vs. objective: 54
Universe of action: 282, 284

Universe of discourse: 268
Univocal: 186, 308
Unlimited semiosis: 131, 168, 238, 252, (*see also* Infinite process; Infinity; Progress to the infinite)
Unlimited semiosis, source of: 138, 218, 243-244, G21
Unlimited semiosis realized only through anthroposemiosis: 138
Unmoved mover: G33
Unreal: 144-145, 196, 300, 308
Unreasonable strictly speaking: 40, 50
Ut significata: 240
Utopia (More): 126

Vagueness: 223-224, G37
Validity: 271
Vampire: 33
Verbal markers: 121
Verifiable: 16
Verification, verify: 7, 10, 96, 107, 243, 298
Vicarious subordination of causes: 211
Viking Lander: 49
Virtual: 3, 20, 25, 26, 70, 110, 112, 113, 127, 130, 151, 155, 167, 168, 172, 179, 200, 226, 229, 280, 286, G1, G15
Virtual acquaintance (Peirce): 155
Virtual action of signs outside experience: 112
Virtual inclusion of zoösemiosis in anthroposemiosis: 179
Virtual operation of codes: 200, 280
Virtual secondness: 229
Virtual semiosis: 20, 70, 110, 112, 113, 127, 130, 200, G15
Virtual textuality: 25, 280
Virtual universality: 167, 172
Virtualities: 3, 110, 151
Virtualities, physical: 168
Virtualities of zoösemiotic influence: 286
Virtuality: 286
Virtus intellectus: G46

Vitalism: G17

Web: 4, 16, 18, 19, 22, 110, 115, 167, 168, 181, 273-275
Web of renvoi: 274
What can be said but not thought: 227, G36
What is that question, motivation of: 297-298
What makes an object a sign: 73
Will of interpreter: 84, 89, 108, 148, 294, G8, G17
Will of interpreter in deconstruction: G8
Word, capacity of for learning: G27
Word, life of: G27
Word, path of: G27
Word spoken contrasted to written: 143
World as Lebenswelt: 200
World of experience: 25, 54, 63, 115, 123, 128, 172 (*see further* Experience; Objective world; Umwelt)
World of experience as through and through objective: 54
World of fancies: 155
World of language: 172
World of things: 147
Written language: 74

Xenophobia: 229

Yahweh: 62
Yoruba: 28
Youthful conception of Bakhtin: G39
Yugoslavia: G24

Zone of already-understood: 197
Zoösemiosic: 199
Zoösemiosis: 14, 19, 24, 120, 127, 137, 150, 151, 161, 164, 169, 174, 177-179, 181, 182, 185, 186, 188, 189, 195, 199, 220, 229, 232, 233, 246, 262, 263, 281, 282, 283, 285, 286, G2, G21, G25
Zoösemiotic objectivity: 178

About the Author

John Deely is the author of many scholarly articles and books, including notably *Introducing Semiotic* and *Basics of Semiotics*. He is also the editor of many volumes, including the *Semiotics 1981-1992* Proceedings volumes of the Semiotic Society of America, *Frontiers in Semiotics*, and the bilingual critical edition of the earliest systematic treatise on the foundations of the doctrine of signs, John Poinsot's 1632 *Tractatus de Signis*. He is currently completing a monograph on *Logic within Semiotics* for the Indiana University Press and expects to bring to publication in 1994 a work titled *New Beginnings, Early Modern Philosophy and Postmodern Thought*.

Lightning Source UK Ltd.
Milton Keynes UK
UKHW052115270422
402142UK00018B/612